KENYA
& NORTHERN TANZANIA

A Travellers' Guide

KENYA

TANZANIA

KENYA
& NORTHERN TANZANIA

A Travellers' Guide

RICHARD COX

HIPPOCRENE
BOOKS, INC.

Distribution:
Distributed in Great Britain and the Commonwealth by
Roger Lascelles, 47 York Road, Brentford, Middlesex TW8 0QP
Telephone: (01) 847 0935

ISBN 0 902726 38 2

Distributed in the United States and Canada by
Hippocrene Books Inc., 171 Madison Avenue, New York NY 10016

US ISBN 0 87052 495 X

Published by Thornton Cox (1986) Ltd,
Epworth House, 23-35 City Road, London EC1Y 1AA

Published in the United States and Canada by
Hippocrene Books Inc., 171 Madison Avenue, New York NY 10016

First published as The Travellers' Guide to East Africa 1966.
Revised editions 1968, 1970, 1972, 1980. Republished under this
title by Geographia Ltd 1984. This edition, fully
revised, January 1988.

Drawings by RENA FENNESSY
Maps by Tom Stalker-Miller, MSIA
Cover: Zebra on the Mara River. Copyright Jonathan Scott

Printed in Great Britain by The Guernsey Press Company Limited,
Guernsey, Channel Islands

© Thornton Cox (1986) Ltd, 1988

Thornton Cox Guides:

Titles in print in this series include:

Southern France	**Majorca**
Greece	**Portugal**
Ireland	

View of Mount Longonot across Lake Naivasha

Contents

Foreword	7
General Information	9
Safaris	29
Kenya	35
Northern Tanzania	151
East Africa's Wildlife	174
Bibliography	185
Maps	188
Index	192

Acknowledgements

The author gratefully acknowledges the assistance of Tina Behrens and of many tour operators in Kenya, notably Abercrombie and Kent, Bunson Travel Service and Let's Go Travel, during research work for the revision of this guide. The author also wishes to thank the Tanzania Tourist Corporation and the African Wildlife Foundation for their co-operation in providing information.

Foreword

Recent years have witnessed a surge of interest in East Africa, partly given impetus by the magnificent photography in the film 'Out of Africa.' The word *safari,* which in the Swahili language simply means journey, has become internationalised, epitomising adventure, and mass tourism to Kenya has developed to the point where the main package tour circuits are laden with herds of mini-buses. In consequence, more discriminating travellers increasingly try to plan their own itinerary, or at least get tour operators to book them individual safaris. This book is primarily written for such people and is the successor to our 'Travellers Guide to East Africa', originally published in 1966.

Geographically, Kenya and Tanzania are neighbours and, since animals and birds do not recognise national frontiers, and the region has its own characteristics, the area is still referred to as East Africa occasionally in the text. Overall, the backdrop of East Africa's scenery is of epic proportions and remarkable variety. It is bounded to the east by the Indian Ocean, where the dhows of Arabia ply down to Zanzibar, Dar es Salaam and beyond, and the coral lagoons and big game fishing rival the Bahamas. To the west it reaches inland 715 kilometres (446 miles) to the second deepest lake in the world, Lake Tanganyika, and includes Lake Victoria, the second largest. To the north lie the highlands of Ethiopia, a 3,000 year-old state with ancient castles and rock-hewn churches.

Striking down through the centre of this area goes the Rift, the great valley of Africa, part of a geological fault in the earth's surface that runs from the USSR to Zimbabwe, and cuts the channel of the Red Sea on the way. In Kenya the Rift is 80 kilometres (50 miles) across in places and 2,000 ft deep. Its bed is pitted with extinct volcanoes, while not far from it rise the two highest peaks in the African continent, Kenya and Kilimanjaro, both volcanic, both permanently topped with snow. Either of these may have been the original 'Mountains of the Moon' although the name and the legends now attach to a third snowcapped range, the Ruwenzori in Uganda, near the border of Zaire. Ice and frost are no rarity in other continents, but here they are made dramatic, and even frightening, by the incongruity of their existence above the vast, hot plains below.

Much of the recorded history of both Kenya and Tanzania centres on the coast. Ptolemy, the great geographer, wrote in the second century AD, about Mombasa under the name of Tonike, and the long white coral beaches of both countries, verged with palm trees, were familiar to Indian, Arab and Portuguese adventurers and traders. Until a hundred years ago, the principal trade was with

Foreword

Arabs and Muslim Persians (known as *Shirazi),* who sailed down in the dhows to exchange their cloth, beads and wooden chests, for ivory, rhino horn and spices. Indeed the dhows still sail down today, although the Arab Sultanates of the coast are long extinct.

When the early European explorers trekked inland, they found a landscape of bewildering beauty, teeming with game. Today the plains of the Serengeti, which seem as wide as an ocean, are still the scene twice a year of the greatest game migration in the world, and giraffe and gazelle are still as familiar a sight as cattle, while the profusion of birdlife is as breathtaking as the landscape.

Despite the demand for land for the rapidly increasing populations there is still awareness of the need to conserve the game. President Nyerere's 'Arusha Manifesto of 1961' stated, 'Wildlife is an integral part of our resources and of our future livelihood and wellbeing'. Unhappily this sentiment has not always been backed up by governments. Although instituting improvements, like charting the great annual migrations of game, the authorities failed to stop massive depredations by poachers, especially of elephant and rhino. The effects of this were at last realised in the late 1970s. In Kenya hunting, the sale of game trophies, and the export of sea shells are banned although it can be argued that controlled hunting has the side effect of keeping poachers out of the game areas. But the heavy fines facing poachers have not prevented the rhino becoming an endangered species, able to survive only in special sanctuaries, while the coastal reefs are largely denuded of shells. The preservation of the natural heritage has needed outside help, most notably from the World Wildlife Fund, which has given generous assistance to the game departments concerned and to the development of parks and reserves, while the African Wildlife Foundation and the East African Wildlife Society have also contributed substantially to local conservation of wildlife and its habitat.

Finally, it should be explained that although surface and air communications within Kenya have improved dramatically in the past few years, there are certain restrictions on transit into Tanzania. It is, for example, illegal to take a hired vehicle across the border without special permission. This is dealt with in the General Information section which follows.

General
Information

How to get there

By Air — Kenya

Some 36 international airlines operate to Nairobi, including Aeroflot, Air France, Air India, Air Tanzania, Alitalia, British Airways, Egyptian Airlines, Ethiopian Airlines, El-Al Israel Airlines, Japan Airlines, KLM, Lufthansa, Olympic, PIA, Pan Am, Sabena, Scandinavian, Sudan Airways, Swissair, TWA, Varig and Zambia Airways. Many of these also serve Tanzania, but seldom via Nairobi.

Kenya Airways operates international services to Nairobi and Mombasa from London (Heathrow), Athens, Copenhagen, Dar es Salaam, Frankfurt, Kilimanjaro (Arusha) and Paris, as well as from Cairo, Khartoum, Jeddah, Bombay, Karachi and other Middle Eastern and Asian capitals.

Among the few airlines linking East and West Africa are Ethiopian Airlines, Nigeria Airways, Air Zaire and Cameroon Airlines. Pan Am used to serve West Africa but now flies New York - Frankfurt - Nairobi on Fridays, returning on Mondays.

Possession of a return ticket and adequate funds are liable to be a condition of entry for visitors.

Kenya's two international airports are Jomo Kenyatta, 13 kilometres (8 miles) south east of Nairobi, and Moi International 13 kilometres (8 miles) from the centre of Mombasa. Customs and Immigration facilities are also available for charter flights at Nairobi's Wilson airport, close to the city centre.

Check-in time for most international flights is officially 60 minutes before departure, but 90 minutes is safer, and some airlines, such as Air India and Sudan Airways demand 2 hours. Check-in time for local flights is 30 minutes. Again, allow longer.

On arrival at both Nairobi and Mombasa you have to complete a currency declaration form at the Customs, detailing the foreign currency you are bringing in. This form, stamped by banks or hotels where you change money, will be required when you leave. See

General Information

below for Customs allowances. There are banks in the arrival areas at both airports and also snack bars.

After Customs you will find taxi touts waiting at the exit. If you accept a taxi offer agree the price beforehand. The fare into the town centres should be around Shs. 175/-. A reliable taxi firm is Kenatco, which has airport offices and will charge at the official fixed rate, at the time of writing Shs. 11/- per kilometre.

There is an airport bus service from both airports at roughly hourly intervals to the Kenya Airways town terminals for a fare of Shs. 40/-.

Buses for Jomo Kenyatta airport leave the Kenya Airways terminal in Koinanange Street in central Nairobi at 0800, 0900, 1000, 1130, 1245, 1430, 1645, 1830 and 2000. The journey time is around 25 minutes.

On departure there is a set procedure. First you check in at the airline desk, then pay the $10 departure tax at a separate counter (some airlines do this for you). It can be paid in other currencies, but not in Kenya shillings. After this go past the check-in desks to identify your baggage with the Customs. Here you must hand in your currency declaration form. You are not allowed to take out more than Shs. 100/- of Kenya currency. Change any surplus at the airport bank. Signs warn against destroying surplus notes or trying to bribe officials: both are criminal offences. But, provided you obey the regulations, there will be no problem and you will be allowed through to where your ticket and departure tax stamp are checked, followed by normal immigration and hand baggage security routines. If your flight is delayed both Jomo Kenyatta and Moi airports have good 'Simba' restaurants in the departure areas, as well as duty-free shops selling liquor, cameras, watches and such local produce as coffee beans.

Note that local Kenya currency is not accepted for purchases in airport duty-free shops nor on board aircraft. However it is usable in the departure area to pay for snacks and meals and to buy local handicrafts, produce and magazines.

By Air — Tanzania
Among international airlines serving Tanzania are Aeroflot, Air France, Air Tanzania, British Airways, Ethiopian Airlines, Kenya Airways, KLM, PIA, Lufthansa, Pakistan International, Swissair, Uganda Airlines and Zambia Airways.

Air Tanzania's internal network is detailed in the Northern Tanzania chapter.

Possession of a return ticket and adequate funds are a condition of entry. Visitors with South African stamps in their passports are not admitted.

The two international airports are Dar es Salaam, 13 kilometres (8 miles) outside the city and Kilimanjaro, approximately 50 kilometres (31 miles) from Arusha.

Check-in time for international flights is officially 65 minutes. It is wise to allow 90 minutes. Check-in time for local flights is 30 minutes. Again, allow more.

Procedures on arrival are similar to Kenya's except that it is compulsory to change US$50 on arrival. Other currencies are acceptable, but since the US$10 departure tax has to be paid in dollars it is worth bringing at least US$100 in notes for these and other purposes. No taxis are available at the airport. The State Travel Service runs a bus shuttle into Arusha for a fare of Shs. 200/-. Tour operators normally arrange their own transfers.

Departure procedures are also similar to Kenya's, except that you are only allowed to take out Shs. 40/- in local currency and you can have difficulty changing it back at the airport: better to leave yourself with the minimum at the end of your stay. Refreshments are available at the airports. The duty-free shops are not up to the Kenyan standard.

Airline Fares

It is difficult to quote fares sensibly. APEX excursion fares on British Airways run as low as £412 from London to Nairobi, rising to £592 in the high season (July to September, December and January) and £44 from Nairobi to Kilimanjaro return fare at any time of year. APEX fares can have a validity of from 14 days to one year and must be bought 21 days in advance and do not permit change of bookings. The three-month economy return fare at the time of writing was £923 London to Nairobi and £930 London to Kilimanjaro. However, discount travel agents, or 'bucket shops', could provide one year open return tickets on reputable airlines for £500. The very cheapest tickets are usually available on Aeroflot, Egyptair and Sudan Airways. The Aeroflot flight can take up to 30 hours via Moscow and the schedules of the other two are frankly unreliable.

From New York the basic economy fare to Nairobi at the time of writing was US$1,392 each way. Much cheaper fares are available. Consult a travel agent.

Remember that if you do pay the full fare you can add internal sectors, such as Nairobi to the coast, at very little cost.

11

General Information

A large number of travel agents offer package tours to Kenya and a growing number to Tanzania. In Britain these include Bales, Thomas Cook & Son, Hayes and Jarvis, Nilestar, Flamingo, Swan-Hellenic, Kuoni Travel Ltd, Lunn-Poly, Houlder Brothers, Inghams, Lord Brothers, Speedbird and Wings, all in London; in the United States they include Lindblad Travel Inc of Westport, Connecticut, Intrav in St Louis, Percival Tours in Los Angeles and Blue World Travel in San Francisco.

By Sea
In recent years virtually all passenger traffic by sea has ceased. Even cargo ships rarely take passengers, and their schedules are anyway extremely unreliable.

Overland
Overland treks are arranged by a number of specialist firms, as well as often being organised privately. The normal route crosses the western Sahara to West Africa and goes through the Central African Republic and northern Zaire. It takes up to four months and is governed by the rainy seasons encountered on the journey. Around 20 people travel in a truck. You camp en route and it is vital to have an experienced leader. Two firms which organise trips are Encounter Overland Ltd (267 Old Brompton Road, London SW5 91A; telephone 01-370-6845) and Trail Finders Ltd (46 Earls Court Road, London W8; telephone 01-937-9631). Encounter Overland's trip to Dar es Salaam and then Nairobi takes sixteen weeks and costs £1,845. The expedition then returns to London. Trail Finders trek to Nairobi costs from £1,500. At the time of writing the alternative route down the Nile through Sudan was not feasible because of the rebellion in southern Sudan.

Travel within the Country

Air
Kenya Airways and Air Tanzania operate scheduled services between Nairobi, Dar es Salaam and Kilimanjaro (Arusha). Recently Kenya Airways has revived a near-historic route from Mombasa to Zanzibar. Both these national carriers operate their own internal network of routes on which fares are very reasonable by European standards. Furthermore, in Kenya a number of private charter companies operate internal scheduled services. These are listed, with fares and private charter details, in the Transport and Tours chapter of the Kenya section. No private scheduled services exist in Tanzania, but Air Tanzania's routes serve most parts of the country, as listed in the Tanzania section, together with private charter rates.

Local air charters
There are several hundred airstrips in Kenya and Tanzania, including ones in all the national parks and most reserves. In consequence

flying is an accepted way of getting about and, given that you go direct, can often rival car hire costs. Nairobi to the Masai Mara Game Reserve, for example, is less than one hour by air against six hours by road.

However, although communications between Kenya and Tanzania are now more free than for many years, there are still restrictions on private flying between the two countries. Permission has to be sought from the Ministry of Transport and Communications in Nairobi as well as from the Directorate of Civil Aviation in Dar es Salaam, and it takes a week to obtain the entry and exit permits. The points of entry are the international airports, although there are Customs and Immigration facilities at Wilson airport, Nairobi and at Kisumu. Tanzania has also made entry facilities available at Lake Manyara and at Seronera Lodge in the Serengeti.

Car Hire and Driving
Avis and Hertz are both represented in Kenya, which means you can book through their international reservation systems. But there are reliable cheaper local firms. For fuller information, please refer to the Transport and Safaris sections of the Kenya and Tanzania chapters.

You drive on the left and in Kenya you can use your home licence for up to six months. Both countries have speed limits: 88 kph (55 mph) in Tanzania; 100 kph (62 mph) in Kenya. Distances are measured in kilometres.

If you are setting out on a self-drive safari there are certain basic precautions to take beforehand. If your vehicle has not got four-wheel drive check that the routes you intend to take are passable without it, especially during the rains. If possible take two spare wheels. Always carry some food and water, a torch and a spare can of fuel. If you do break down outside a populated area keep a look-out for animals. In general, if you are in any kind of trouble passing drivers will usually stop and help. Finally, remember there are regulations on driving in the National Parks and Reserves. These are outlined in the National Parks and Reserves chapter for Kenya and are similar in Tanzania, where you are in any case unlikely to be able to hire a self-drive vehicle.

It is illegal to take a hired car across the Kenya/Tanzania frontier except by special arrangement. Private vehicles may cross provided they have an export permit for the export of the fuel they are carrying from the Central Bank of Kenya. A 'Foreign Registered Vehicle' fee of US$60 is payable on the Tanzania side, with appropriate documentation and possible Tanzanian road taxes. Consult the AA of Kenya (PO Box 40087, Nairobi; telephone 730382) on the current situation. If you do go, take as much fuel as possible in case of shortages in Tanzania.

Kenyan buses go to the border at Namanga and you can then cross and board a Tanzanian bus.

Accommodation

Please refer to the sections on Hotels and Game Lodges in the Kenya and Tanzania chapters. There are an increasing number of very cheap hotels, offering basic facilities which are not up to normal European standards but are perfectly adequate if you do not mind roughing it. There are also excellent youth hostels in many towns.

Altitude and Climate

Being on the Equator most of East Africa has no summer or winter and the days vary little in length. Sunrise is between 0600 and 0630 and sunset between 1830 and 1900. The sun rises and sets much faster than in temperate latitudes.

The climate is warm throughout the year, varying according to the altitude above sea level of the place you are at. At the coast daytime temperatures average between 24°C and 29°C (75°F and 85°F) with an average humidity of 75 per cent. If there is no wind it can feel decidedly sticky, though at night it can be cool enough to wear a light pullover. Inland the humidity declines as you go higher up, and the nights become appreciably cooler. At 5,000 ft the average daytime temperatures are only slightly less than the coast's, but at night they fall to around 10°C (50°F). In the mountains the temperature drops to freezing point.

The sun is often hotter than it feels and you can all too easily get sunburnt, or find yourself suffering from heat exhaustion. In this climate your body needs more liquid than it does in temperate latitudes, which means drinking more, though not necessarily more alcohol! It is sensible to take water with you when driving a long distance. Finally, the sunlight is strong and you need good-quality sunglasses to protect your eyes.

Rain usually comes down in short downpours, after which the sun comes out again. Broadly speaking the long rains come to Kenya, and Northern Tanzania in April/May and the short rains in November and early December. However, in recent years the rainy seasons have been disobligingly erratic, so do not be surprised if you find it raining at some other time.

Complaints

If you have a complaint about a hotel or restaurant, address it to the Kenya Association of Hotelkeepers and Caterers (PO Box 46406, Nairobi; telephone 330865). Equally the Kenya Association of Tour Operators (PO Box 48461, Nairobi; telephone 25570) can help with safari or car rental problems. You could also approach the Ministry of Tourism and Wildlife (PO Box 30027, Nairobi; telephone 331030).

In Tanzania contact the Tanzania Tourist Corporation (PO Box 2485, Dar es Salaam; telephone 27671).

Currency and Banking

Kenya and Tanzania each issue their own shillings as the basic unit. The shilling is a silver-coloured round coin, divided into 100 cents. Lesser coins of ten and five cents are made of brassy, yellow metal.

In Kenya notes come in denominations of Shs 5/-, Shs 10/-, Shs 20/-, Shs 50/-, Shs 100/- and Shs 200/-. The Shs 5/- note is going out of use and being replaced by a silver-coloured coin.

In Tanzania the denominations are similar.

The international exchange ratios of both currencies fluctuate. The Kenya shilling is the strongest currency and at the time of writing was at Shs 26/70 to the pound sterling, Shs 16/35 to the US dollar and Shs 8/95 to the Deutschmark. Large amounts are commonly expressed in pounds with 20 shillings making £1.

The Tanzania shilling, at the time of writing, was around Shs 100/- to £1 sterling and Shs 62/- to US $1.00. Check with a bank or travel agent for up-to-date rates.

Both countries have strict currency regulations, requiring a customs declaration to be completed on arrival. This form must be filled in and stamped by any hotel or bank which changes your money. It is then handed in to the customs on departure, though not always checked. Inevitably there is a considerable black market in both currencies and tourists are frequently accosted by touts on the streets. Quite apart from such men being adept at cheating by handing over the 'currency' in an envelope containing only ordinary paper, there are severe penalties if you are caught infringing the currency regulations and your passport will be impounded until after trial. Unspent foreign currency can, of course, be taken out. Local currency must be exchanged before departure and you should allow time for this at the airport bank. Note that although the bank at Jomo Kenyatta airport is open 24 hours a day, banks at other airports may not be open at night when international flights leave.

General Information

Banking hours in Kenya are from 0900 to 1400 Mondays to Fridays, and 0900 to 1100 on the first and last Saturdays of the month. Most hotels will change currency and travellers' cheques. The principal banks are Barclays Bank International, Kenya Commercial Bank, Commercial Bank of Africa and Standard Bank Ltd.

In Tanzania banking hours are 0830 to 1230 Mondays to Fridays, and 0830 to 1200 on Saturdays. Banking facilities are provided by the National Bank of Commerce. Hotels are authorised to change foreign currency.

Customs Duties

Visitors are allowed to bring in duty free all bona fide personal effects, provided they are declared on arrival and the proposed stay is not over six months. This includes cameras, binoculars, portable typewriters; one bottle of spirits or perfume; 50 cigars, or 200 cigarettes or ½lb tobacco.

On certain articles a customs deposit can be demanded which is refunded on departure. Motor vehicles covered by a triptique or carnet will be allowed duty free for the period of validity of the document.

Items that the customs tend to pounce on include transistor radios and tape recorders, though if they are demonstrably personal property they are normally let through. Gifts or anything intended for sale or exchange are liable to duty. Guns and ammunition must be declared, and need a firearms certificate from the police which safari organisers can obtain for you in advance.

Almost anything that is posted to you while you are in East Africa will have duty levied on it, usually at 30 per cent of the estimated value, while some items like perfume attract 100 per cent duty. Even personal clothing has to be visibly used to escape duty if it comes by post. It is preferable to send one's belongings by air freight.

The sale of game trophies is illegal in Kenya, with very rare exceptions. In Tanzania their sale is legal, since hunting is permitted. However in both countries the main restriction when you leave is on taking out hides, skins and ivory. Anything made from animals, from zebra-decorated sandals to a whole mounted leopard skin, must have a Game Department Certificate, which shops should provide for you at the time of purchase. This is to prevent the sale and export of illegally trapped animal skins.

Diplomatic Representation

There are Kenyan diplomatic missions in Addis Ababa, Beijing,

Bonn, Brussels, Cairo, Jeddah, Kinshasa, Lagos, Lusaka, London, Mogadishu, Moscow, New Delhi, Ottawa, Paris, Rome, Stockholm, Tokyo, Vienna and Washington. Visas or Visitor's Passes can be obtained from them (see Immigration below).

Over 60 countries maintain embassies or consulates in Nairobi, including Australia, Austria, Belgium, Brazil, Canada, People's Republic of China, Colombia, Cyprus, Czechoslovakia, Denmark, Ethiopia, Finland, France, German Federal Republic, Ghana, Great Britain, Greece, Hungary, India, Iran, Ireland, Italy, Japan, Korean Republic, Kuwait, Lesotho, Liberia, Malagasy Republic, Malasia, Malawi, Netherlands, Nigeria, Norway, Pakistan, Poland, Portugal, Rwanda, Somalia, Spain, Sri Lanka, Sudan, Sweden, Switzerland, Swaziland, Tanzania, Thailand, Turkey, UAR, Uganda, USA, USSR, Yugoslavia, Zaire and Zambia.

Belgium, France, India, The Netherlands and Sweden maintain consulates in Mombasa.

A growing number of international organisations have offices in Nairobi, including UNDP, UNESCO, UNICEF, FAO, the EEC and UNEP which has its headquarters just outside the city.

Tanzania has diplomatic missions in Addis Ababa, Beijing, Bonn, Brussels, Cairo, Conakry, Geneva, The Hague, Harare, Khartoum, Kigali, Kinshasa, Lagos, London, Luanda, Lusaka, Maputo, Moscow, New Delhi, Ottawa, Paris, Rome, Stockholm, Tokyo, Washington and the United Nations.

Countries which maintain embassies or consulates in Tanzania, where the capital was due to be transferred from Dar es Salaam to Dodoma in the late 1980s, include Algeria, Angola, Australia, Austria, Belgium, Burundi, Canada, People's Republic of China, Cuba, Czechoslovakia, Denmark, Ethiopia, Finland, France, German Democratic Republic, German Federal Republic, Great Britain, Guinea, Hungary, India, Indonesia, Italy, Ivory Coast, Japan, Kenya, Korean Republic, Morocco, Netherlands, Nigeria, Norway, Pakistan, Romania, Rwanda, Somali Republic (through Nairobi), Spain, Sudan, Sweden, Switzerland, Tanzania, Turkey, UAR, USA, USSR, Yugoslavia, Zaire, Zambia.

Dress and Cosmetics

Comfortable clothes matter a lot, as in all tropical climates and most visitors dress very informally. For women a woollen jumper or cardigan is essential for cool evenings up country. At the coast during the day light cottons and linens are the thing, preferably washable, and slacks and shirts for safaris. Sandals can be bought in holiday centres. Swimsuits and beachwear are useful. So are one pair of flattish shoes, and a raincoat, preferably a lightweight one. Sunglasses and a sunhat (obtainable locally) are all but vital.

For men a lightweight suit is useful in the cities if local business or social occasions are included in the trip. Bring plenty of shirts — incidentally in our experience synthetic fabrics can become very sticky and there is no substitute for cotton if you want to stay cool. Several pairs of washable trousers will be handy and so will both long-and short-sleeved sweaters.

Hotels and clubs are not excessively formal and a dinner jacket is rarely needed, but clubs and the best restaurants will insist that men wear a jacket and a tie. In general a dark light-to medium-weight lounge suit for a man, and a smart dress for a woman, will be enough for formal occasions, even if you are at a gathering when the African leaders are in national dress. This latter incidentally is both dignified and colourful. Tanzania's is reminiscent of the Roman toga.

Anyone going on safari will feel more at home in neutral-coloured clothes. Jungle green or khaki bush shirts, trousers and skirts can be made locally, or bought off the peg. You will look right in them and they will be cheaper both in tailoring charges and air freight than any similar clothes you bring with you.

Quite a number of internationally known beauty preparations are sold in the cities. Sun lotions and moisturising creams are vital in this climate, though they are expensive. Equally razor blades, shaving soaps etc are available. Most hotels have plug sockets for electric razors in their bathrooms.

Electricity

The electricity supply in East Africa is 240 volts, 50 cycles, AC. Most hotels provide adaptor plugs for 220 volt and 110 volt appliances.

Etiquette

In general the welcome you get in Africa is refreshing, and Africans will often stop to talk to the foreign visitor. They are relaxed and informal people. It's fair to say, however, that they are sensitive on several points, notably religion, colonialism and photography.

Both Kenya and Tanzania have Moslem communities. Their mosques can be visited but it is best to ask the guardian of the mosque if you may venture inside. Before going in you must remove your shoes and please be fully dressed in all other respects.

Nude or topless bathing is very much frowned upon by both the

Government and the local people. The coastal Africans are a strict Moslem community and their women are expected to cover themselves completely, only allowing their eyes to show.

While politics do not impinge on the visitor at all, do remember that these countries have only fairly recently become independent of British rule and dislike rude remarks about their newly won freedom. The old habit of addressing servants and waiters as 'boy' has gone for ever. Some restaurants and hotels give their staff lapel name badges. In Tanzania one officially approved word for calling for service is *Rafiki* — Swahili for 'friend'. Otherwise call out 'Steward' or 'Waiter'. Using occasional Swahili words (see page 23) will pay dividends in terms of service, even if you only learn *Jambo* and *Asante sana.* Some Africans, especially Moslems, do not like being photographed. It is often believed that by taking a picture of a man you gain control over his soul. If there is obvious hostility then be sensible and put your camera away, or ask the person concerned for his or her agreement. This may lead to a demand for money — in areas near Amboseli, for example, to outrageous demands. A few shillings should normally be enough.

Food and Drink

In hotels and restaurants, in both Kenya and Tanzania, the cooking is basically English, with standard 'international' grills, roasts and other dishes. There are Chinese, French, Indian, Italian, Japanese and Korean restaurants in the cities. In country towns menus are more basic. There is plentiful use of local fruit — such as avocado pears, bananas, mangoes, oranges, paw-paws and pineapples. In Kenya, beef, lamb and pork are abundant and fish is readily available: Nile perch, tilapia and trout from fresh water lakes and rivers, seafish, lobster and prawns from the coast. Kenya cheeses include locally made camembert, cheddar and gouda.

Until recently hotel menus did not include indigenous African foods or cooking. However these are increasingly being put on offer. Some of the ingredients and dishes with their Swahili names in italics, are as follows:

Samaki	fish, of any kind
Nyama	meat
Kuku	chicken
Pilao	Indian style rice with meat or vegetables
Githeri	beans and maize cooked together whole
Irio	beans or peas and maize and sometimes potatoes boiled together, seasoned and mashed
Matoke	plaintain bananas steamed, sometimes with coconut sauce

General Information

Mseto	boiled lentils and rice with onions, coconut and milk
Ndizi	plaintain bananas *(matoke)* fried with onions
Sukuma wiki	a hard variety of spinach, boiled and mixed with whatever leftovers are available. The name means 'make the week last', it's a stand-by when money is running out
Ugali	a very thick maize porridge. Often eaten as the accompaniment to meat or stew

At the coast Swahili cooking, influenced by Arabian traditions, utilises exotic spices and coconut milk, often with grilled fish.

Additionally various Indian specialities have become widely adopted, for instance *samosas* which are small triangles of crisp pastry filled with minced meat and vegetables, and curries.

If you want to know about Kenyan menus, look for Kathy Eldon's book *Tastes of Kenya* published by Kenway Publications, Nairobi.

Drink
Drinks of all kinds are at least twice as expensive in Tanzania as they are in Kenya, even allowing for the substantial exchange rate differences between the two countries.

Local beers are lager style and a normal bottle is enough to fill two large glasses. The Kenyan fixed price is Shs 10/50 a bottle. White Cap and Tusker are the most popular brands. Tusker Export and Tusker Premium are superior brews sold in smaller bottles at a slightly higher price. Guinness Stout is also brewed locally.

In Kenya soft drinks such as Coca Cola, Fanta, Sprite and local lemonades are sold everywhere and are very cheap. Spirits are expensive, the best bargains being gin and vodka which are distilled locally. There are also local whiskies and brandies, created by mixing local and imported spirit. Scotch whisky costs whatever the shop thinks it can charge. At the time of writing this was never less than Shs 290/- and likely to rise.

Wine is expensive in Kenyan hotels and restaurants, although usually available. Italian wines like Chianti or Soave appear to travel best, but even they can suffer from secondary fermentation during shipment from Europe. This, coupled with import costs, has stimulated the establishment of local wine making. The Lake Naivasha Vineyards, for instance, produce a Sauvignon Blanc and a Colombard, which sell in shops at around Shs 70/-, if you can get them. On a larger scale the Kenya Wine Agencies have developed a local white Riesling style wine made not from grapes but from paw-paw juice.

This is called 'Papaya', costs around Shs 40/- in a shop and is drink-able if properly chilled. Ordinary Italian wines will be upwards of Shs 90/- in a shop and French wines substantially more. But in a restaurant the only bottle priced at under Shs 300/- will be the 'Papaya'.

Tanzania is a completely different story, though the situation may improve. Spirits, when available, costs Shs 120/- a shot in a bar and mixers are in very short supply. Wine is rare, though mission-aries at Dodoma have long produced a rather heavy Dodoma red and rosé. Beer, probably in an unlabelled bottle will cost Shs 80/-. You go to Tanzania for the wildlife not the drinking, and you'll never value the duty-free whisky you bring in more.

Normal bar opening hours in Kenya are 1100 to 1400 and 1700 to 2300.

In Tanzania the hours in hotels and restaurants are 1200 to 1400 and 1800 to 2300 weekdays, and midnight at weekends.

Water
Tap water is normally drinkable, though in some areas it is naturally highly fluorine and not suitable for pregnant women or young children. When tap water is not drinkable hotels leave a Thermos flask of cold drinking water in your room.

Cigarettes
Locally made Kenyan cigarettes include Crown Bird Filter, a mild brand, Sportsman, which is stronger, and Embassy, the closest to an ordinary Virginia type. The tar content of cigarettes is not officially controlled.

Gratuities
Sometimes gratuities are added to hotel and restaurant bills. Otherwise about 10 per cent of the bill is fair, or 15 per cent if you have had especially good service. Shs 5/- is normal for a luggage porter and Shs 10/- for the room servant after one or two nights, depending on how helpful he has been. If you are staying in a private house then Shs 20/- per day for each servant is appropriate. Drivers should be given around Shs 30/- per day and game rangers the same after a game drive.

There is a 5 per cent service charge added to all bills in Kenya.

Health
Officially, if you are coming from Europe or other countries where such diseases as cholera are not endemic you no longer require

international certificates of vaccination against smallpox and inoculation against yellow fever. In practice, it is extremely unwise not to be immunised against yellow fever, cholera and typhoid; equally it is wise to take anti-malarial pills, starting before you arrive, even though up-country areas are not malarial. Nivaquin, Paludrine and Sensida are among the best anti-malarial tablets. These can be bought locally and taken in the evenings for better effect.

If you are going to Tanzania it is obligatory to have cholera and yellow fever immunization.

There are chemists' shops throughout East Africa, experienced doctors practise in most towns and there are good hospitals in the cities.

Do not swim in the inland lakes and rivers, unless you are told it is safe, since they are often infested with bilharzia (a disease carried by water snails). Beware of over-exposure to the sun, which can definitely be injurious.

The Flying Doctor Service (PO Box 30125, Nairobi; telephone 501301) is based at Wilson Airport. Most tour operators subscribe to it so that their clients can be flown back from anywhere in Kenya to a medical centre. Alternatively visitors can obtain one month's temporary membership for £5, US$8 or, strangely, only Shs 50/-. There is also a Flying Doctor service in Tanzania.

Immigration

Visitors to both Kenya and Tanzania must have a Visitor's Pass, which can normally be obtained on arrival, subject where necessary to the possession of a valid visa.

Kenya does not require visas from citizens of Denmark, Ethiopia, Italy, Norway, San Marino, Spain, Sweden, Turkey, Uruguay, West Germany and the British Commonwealth (except Australia, Nigeria, Sri Lanka and British passport holders of Bangladeshi, Indian or Pakistani origin). Visas can be obtained from the Kenyan embassies listed in the Diplomatic Representation section above, or from British embassies abroad. They should be applied for 30 days in advance. Visitor's Passes are granted for a maximum of three months, but can be extended by application to the Immigration Department, Nyayo House, Kenyatta Avenue, Nairobi; telephone 333551. Visitors are not allowed to accept work, either paid or unpaid.

Tanzania does not require visas from Commonwealth citizens. Nor does it need visas from citizens of Bangladesh, Denmark, Ireland, Norway, Rumania, Rwanda, Sudan and Sweden under the mutual Visa Abolition Agreement' between itself and these countries.

However it is always wise to check on visa requirements since they not infrequently change. Visas can be obtained from Tanzanian diplomatic missions abroad or by direct application to the Principal Immigration Officer, PO Box 512, Dar es Salaam. Visitors Passes are granted at the main entry points to the country. As in Kenya, visitors are not permitted to accept employment.

Language

English is spoken widely and is the accepted language in the cities, hotels, restaurants etc. However, as well as numerous tribal languages, East Africa has its own lingua franca, called Swahili. This is the official language of Tanzania and has its origin at the coast. Although you can manage perfectly well without knowing any Swahili, the following words and phrases will be useful. Swahili Grammars are available in East African bookshops.

Hello	Jambo	Beer	Beer or Tembo
How are you?	Habari		(lit: elephant) in Kenya
Goodbye	Kwaheri	Argument, problem	Shauri
Please	Tafadhali	Hot	Moto
Thank you	Asante	Cold	Baridi
Thank you very much	Asante sana	One	Moja
		Two	Mbili
Today	Leo	Three	Tatu
Tomorrow	Kesho	Four	Ine
Lion	Simba	Five	Tano
Quickly	Upesi	Six	Sita
Slowly	Polepole	Seven	Saba
Food	Chakula	Eight	Nane
Tea	Chai	Nine	Tisa
Coffee	Kahawa	Ten	Kumi

Where is the nearest garage?	Wapi garage karibu zaidi?
Is the road ahead passable?	Naweza pita njia mbele?
Where is the nearest police station?	Wapi stesheni polisi karibu?
Where is the nearest telephone?	Wapi simu karibu?
Where does this road lead to?	Njia hii inakwenda wapi?
Do you know anyone who speaks English?	Unajua mtu anayesema kiingereza?
I want a room for one night with a bath	Nataka nyumba na bafu pamoja kwa siku moja
What time is it?	Saa ngapi?
Where is the nearest doctor?	Wapi dakitari karibu?
Where is the nearest hospital?	Wapi hospitali karibu?

Where is the German/French/ Danish/English/Swedish/ American Consulate?	Wapi Consul ya Gerumani/ Faranza/Denmark/Ingereza/ Sueden/Marekani?
Please direct me to a good hotel	Wapi hoteli mzuri?
How much?	Pesa ngapi?
What time will food be ready?	Chakula tayari saa ngapi?
I want a cold beer	Nataka tembo baridi.

Pronunciation is important but easy. Every letter must be sounded. The consonant 'G' is always hard like the G in 'got'; 'CH' and 'SH' have the same sounds as in English. There are no diphthongs; vowels are pronounced as shown below.

a is like the a	in 'father'
e is like the a	in 'say'
i is like the e	in 'be'
o is like the o	in 'hoe'
u is like the oo	in 'too'

Lavatories

Public lavatories are very few even in cities. In classified hotels they are usually of the European kind with seats, and reasonably clean. Elsewhere they may be of the 'squat john' variety and smelly.

Maps

The most easily available and accurate road maps are the 'Road Map of Kenya' produced by BP and approved by the AA Kenya, usually priced at around Shs 42/-; and the 'Shell Map of Tanzania', if available. The official map of Kenya is the 'Survey of Kenya'. Nissan and D. T. Dobie, the car company, sponsor a series of 12 'Game Park Maps' obtainable free from any D. T. Dobie/Datsun dealer. The main office is in Koinange Street, Nairobi. The best map of Nairobi is the 'A to Z' pocket street atlas published by Kenway Publications. A good city map of Dar es Salaam can be had free from the Tanzania Tourist Corporation.

Photography

The sunlight is intense and you should allow a faster exposure than you would in Europe. The DIN, ASA and Weston meter settings recommended by film manufacturers are now for the minimum exposure, not the average, and so are just about right for East African conditions. However, where there is a lot of refracted light, as on the dazzling white sands of the coast or some of the open plains, you will need a still shorter exposure. A lens hood is invaluable, while an ultraviolet filter cuts down the effects of glare. It is advisable to buy film before you arrive as it is expensive locally.

Allow yourself two rolls of film a day while on safari, including fast film for dawn and dusk game runs.

Photographing game you are obviously unlikely to get close enough to take a meter reading off the animal itself, which will need a greater exposure than the landscape it is in. A good way to check is by taking a reading off a dull-coloured piece of clothing, remembering to take a reading in shade if the animal you are about to photograph is lying in the shade. When using a telephoto lens, especially one you have not used before, it is wise to open the aperture an extra half stop.

Photographing Africans, whose dark skins reflect very little light, you need to open the aperture by at least one stop (eg f8 to f5.6). Or of course you can halve the shutter speed (eg from 1/250th down to 1/125th sec).

Finally, be careful how you use a camera (see under Etiquette above). Never, in any circumstances, photograph government buildings, military camps and vehicles, or airports. Kenya is otherwise liberal towards photographers. In Tanzania, however, it is unwise to use a camera anywhere outside the game parks. The author of this book was arrested while revising it.

Posts, Telegraphs and Telephone

There are no house-to-house deliveries of mail, so all postal addresses are Post Office box numbers. In Kenya and Tanzania internal letters cost Shs 1/-. Overseas airletter forms cost Shs 3/-. Airmail letters cost Shs 5/- for every 10 grammes weight to Europe and Shs 7/- to America. Postcards cost Shs 3/50 airmail to Europe and Shs 5/- to America.

A local telephone call costs Shs 1/-. Trunk call charges vary with distance. Subscriber trunk dialling has been introduced between the major East African cities and towns but is overloaded, and there is a shortage of public call boxes. This said, the service is vastly better than in most of Africa. Some of the STD codes are:

Arusha 057, Dar es Salaam 051, Diani Beach 01261, Malindi 0123, Mombasa 011, Nairobi 02, Nanyuki 0176, Nyeri 0171.

From some areas you can dial international calls direct. The international access code is 000 or 001. Thus for Britain you dial 000-44 followed by the exchange and number. For North America you dial 000-1 followed by the area code and number. The Kenya telephone directory has a table of international codes and charges. Alternatively international calls can be booked in Kenya by dialling 0196. The minimum charge is Shs 174/- for Great Britain for 3 minutes plus

Shs 58/- for each additional minute. For the United States and Canada the charge is Shs 175/- for a minimum of three minutes plus Shs 58/- for each additional minute. For personal calls there is also an extra charge of Shs 116/- added. Cheap rate is between 2200 and 1000.

Public Holidays

Kenyan public holidays, when banks, shops and government offices close, are Christmas Day, Boxing Day, New Year's Day, Good Friday, Easter Monday, Labour Day (May 1), Madaraka Day (June 1 or the following day if June 1 falls on a Sunday), Kenyatta Day (October 20), Jamhuri (Independence) Day (December 12). Additionally the Moslem holidays of Idd-ul-Fitr and Idd-ul-Haj are observed by all people of the Islamic Faith. (See Tanzania below.)

In Tanzania official public holidays, when government offices, banks and shops close, are Christmas Day, Zanzibar Revolution Day (January 12), CCM Day (February 5) Good Friday, Easter Monday, International Workers Day (May 1), Union Day (April 26), Maulid Day (mid-June), Farmers Day (July 7), Independence and Republic Day (December 9), Idd-ul-Fitr, Idd-ul-Haj. These last two are Moslem religious festivals and the actual dates vary from year to year.

Security

Cities pose obvious dangers of theft. Do not carry large amounts of cash or valuables with you, especially not wallets in hip pockets. No matter where you are, do not leave money or travellers cheques in hotel rooms or in vehicles: indeed never leave anything of value in a vehicle, even out in the bush. Do not walk alone along deserted parts of the beach carrying valuables, whether cameras or rings or watches, and be careful in city streets at night. Beach and camping site thefts are commonplace and visitors should be wary.

Shopping

Shopping in Kenya and Tanzania can broadly be divided into three kinds: first there are the European type products you need on safari, like film and suncream; secondly souvenirs; and thirdly artefacts which are works of art, as opposed to mass produced souvenirs.

In the first category, toiletries, medicines, camera film and clothing are all easily available in Kenyan tourist centres and cities, though they are expensive by comparison to Europe or the USA. In Tanzania they are in very short supply. In either case, it is advisable to stock up before you come out, with the one exception that safari clothing is not expensive in Kenya and it is much easier to buy suitable bush jackets, hats and boots there than abroad. The Bata Shoe Company manufactures suede ankle boots and shoes which are hard wearing, comfortable and cheap at around Shs 350/- a pair. There are Bata stockists all over Kenya. It is also easy to get wildlife reference books.

Mass production sounds an odd word to apply to African souvenirs. However the handcarved stools, figurines, heads, animals, flywhisks, boxes, woven baskets, decorated gourds, copper bracelets and 'primitive' paintings which you see everywhere are turned out in huge quantities, albeit handmade because labour is cheaper in Africa than machinery. Among the best buys are baskets, ebony salad spoons, Arab inlaid boxes and the work of the Makonde carvers of Tanzania. Items not specifically made for tourists – like the baskets – include various kinds of cloth. There are Indian saris, African *kangas* (gaily printed lengths of cotton which make up well into summer dresses) and African *kikois* (a length of usually plain coloured cloth worn by men at the coast as a loincloth, but which can equally be made up). Both *kangas* and *kikois* are softer if they have been washed and cleaned; used ones can cost more than new ones. *Kikois* have a fringe which it is usual to tie into knotted strands. Always bargain over prices.

The third category of artefacts include the finer, individual, work of Makonde carvers, old African masks (if genuine), Ethiopian silver, old brass-bound and decorated chests, batiks by known African artists, soapstone ornaments and meerschaum pipes. The soapstone from Kisii in Kenya furnishes both articles of considerable vulgarity and some fine work. Semi-precious stones are mined in both countries. Tanzanite is a sapphire-like blue stone. Tsavorite is a green garnet. Rubies are mined in Kenya and diamonds in Tanzania. Aquamarines, tourmalines, amethysts, and sapphires are available. But prices are seldom low. The names of jewellers and of shops specialising in African handcrafts are given in the text under the appropriate towns.

Shopping hours in Kenya are from 0830 to 1230 and 1400 to 1700 Mondays to Fridays and 0830 to 1230 on Saturdays. Officially shops are closed on Saturday afternoons and Sundays, but in practice many stay open part of the weekend in Nairobi. There are shops selling film, curios, books and basic toiletries at most game lodges.

In Tanzania shopping hours are from 0730 to 1230 and 1400 to 1700 on weekdays.

Sport

Golf, tennis, fishing, climbing, polo, racing, football and cricket are all widely available in Kenya. The skin-diving at the coast, called goggling locally, and the scuba-diving are superb, and there is surfing, water-skiing, sailing and big game fishing.

Time

Local time in Kenya and Tanzania is three hours ahead of GMT. Thus in the European winter when it is midday (1200) in Kenya it will be 0900 in Britain and, allowing for the exact date of change to summer time, 1000 in Europe. In summer, when BST is in force, it will be 1000 in Britain and 1100 in Europe when it is midday in Kenya. In New York the time will be 0100 when it is midday in Kenya.

Weights and Measures

Kenya and Tanzania have converted to the metric system.

Safaris

The glamorous international image of the safari was originally created back in the days before the 1914-18 war when legendary hunters like Karamoja Bell and F. C. Selous roamed the plains after elephant, lion and the other three of the 'Big Five': leopard, buffalo and rhino. The great American sporting connection with East Africa began when President Theodore Roosevelt spent three months in Kenya in 1911, after his term of office. His famous safari set off from Nairobi's Norfolk Hotel with 100 African porters, all in blue sweaters, carrying everything needed in the bush from gifts to ammunition. A complete entourage of professional hunters went with him. This sporting tradition, which inspired Hemingway's 'Green Hills of Africa' and many other novels, was carried on by hunters as diverse as Bill Ryan, who shot his first lion when he was 11, and Eric Rundgren — who once fought off and killed a leopard with his bare hands. Clients came from America and Europe for the modern equivalent of Roosevelt's safari: much shorter in time, with hunting cars and trucks instead of porters, and with sprung mattresses, refrigerators and two-way radio in the camps set up for them in the bush.

Today public awareness of the need for game conservation has greatly reduced the scope for hunting, which is banned in Kenya, though permitted in some areas of Tanzania. Restricted bird shooting is allowed in Kenya.

None the less the tradition of the field safari not only dies hard, it has been given a boost by the film 'Out of Africa' and there is a strong demand for photographic safaris in the old style. A number of former professional hunters have originated specialist safaris, for example for bird watching, with camels and on horseback. It remains true that only by pitching camp in the wild can you get the proper feel of Africa and only with patience and the aid of skilled African trackers can you learn how it feels to follow game on foot. To walk for a week through the bush, as the author has done, is to find a very different world from the minibus game viewing of the national parks: and his was a very short safari. The real minimum is 14 days.

However, the vast majority of people who go 'on safari' will do so on a tour of game lodges in the national parks, so we will deal with these lodge safaris first.

Safaris

Lodge Safaris
In both Kenya and Tanzania there are a series of well-established tourist circuits, with overnight stops in permanent game lodges or hotels, which are offered by travel agents and tour operators in every form from a one-day trip out of Nairobi to a full 14-day tour. In Kenya the best known are west to the Masai Mara Reserve; north west to Lake Naivasha, Lake Nakuru and Lake Baringo; north to the 'tree hotels' like Treetops and the Ark, the Mount Kenya Safari Club and the Samburu National Reserve, possibly taking in the Meru National Park as well; south to the Amboseli National Park and the Tsavo National Park. A more adventurous journey would take you to Lake Turkana in the far north. These circuits are criss-crossed and interlinked in many ways: for example by flying safaris from the coast hotels to the Mara. They are the mainstay of Kenya's tourism and arrangement of this book is based on them, although we also cover a great many out-of-the-way places. Similarly Tanzania has its famous northern circuit based on Arusha and taking in Lake Manyara, the Ngorongoro Crater and the great Serengeti National Park or sometimes only covering part of this huge area.

The remainder of this chapter on Safaris is devoted to the more off-beat and expensive kind of individually tailored safari, setting up camp according to the client's wishes and with private staff and vehicles.

Bird Shooting Safaris
The bird shooting season in Kenya is from June 1 to the end of October. The species which may be shot include duck, francolin, geese, grouse, guineafowl, pigeons, sandgrouse and spurfowl. But this is only allowed in certain designated controlled areas. A visitor's bird shooting licence costs around Shs 3,000/- and the controlled area fees are Shs 300/- per area. One safari company which organises bird shooting is Ker and Downey Safaris Ltd. (PO Box 41822, Nairobi; telephone 556466; telex KULIA 22959).

Bird shooting in Tanzania can be arranged by the companies mentioned below.

Hunting
As mentioned above, no hunting is allowed in Kenya. In Tanzania it is under the control of the Tanzania Wildlife Corporation in Arusha, contactable through any branch of the Tanzania Tourist Corporation, which licenses a number of private hunting firms to operate. The main hunting areas are in the centre and west of the country, ranging from open savannah to forest and swamp. As well as a variety of plains game, Tanzania is known for its very large buffalo, large leopard, good maned lion, kudu, oryx and sable antelope. Trophies can be prepared and shipped from Arusha.

However Tanzania is an expensive country to operate in. Clients on a hunting safari, which is likely to spend a minimum of fourteen days in the field, will pay from US$800 to US$1,100 per person per day, excluding air fares and hunting licences. The average costs of licences (payable to the Wildlife Corporation) will be US$5,000. The companies operating hunting safaris include Tanzania Gametracker Safaris Ltd (Private Bag, Arusha; telephone 057-6986). This firm is American owned and safaris can be booked from its office at 7701 Wilshire Place Drive, Suite 504, Houston, Texas 77040; telephone 713-744-3527. Or through PO Box 24988, Nairobi, Kenya; telephone 882826. Two other American companies operating in conjunction with the Wildlife Corporation are Safari Outfitters Inc (85 Michigan Avenue, Chicago, Illinois 60603; telephone 312-346-9631) and International Big Game Safaris (100 South Waverly Road, Holland, Michigan 49423; telephone 616-392-6458).

Photographic and Specialist Safaris

The most renowned firm operating in Kenya is Ker and Downey Safaris Ltd (PO Box 41822, Nairobi; telephone 556466). One of the region's professional hunting firms for many decades, they turned to full-scale photographic field safaris after hunting was banned in Kenya, though they can still arrange hunting in other countries. Robin Hurt Safaris Ltd (PO Box 24988, Nairobi; telephone 882826; telex 25583 ROBINHURT) does luxury tented safaris. Abercrombie and Kent Ltd (Box 59749, Nairobi; telephone 334955) combines camping safaris with occasional nights in lodges and operates in a number of other African countries, including Tanzania (PO Box 427, Arusha, Tanzania; telephone Arusha 7803). Among a number of smaller firms one of the best is Robert Lowis' Trans African Guides (PO Box 49538, Nairobi; telephone 891172) which specialises in birdwatching safaris. All these firms have been personally recommended to us by former clients. They all provide complete camp staff, tentage, vehicles and such useful luxuries as hot showers in the evenings. Prices vary. Robert Lowis charges US$12,000 for four people for the first ten days and $1,000 per day thereafter. This is less than Ker and Downey or Robin Hurt, though more expensive than Abercrombie and Kent's 14-day *Kenya under Canvas* at US$2,495 per person double occupancy for 14 days in a larger group. It all depends on the degree of luxury you want in the bush. At the other end of the scale Kimbla (K) Ltd (PO Box 40089, Nairobi; telephone 337695) offers individual camping safaris at from only US$40 to US$300 per person per day. Finally, the African Wildlife Foundation arranges special safaris for those interested in conservation, notably camping in the Serengeti. Its addresses are PO Box 48177, Nairobi, and 1717 Massachusetts Avenue NW, Washington, DC 20036, USA.

Camel and Riding Safaris

Julian McKeand, a former game warden with unrivalled knowledge of the Samburu country organises six-day camel safaris there

Safaris

(described in more detail in the Northern Kenya chapter). They start from a private ranch near Mount Kenya and can be booked through Flamingo Travel Ltd (PO Box 45070, Nairobi; telephone 27927). The six days cost Shs 6,000/- plus Shs 300/- for transport to the ranch. Riding safaris in the Rift Valley and elsewhere have been developed over the past fourteen years by Safaris Unlimited Africa Ltd (PO Box 20138, Nairobi; telephone 332132) whose rates for individually arranged camping safaris are around US$295 per day for each of four people. Riding safaris to the Aberdare Mountains, Mount Kenya and the Northern Frontier are organised by Jane and Mike Prettejohn from their Sangare Ranch at Mweiga. (PO Box 24, Mweiga; telephone 20) using zebroids as pack animals. The zebroid is a cross between a zebra and a horse. Prices range from US$135 per day for each of six people. Curiously, it is possible to get much closer to game on horseback than it is on foot.

Fishing Safaris
Fishing safaris can be arranged by Ker and Downey Ltd (see above) and the other firms. Kenya offers four main types of fishing: for trout in the upland streams; for black bass at Lake Naivasha; for Nile perch and tiger fish at Lake Turkana in the north; and big game fishing at the coast, described further in the chapter on Kenya's Coast. Good quality dry flies are tied and sold in Nairobi.

Private Ranches
Recently several private ranches and farms have been equipped to accept guests on an individual basis. One of the best is run by Galana Game and Ranching Safaris, which has a private lodge on its 1½ million acre- (this is not a misprint, 1½ million acre-) ranch on the Galana River between the Tsavo East National Park and Malindi. It is further described in the Southern Kenya chapter. Bookings can be made either through Box 76 Malindi (telephone 20394) or through the Pan African Travel Organisation (PO Box 44209, Nairobi; telephone 333281). Galana prices are US$250 per night for two people, including transport from Malindi.

Up-country, near Mount Kenya, is the 6,500-acre Sangare Ranch at Mweiga (PO Box 24, Mweiga; telephone Mweiga 20) with a private lodge by a lake accommodating four people. The charge per night is Shs 950/- per person. Both Galana and Sangare have considerable quantities of game. Both can be booked in Britain through Safari Consultants Ltd, 83 Gloucester Place, London W1H 3PG; telephone 01-935-8996; telex 264690 SAFARI G.

Stays at other private ranches can be arranged through Abercrombie and Kent (PO Box 59749, Nairobi; telephone 334955 or Sloane Square House, Holbein Place, London SW1; telephone 01-730-9600). In Tanzania they act for the very pleasant Gibbs Farm near Lake Manyara (see the Lake Manyara chapter).

There are further details of safari operations in Tanzania at the start of the Northern Tanzania chapter. In general there are fewer options in Tanzania than in Kenya and prices tend to be higher, though the game viewing is unsurpassed. An increasing number of safaris are now being split between Kenya and Northern Tanzania, with clients spending a week or ten days in each country.

Air Rescue
Most safari firms will recommend that if you are camping in the wild you should take out a policy with either Africa Air Rescue (K) Ltd (PO Box 41766 Nairobi; telephone 337766) or the famous Flying Doctor Service (PO Box 30125, Nairobi; telephone 501301). As already mentioned in the General Information section the latter charges only £5 or US$8.00 per month. Both will send medically equipped rescue aircraft to any part of Kenya or Tanzania in emergency. Many safari firms provide this cover for their clients automatically.

Driving yourself
There is advice on car hire in the country chapters. Many visitors now hire vehicles to drive themselves around the National Parks. See also under Car Hire and Driving in the General Information chapter.

Treetops — the hotel in a tree

Kenya

The Country	36
Hotels and Game Lodges	39
National Parks and Reserves	41
Transport and Tours	43
Do-it-yourself Safaris and Camps	49
Nairobi	50
The Great Rift Valley: Lakes Naivasha and Nakuru	60
Lakes Bogoria and Baringo	73
The Masai Mara	76
Western Kenya	83
Nyeri and the Aberdares	88
Mount Kenya, Meru and Embu, Isiolo	93
Northern Kenya: Maralal, the Samburu	99
Northern Kenya: Marsabit, Lake Turkana	103
Eastern Kenya and the Tana River	106
Southern Kenya: Masailand, Amboseli, Tsavo	108
The Coast	120
Mombasa	122
The Coast North of Mombasa	129
The Coast South of Mombasa	146

The Country

Kenya is a land of kaleidoscopic contrasts. Most visitor's first impressions are of the modern semi-skyscrapers of Nairobi, the sweeping Athi plains outside the city, and game straying among the thorn bushes of the Nairobi National Park. Going up-country, you will see the splendour of the Rift Valley, or pass coffee farms on the way towards the thick rain forests of the Aberdares, perhaps glimpsing the snow on the deceptively unimpressive peaks of Mount Kenya. These mountain forests harbour elephant, rhino, buffalo and that elusive antelope, the bongo. Beyond Mount Kenya lie the vast semi-deserts of the north, the magnificent Samburu and Turkana peoples and the 'jade sea' of Lake Turkana. The 'up country' landscapes are one of the great attractions of Kenya. The other is the coast, with its perfect white coral beaches, Arab traditions and resort hotels. It is not surprising that Kenya fires the imagination of everyone who goes there and that since Independence in 1963 it has become internationally recognised as one of the most magnificent and exciting holiday areas anywhere.

Geographically the country covers 582,647 sq kilometres (225,000 sq miles) and lies across the Equator. Its Indian Ocean coastline is 608 kilometres (380 miles) long, while its centre is cut by the Great Rift Valley, running north to south and containing a variety of lakes. The largest river is the Tana, which flows in a wide curve eastwards from the slopes of Mount Kenya (17,058 ft) to the Indian Ocean. The climate is described in the General Information section.

Historically more has been discovered about Kenya in the years since Independence than ever before. The earliest inhabitants left no written records and Independence has generated keen interest in the country's heritage. Recent investigations by Richard Leakey, Director of the Nairobi Museum, and others have revealed fossilised remains of hominids at Koobi Fora on the eastern shore of Lake Turkana which are approximately 3 million years old: these bones of early men are so old that they suggest Kenya was the cradle of mankind. There are also a variety of hand-axe, or Acheulean sites dating from 1.4 million years ago to 150,000 years ago, which show the continuity of human descent in this part of Africa.

However, the present African population owes its origin to far more recent migrations: of Cushites from the north some 9,000 years back whose descendants are still nomadic; of Bantu from the west 1,000 years ago; and of Nilotics from what is now the Sudan, some 400 years ago. The earlier inhabitants survive in only three tiny groups: the Ndorobo of the forests, the Boni and the Sanye.

The ancient Greeks called the coast 'Azania', the 'dry country' and Ptolemy, the great Egyptian geographer, marked Mombasa on his maps as Tonike around AD 160. More than a thousand years ago Arab traders and conquerors from Oman sailed south in their dhows, bringing Islamic religion and its culture, which are still predominant today despite the later influence of Chinese, Portuguese and British explorers, traders and colonists. All down the coast lie the mouldering remains of the Arab Sultanates established here from about 900 AD onwards. Suprisingly their tenure only officially ended on Kenya's and Zanzibar's Independence, when the Sultan of Zanzibar, subsequently deposed, surrendered his legal right to the 16 kilometre (10 miles) wide 'coastal strip'. The British had recognised this claim throughout their rule of the two countries. The Arab colonisers exported ivory, Ethiopian gold, leopard skins and rhino horn from the interior, and also slaves, a practice that has left its mark on Arab-African relationships today, even though the slave trade was put down by the British in the 1870s. However, Arab culture has also imparted a well-mannered, unhurried aura to the coastal way of life. Indeed Arab intermarriage with the Giriama, Bajun and other African coastal tribes produced the Swahili people and their language, which has spread to become the lingua franca of all eastern Africa. Links with Arabia are still maintained by the dhow fleets that ply down to Mombasa and Dar es Salaam on the north east monsoon, the Kaskasi, in January; and return to the Arabian Gulf and India in May on the south east monsoon, the Kuzi.

Today Kenya is home to Arabs, Asians and Europeans as well as more than 48 main African tribes. Overall, the African population is increasing at around 4% a year. At the last census in 1985 it was 20.3 million and half the people were under fifteen years old: wherever you go in Kenya you will see schoolchildren. Some tribes, like the Masai, are famous as warriors. Others, like the El Molo up at Lake Turkana or the Waliangulu elephant hunters near Tsavo Park, are few in number, shy and still backward. The largest are the Kikuyu, whose homelands lie between Nairobi and Nyeri, followed by the Luya of the Kisumu area on Lake Victoria and the Kamba centred on Machakos and Kitui. President Daniel arap Moi comes from the small Kalenjin tribe of western Kenya. A century ago there was great rivalry between the tribes, but today everything is concentrated on collaboration and Kenya's motto is Harambee, which means 'Let's pull together'.

Nonetheless traditional dances and costumes are cherished as part of the country's cultural heritage. Their innate vitality always improsses, and the Chuka drummers, for instance, have drawn crowds to overseas performances in London and elsewhere. Broadly-speaking, there are two ways of getting to see traditional dancing. First if there is a celebration on, such as Independence Day (December 12), there are likely to be public performances. Secondly, if you are on tour, you may find an exhibition arranged

37

at some point, for instance at Bomas of Kenya in Langata outside Nairobi or Mayer's Ranch near Kijabe in the Rift Valley. Many hotels have performances — indeed the fierce dancer wielding a spear may be the same man who earlier carried your suitcase to your room! One word of warning here. If you happen accidentally upon a local *ngoma,* which is Swahili for a dance or celebration, make sure to ask if you may stay and watch, especially before taking photographs. These are private affairs.

Equally, if you want to see a representative selection of traditional huts, implements and crafts you should visit the Bomas of Kenya.

When the British colonised and developed Kenya they introduced both Asian and European minorities. The Asians came mostly to work on the railway, then branched into trade. Since Independence many have left and there are now about 80,000 of them, mainly in the cities, and you will notice their mosques, temples and bazaars, the Sikhs' turbans, and the women's brightly coloured saris.

The European settlers have progressively been replaced by African farmers. However, their influence remains evident both socially and in business, reinforced by a large influx of businessmen and officials from many international agencies. The European population is about 20,000 and many are Kenya citizens. Down at the coast there is a sizeable Arab community.

Independence day was on December 12, 1963, and a year later Kenya became a Republic in the Commonwealth, under the Presidency of Mzee Jomo Kenyatta *(Mzee* is an honorific title, roughly translatable as 'wise old man'). He died in 1978 and his successor is the Hon. Daniel arap Moi. The National Assembly sits in Nairobi. Administratively Kenya is divided into seven provinces — The Coast, Rift Valley, Central, Nyanza, Western, Eastern and North Eastern.

A glance at the map shows that Nairobi is at the centre of a spider's web of communications, with roads that have been enormously improved in recent years. To the west and north west, road and rail lead to the Rift Valley, Lakes Naivasha and Nakuru, then over the Mau Summit to Kisumu and Lake Victoria. Branching from the main road is one to Narok and the Masai Mara Game Reserve. North, both road and rail run along the eastern side of the Aberdare Mountains to Nyeri and Nanyuki, passing the vast bulk of Mount Kenya. The railway stops at Nanyuki, but the road goes on to descend the dramatic escarpment to Isiolo and the vast semi-desert of the North Eastern Province — the Northern Frontier District of former days — with the 'jade sea' of Lake Turkana. South east, road and rail march side by side to Mombasa and the coast via the Tsavo Park, while directly south is the road through Kajiado and Masailand to Arusha in Tanzania. For convenience we will divide Kenya into the areas to which these major routes lead, but dealing first with the national parks and game reserves and the capital city itself.

Hotels and Game Lodges

In recent years Kenya's tourist facilities have been enormously improved, both in the number and quality of hotels and in the roads that serve them. The coast, especially around Mombasa and Diani Beach, has seen great expansion and the demand for accommodation in or near the national parks has led to a number of first-class tented camps being established. At the other end of the scale, there is a good chain of youth hostels which charge only Shs 140/- a night and a large number of cheap, basic hotels, which cater equally for less well-off African travellers and overseas visitors. Thus the range of facilities is now far wider than it was ten years ago, and we only mention establishments in the text which can be recommended relative to their status.

There is a classification system for hotels, lodges and camps, originally introduced by the Kenya Association of Hotelkeepers and Caterers (PO Box 46406, Nairobi) and revised in 1987 in collaboration with the Ministry of Tourism and Wildlife. We give this 'star' grading in brackets after each hotel we name, although it is still little known locally. Broadly speaking Five Star equates to an international standard, Four Star to 'clean and good', Three Star to 'acceptable' and Two Stars to a basic standard that a Western visitor would tolerate when staying from choice as opposed to necessity.

The official listings do not include prices and we have compiled an approximate price guide for this book. These prices are not official. They are based on the 1988 high season and include the accommodation tax of 17.5 per cent. Expect a ten per cent price rise each year. The high season is January to March and the low season April to mid-July, with 'shoulder' months in between. In the low season many coast hotels offer discounts.

Hotels	**Town and Business**	
5 Star	Double, room only	Shs 1,500/- to Shs 2,000/-
(Class A)	Single, room only	Shs 1,100/- to Shs 1,700/-
4 Star	Double, with breakfast	Shs 1,000/- to Shs 1,500/-
(Class B)	Single, with breakfast	Shs 500/- to Shs 800/-
3 Star	Double, with breakfast	Shs 500/- to Shs 750/-
(Class C)	Single, with breakfast	Shs 300/- to Shs 500/-
2 Star	Double, with breakfast	Shs 425/- to Shs 600/-
(Class D)	Single, with breakfast	Shs 265/- to Shs 365/-

Kenya

1 Star Cheap hotels, only mentioned when there is no other hotel in town.

Hotels	Vacation	
5 Star	Double, full board	Shs 2,000/- to Shs 3,000/-
(Class A)	Single, full board	Shs 900/- to Shs 2,000/-
4 Star	Double, full board	Shs 1,500/- to Shs 2,000/-
(Class B)	Single, full board	Shs 1,000/- to Shs 1,800/-
3 Star	Double, full board	Shs 760/- to Shs 1,300/-
(Class C)	Single, full board	Shs 500/- to Shs 800/-
2 Star	Double, full board	Shs 600/- to Shs 1,000/-
(Class D)	Single, full board	Shs 350/- to Shs 600/-
1 Star	Double, full board	around Shs 500/-
(Class E)	Single, full board	around Shs 350/-

Most of the coastal hotels are basically package tour hotels. Many only quote prices on application. Bed and breakfast or half board terms are not always available.

Lodges

5 Star	Double, full board	Shs 2,000/- to Shs 3,000/-
(Class A)	Single, full board	Shs 1,100/- to Shs 2,000/-
3 Star	Double, full board	Shs 1,500/- to Shs 2,500/-
(Class B)	Single, full board	Shs 1,000/- to Shs 1,500/-
1 Star	Double, full board	Shs 1,500/- to Shs 2,000/-
(Class C)	Single, full board	around Shs 900/-

Note that lodge (and tented camp) prices may seem high compared to their grading, but they are invariably in remote places where the costs of supplies and administration are high. Lodges which are called 'clubs' by their owners are not always granted a classification, even though visitors can be freely booked in by travel agents. Tented camps are not given star ratings.

Tented Camps

Class A	Double, full board	Shs 2,000/- to Shs 3,000/-
	Single, full board	Shs 1,500/- to Shs 2,500/-
Class B	Prices are little less than for Class A	

General Advice
In Kenyan hotels the standard check out time is 1000. Double rooms are normally twin-bedded, and triple rooms are generally available. You should note that while hotels offer broadly international standards, accommodation in the wild is of necessity different. Lodges and camps are usually sited so as not to interfere with the natural surroundings, using local stone and timber. Rooms tend to be small and simply furnished, though comfortable, with private toilet facilities. Tented camps normally provide full-sized beds in insect-proofed tents, often with private showers and lavatories. The forest lodges, often called 'tree hotels', are effectively luxury game lookouts, operated in conjunction with base hotels; thus Treetops in the Aberdares works in conjuction with the Outspan Hotel in Nyeri. Rooms in the tree hotels are very small and you should only take a small overnight bag with you. Self-help lodges usually have basic furnishings and a stove, but you have to bring your own food and there in no service. They are mainly used by local residents and cost around Shs 170/- per person per night.

Lodges and camps — except the self-help ones — have restaurant and bar facilities, normally with a set menu. The larger ones have swimming pools. There is seldom any organised entertainment apart from game drives, which on average cost Shs 1,155/- for a vehicle for a morning or afternoon. Remember that you are out in the wild and it is dangerous to wander away from the lodge unescorted.

National Parks and Reserves

These are the two kinds of area in which game is protected and facilities are maintained for visitors to see and enjoy it. There are over 40 of them, large and small. All have roads and most have airstrips and are open throughout the year, except for the mountain parks, which may be inaccessible in wet weather. Entrance fees are Shs 80/- per person and Shs 50/- per car or light aircraft except where otherwise stated. Season tickets are available to Kenya residents. The gates are open approximately from dawn to dusk and regulations include a ban on travel at night — you must then be either out of the park or at a game lodge. You can only move about by vehicle and the speed limit is 20 mph, which is commonsense because you see nothing if you hurry, while roads are deliberately kept rough to slow down traffic. Nor may you leave the vehicle except at clearly indicated places, again commonsense because big game, though often used to cars, is still dangerous. Indeed, animals are less shy of cars than of human beings.

In some areas, such as the Masai Mara, you are allowed to leave the Park roads and drive cross-country, but it is not advisable to do so without four-wheel drive. There are some other unwritten rules which it makes sense to observe. If photographing elephant, buffalo or rhino make sure you are in a position to drive away fast if the animal charges. If you have a serious breakdown stay in the vehicle until someone comes past. Don't switch off the engine the moment you stop as it frightens some animals. Don't talk loudly when game watching as that does the same. Remember the best times of day for game viewing are at dawn and in the late afternoon/early evening.

There are no restrictions on photography, but professional work requires a licence. High speed film is essential on dawn game runs. See also the advice on photography in the General Information chapter.

The parks are run by the Wildlife Conservation and Management Department of the Ministry of Tourism and Wildlife. The Department's HQ is on the Langata Road, near the entrance to the Nairobi National Park (Box 40241 Nairobi; telephone 501081). Each park has wardens and a staff of rangers. These rangers wear green uniforms and sometimes a Foreign Legion type of hat. National reserves are run by local authorities on similar lines with game scouts, though (unlike the national parks) the indigenous tribes continue to live in them. Forest reserves are simply areas of planned afforestation.

Although the game lodges all have special booking agents, listed as they occur in the text, any travel agent can make your reservations. Camping is allowed at designated sites in most parks.

The increasing awareness of the need to protect special habitats and flora as well as fauna — not to mention tropical fish and coral — has led to the establishment of many new parks. A complete list is in the index, and all are mentioned in the text. Among the best known are:

Amboseli National Park
380 sq kilometres (147 sq miles) of swamps and plains country inside a 3,260 sq kilometres reserve, dominated by the snowcapped peak of Kilimanjaro. About 3,500 ft above sea level.

Masai Mara Game Reserve
1,813 sq kilometres (700 sq miles) round the Mara River in SW Kenya. Mostly 5,000 ft up. One of the best parts of Kenya in which to see plains game.

Meru National Park
Some 60 miles NE of Mount Kenya, 1,000 to 3,400 ft up, 870 sq kilometres (336 sq miles). Noted for Grevy's zebra and reticulated giraffe.

Mount Kenya National Park

717 sq kilometres (277 sq miles) round the upper slopes of snow-topped Mount Kenya, starting at 11,000 ft. Big game in the forests. Climbers' huts for mountaineers.

Nairobi National Park

Unique in being only five miles from the city centre. 114 sq kilometres (44 sq miles). Lions are the speciality. Open all year round.

Lake Nakuru National Park

A bird sanctury on Lake Nakuru, 100 miles from Nairobi in the Rift Valley. Thousands of flamingoes make the water seem pink from a distance. Altitude 5,765 ft.

Samburu National Reserve

Near Isiolo in the north, 3,000 ft above sea level and therefore hot. Only 101 sq kilometres (39 sq miles) of fairly dense bush but wildlife congregates at the river, where the main lodge is.

Tsavo National Park

20,780 sq kilometres (8,024 sq miles) of bush and occasional hills on the plains east of Kilimanjaro. Mostly 2,000-4,000 ft up. Divided into two sections, East and West, by the Nairobi-Mombasa road. Noted for great herds of elephants.

Game Conservation and Poachers

Finally, a word about poaching. The value of ivory and the Oriental belief that powdered rhino horn is an aphrodisiac, not to mention Western furriers' demands for leopard and other skins, result in the game wardens fighting a constant battle to safeguard Kenya's wildlife from poaching by traps, poisoned arrows and other means. Indeed the rhino is an endangered species decreasingly able to survive outside special fenced sanctuaries. This is why hunting is banned as is the sale of ivory and game trophies. It is illegal to export any game product without a licence — which extends to sea shells and elephant hair bracelets. The East African Wildlife Society (Box 20110, Nairobi) exists to help preserve wildlife and welcomes new members.

Transport and Tours within Kenya

Scheduled Air Services

Kenya Airways runs secluded services daily from Jomo Kenyatta airport, Nairobi, to Kisumu, Malindi and Mombasa. The Nairobi reservations office is in Koinange Street, from which buses go to the airport at 0800, 0900, 1000, 1130, 1245, 1430, 1645, 1830 and 2000. The journey time is 25 minutes. Taxis charge around Shs 175/-from the city centre. Check-in time is 30 minutes before departure. There

43

Kenya

is no departure tax on internal flights and no Customs and Immigration formalities at Jomo Kenyatta airport.

Kenya Airways reservations telephone numbers are as follows: Nairobi 29291, Kisumu 2631, Malindi 20237, Mombasa 21251. The Flight Information numbers are Nairobi 822288 and Mombasa 433400. Airport administration numbers are given in the telephone directory.

Scheduled services are also run by a number of private companies from Wilson airport, ten minutes drive from the city centre on the Langata Road. Check-in time is 30 minutes before departure. The baggage allowance is 15 kilos per passenger. There is no departure tax on internal flights but there are Customs and Immigration formalities which the airline will do for you and which do not normally involve the inspection of either baggage or passport. These are carried out for security reasons. The services from Wilson and their operators are:

Destination	Operator
Amboseli	Air Kenya Aviation Ltd (PO Box 30357, Nairobi; telephone 501421). Daily. Single fare Shs 730/-, return Shs 1,260/-. Flight time 45 minutes.
Eldoret	Air Kenya Aviation, as above. Mon, Tues, Thurs, Fri. Single fare Shs 950/-, return Shs 1,750/-. Flight time 75 minutes.
Kiwaiyu	Air Kenya Aviation. Daily. Single fare Shs 2,000/-, return Shs 3,670/-. Flight time approx. 2½ hours.
Lamu	Air Kenya Aviation, as above. Daily. Single fare Shs 1,700/-, return Shs 3,170/- Equator Airlines (PO Box 43356, Nairobi; telephone 21177). Daily. Fare each way Shs 1,700/-. Flight time 2 hours.
Masai Mara	Air Kenya Aviation Ltd as above. Twice daily. Equator Airlines as above. Twice daily. Executive Air Services Ltd (PO Box 42304, Nairobi; telephone 500607). Twice daily. Note that there are several lodge airstrips in the Mara and the sequence in which they are visited will depend on bookings. Fares on all services single Shs 900/- , return Shs 1,600/-. Children half fare. Flight time 1 hour.

Nyeri/Nanyuki/   Air Kenya Aviation Ltd as above. Daily. The service
Samburu   calls at Nyeri and Nanyuki en route to the Samburu
National Reserve and vice versa. Single fare to
Samburu Shs 1,080/-, return Shs 1,960/-. Sector
fares available. Flight time 1 hour 40 minutes.

Lake Turkana   Air Kenya Aviation Ltd as above. Wed, Fri, Sat. This
service goes to Loiangalani, Lodwar and Kalokol.
Single fare Shs 1,700/-, return Shs 3,170/-. Flight
time 3 hours.

There are a small number of private scheduled services operating
at the coast from Moi International airport, Mombasa and from
Malindi.

Destination	Operator

Lamu from   Cooper Skybird Aircharters (telephone Mombasa
Mombasa   21443, Malindi 20860 and care of Bunson Travel,
Nairobi 21992). Daily. Single fare Shs 800/-, return
Shs 1,600/-.
Equator Airlines (telephones Mombasa 432355,
Malindi 20585, Lamu 3139, Nairobi 21177). Daily.
Fare Shs 660/- each way.

Lamu from   Cooper Skybird Aircharters, as above. Daily. Fares
Malindi   single Shs 550/-, return Shs 1,100/-.
Equator Airlines, as above. Daily. Fare Shs 440/-
each way.
Note that Lamu airfield is on Manda Island and you
have to take a boat across to Lamu Island. Malindi
airport is 10 minutes drive from the town.

Air Charters
Air charter companies include those that run the services listed
above. The principal others at Wilson airport are Africair (PO Box
45646, Nairobi; telephone 501210; telex 23061 BOSKY), which has
a good reputation among local businessmen; CMC Aviation (PO
Box 44580, Nairobi; telephone 501221) and Safari Air Services (PO
Box 41951, Nairobi; telephone 501211). At Mombasa the other
charter company is Sunbird-Air Kenya Aviation Ltd (PO Box 84700,
Mombasa; telephone 433320). As already mentioned, flying can rival
car hire for cost on long journeys and is, of course, immensely
quicker where roads are bad. Charter rates run from Shs 16/- per
mile for a single engine Cessna taking three passengers to Shs 42/-
for a twin engined Cessna 404 carrying 13 passengers. A small group
of five people in a Beech Baron would pay Shs 26/- a mile, or only
Shs 5/20 each. (Flying distances are measured in miles, not kilo-

metres). However, rates are certain to increase with fuel costs. They rose 60 per cent between 1983 and 1987. But so did car hire charges.

Self-fly charters are possible at Wilson airport with three organisations: CMC Aviation, as above, Rent-a-Plane Ltd (PO Box 42730, Nairobi; telephone 501431); and the Aero Club of East Africa (PO Box 40813, Nairobi; telephone 501772), which admits overseas members. CMC Aviation and the Aero Club both give flying training. Pilots must obtain a Kenya conversion to their licences from the Civil Aviation Board. Typical rates are Shs 1,020/- for a Piper Warrior or Shs 1,500/- for a Cessna 182 and Shs 750/- for a Cessna 150.

Rail
Kenya Railways' main routes are from Nairobi to Mombasa, which goes overnight daily in both directions, and Nairobi to Kisumu, continuing to the Kenya/Uganda border at Mombasa, which runs three times a week. Other trains serve Nyeri and Nanyuki. Trains going up-country are slow, because of the hills, but fares are low. The Nairobi to Mombasa service is in a class of its own — partly because there is still a vintage restaurant car, but mainly because it saves you a night in a hotel and is therefore competitive with even the cheap express buses. A first class single compartment, one way, costs Shs 454/- and a two-berth one Shs 340/- per person. Bedding, dinner and breakfast costs Shs 130/- per person.

Buses
The Kenya Bus Company serves the whole country and very cheaply, but buses are liable to be very crowded. The Nairobi bus terminal is on Haile Selassie Avenue. A better alternative is the long distance buses which ply between towns, and on which seats can be booked. G.A. Road Services on Racecourse Road, opposite the Esso petrol station, operate coaches daily from Nairobi to Kisumu, Mombasa, Nanyuki and other towns. They are called 'luxury' coaches, which by local standards they are. The service is reliable and fares low: for example Nairobi to Mombasa single is Shs 110/-. The telephone number is Nairobi 27202.

Matatus
The matatu is the African private enterprise answer to local transport. A matatu is a car chassis with a box body built on it, holding a number of seats and normally jammed full of passengers with luggage on the roof. Matatus ply throughout Kenya, stopping to put down and pick up passengers when asked. Their fares are much the same as on the local buses, but standards of driving are poor and accidents frequent. Short of hitch hiking, however, you cannot travel more cheaply.

Car Hire
Car hire is available in all main towns and from most hotels. Hertz

(Box 42196, Nairobi; telephone 331960), Avis Rent a Car (Box 49795, Nairobi; telephone 336794) and Europcar (Box 49420, Nairobi; telephone 332744) are widely represented and you can leave their cars in Nairobi, Malindi or Mombasa at the end of the trip. However some local firms offer lower rates for similar vehicles notably Let's Go Travel (PO Box 60342, Nairobi; telephone 29539), Wheels Car Hire (Box 47173, Nairobi; telephone 336038) and Concorde Car Hire (Box 25053, Nairobi; telephone 743011). There are wide variations when it comes to hiring a Range Rover, a Toyota Land Cruiser, or one of the smaller 4-wheel drive Suzukis. Typical small car charges are from Shs 1,500/- to Shs 2,000/- a week, plus Shs 3/60 to Shs 4/50 per kilometre, and a collision damage waiver of Shs 100/- to Shs 170/- per day. A medium-size Mazda or Peugeot Saloon would cost Shs 3,000/- to Shs 4,000/-a week, plus Shs 5/60 and a damage waiver. A Range Rover or Isuzu Trooper would be Shs 4,800/- a week, plus Shs 8/- per kilometre, while Hertz hire out Mitsubishi minibuses for safaris at Shs 3,900/- a week plus Shs 7/- per kilometre. See also the paragraph on 'Do it yourself safaris' below. Unless you utilise a major credit card, such as American Express or Diners Club you will have to pay a cash deposit of at least Shs 5,000/-. Drivers must be over 23 years old and under 70. You can use your home driving licence for up to six months in Kenya, provided it has not been endorsed for any offence in the past two years.

The fuel used in Kenya is 'gasohol', a blend of petrol and alcohol, sold in 'regular' and 'super' grades. The latter is roughly equivalent to three-star petrol and should be used in cars. It costs Shs 9/50 a litre at the time of writing. Normal diesel is also sold. Shortages do occur, but not often. There are service stations in all towns and at some lodges, though in remoter areas they can be few and far between. On safari you should carry extra jerricans of fuel, as well as drinking water.

The Automobile Association of Kenya
It is well worth joining the AA of Kenya (PO Box 40087, Nairobi; telephone 720382) if you are staying any length of time. It operates an emergency breakdown service and is the only organisation that can give up-to-date information on road conditions. It sells maps and has its own travel agency and car insurance (with American Life). The AA offices are at the Hurlingham shopping centre, one and a half miles from the city centre on Argwings Kodhek Road near its junction with Valley Road.

Hitch Hiking and Giving Lifts
There are two sides to this. Back packers are becoming more familiar in Kenya and often hitch lifts successfully, though it would be extremely unwise for a girl to try it alone. As a driver, you will frequently be asked for a lift by Africans. Regrettably, petty theft from your car can be your reward.

Kenya

Tour Operators and Travel Agents

Travel agents spring up in Kenya as fast as boutiques in Britain. It is important to distinguish between them and tour operators, who are separately licensed by the government, and who specialise in arranging safaris for overseas visitors. The reputable firms in each category have their own trade association.

The main safari firms have already been mentioned in the Safaris section. Among the best tour operators, some of whom have British and US offices, are the following, listed alphabetically: Abercrombie & Kent (PO Box 59749, Nairobi; telephone 334955) are on the fourth floor of Vedic House in Mama Ngina Street and also in Mombasa. They have a London office: Sloane Square House, Holbein Street, London SW1W 8NS (telephone 01-730-9600) and a main US office: Abercrombie & Kent International, 1420 Kensington Road, Oakbrook, Illinois 60521 (telephone 312-954-2944). Across Africa Safaris (PO Box 49420, Nairobi; telephone 332744) are in Standard Street. African Tours and Hotels (Head Office: PO Box 30471, Nairobi; telephone 336858) is in Utalii House opposite the Hilton Hotel. Flamingo Tours (PO Box 44899, Nairobi; telephone 28961) is in Harambee Plaza on the corner of Uhuru Highway and Haile Selassie Avenue and has a British office at 12 New Burlington Street, London W1 (telephone 01-439-7722). Thorn Tree Safaris (PO Box 42475, Nairobi; telephone 25641) is in the Jubilee Insurance Exchange in Kaunda Street. Finally, the largest and one of the oldest established is the United Touring Company (PO Box 42196, Nairobi; telephone 331960) in Muindi Mbingu Street. Known as UTC it has branches in Mombasa and Malindi, in Britain it is known as United Touring International (130 Regent Street, London W1R 6HD; telephone 01-734-4246) and under the same name in the USA (1315 Walnut Street, Suite 800, Philadelphia, PA 19107; telephone 800-223-6486).

These operators all offer a variety of safaris and tours from a half-day to 11 days or more, usually in minibuses and including tours into Tanzania. Another firm that is particularly good for visitors arriving with no definite plans except to go off the well-worn trails is Let's Go Travel (PO Box 60342, Nairobi; telephone 29539) in Caxton House, Standard Street, near the main Post Office. It specialises in camping safaris, also acting as an agent for two of the best-known camping expeditions, the Turkana Bus and the Wildlife Bus. These offer excellent value if you are prepared to rough it: for example travelling in the back of a truck with seating but with little protection from dust. The Turkana Bus is the best known and does a seven-day trip to the famous lake. It leaves every second Saturday and costs Shs 3,800/- per person. Similarly the Wildlife Bus goes for seven days to Lake Nakuru and the Masai Mara at a cost of Shs 4,000/-.

Among the most reliable travel agents are Bunson Travel Service Ltd (PO Box 45456, Nairobi; telephone 21992) in Standard Street;

Pan African Travel Organisation (PO Box 44209, Nairobi; telephone 333281) in Nkrumah Avenue, off Moi Avenue near Harambee Avenue; and AA Travel (PO Box 14982, Nairobi; telephone 339700) in the AA offices at the Hurlingham shopping centre. The best firm specialising in cheap (and legal) airline travel is Air Systems Ltd in Moi Avenue (PO Box 46466, Nairobi; telephone 20171). Travel agents in Mombasa include Abercrombie & Kent and Bunson Travel.

Many lodges and camps are represented in Nairobi by travel agents who accept their bookings and these are quoted where appropriate. But it has long been a feature of the Kenya safari scene that firms change their booking agents – and indeed often their names – more frequently than either a guide book or the telephone directory can keep up with. This is one good reason for making bookings through a well established agent or tour operator.

'Do It Yourself' Safaris and Campsites

There are a large number of campsites in Kenya, both in the National Parks and elsewhere, as well as a small number of self-help lodges, for example at Lake Baringo and in Tsavo National Park East. Most visitors would not consider these because of the problems of getting organised beforehand, though they have always been popular with locals. Hertz/UTC are now offering a self-drive package in a 4-wheel drive vehicle, together with tents, bedding, gas-cooking burners and utensils. Inevitably, although the camp site fees are negligible – from Shs 20/- to Shs 50/- a night – the vehicle hire is not. Cost per person with unlimited mileage runs upwards from around Shs 870/- for each of two people in a small Suzuki Safari. Full details, with a list of campsites, can be had either through Hertz or from UTC at PO Box 42196, Nairobi. Slightly cheaper options on the same principle are provided by Safari Camp Services (PO Box 44801, Nairobi; telephone 891348) in Koinange Street and by Habib's Cars (PO Box 48095, Nairobi; telephone 20463) on Haile Selassie Avenue, who rent out small Suzukis. If you already have a vehicle you can rent tents and other camp gear from Bonar E.A. Ltd (PO Box 42759, Nairobi; telephone 557355) on Addis Ababa Road in the Nairobi Industrial area.

Campsites in National Parks and Reserves are mentioned in the text where the Parks are described. Others are available on Private farms and in the grounds of country hotels, such as the Safariland Club at Lake Naivasha, the Namanga River Hotel and the Naro Moru River Lodge. Security at some campsites is poor with a high risk of theft, even though there may be good facilities, as at the Nairobi Rowallan Camp run by the Boy Scouts Association in Jamhuri Park.

Nairobi

Nairobi lies 139 kilometres (87 miles) south of the Equator and 480 kilometres (300 miles) west of the Indian Ocean; and it is a surprising city, especially to anyone whose ideas of Africa revolve around tropical jungle. Its semi-skyscrapers soar white and dazzling as a mirage out of the surrounding Athi plains. Its avenues are adorned with statues and lined with great stretches of riotously-coloured bougainvillaea. The outer suburbs, occasionally visited by the lions who lived here before, are alive with hibiscus, oleanders and glorious blue-flowering jacaranda trees.

Although a few apartment blocks have been built in central Nairobi, the vast majority of the residents live well outside, normally going home for lunch and so creating four rush hours a day. The city limits include the prestigious suburb of Muthaiga, where government ministers and diplomats congregate in some extraordinary copies of English Tudor mansions and Spanish villas. There is even a replica of the Grand Trianon at Versailles, now the home of the Belgian Ambassador. Other favoured areas are Langata, 13 kilometres (8 miles) out near the Nairobi National Park and Karen, named after Karen Blixen, which has a pleasant country club. The land closer in is rapidly being built over, both with English-sounding areas like Lavington and new African-named housing estates, while elsewhere sprawling shanty towns have sprung up which the visitor is unlikely to see. The city is growing at a phenomenal rate. The population today is one million and is expected to be three million by the year 2000.

However, the city centre remains small and despite all the new building you can still trace all the stages of its hustling growth since it was a railway construction camp and pioneers' town. In 1902 the famous wildlife authority, Colonel Meinertzhagen, recorded in his diary 'The only shop is a small tin hut which sells everything . . . The only hotel here is a wood and tin shanty. It stands on the only "street".' Today the main streets are still wide enough to turn a wagon and team of oxen. You can still find a few small shops – locally known as *dukas* – which have corrugated iron roofs behind one-storey façades. But many hotels are now well up to international standards. There is a wealth of restaurants, and former vacant lots have been transformed by a bloom of modern architecture, like some of the government buildings, the extensions to the City Hall, the fine new buildings of the university and the Kenyatta Conference Centre tower. The city has become a base for many international organisations, including the headquarters of the United Nations Development Programme, while international aid is contributing greatly to Kenya's own progress. The pleasant climate has had a lot to do with Nairobi's booming success.

Shopping

The main shopping streets are Kenyatta Avenue, intersecting Kimathi Street by the New Stanley Hotel, Moi Avenue (formerly Government Road), Standard Street, Kaunda Street, Mama Ngina Street and Tom Mboya Street. Within the central area, in walking distance of the New Stanley, you will find a wide variety of shops and the invariably helpful Information Bureau (telephone 23285), which is close to the Hilton.

Within this small central area of the city there are all the chemists, photographic shops, outfitters and general stores – such as Woolworths diagonally opposite the New Stanley Hotel – which the overseas visitor needs. The other facet of shopping is for local goods and souvenirs, which vary widely in price and quality. Curios are available in countless places, from sidewalk stalls to expensive studios. The main items are carved wooden animals and figurines, often only crudely made, baskets, daggers and spears, miniature drums and beadwork. A good place to look is at the City Market, between Muindi Mbingu Street and Koinange Street. The main building is devoted to fruit and vegetables, while curios are sold in the open air behind. Always bargain. Prices are what you make them. Incidentally, this yellow painted structure may strike you as being a curious shape. It is. It was originally designed as an airship hangar in the 1930s but the R101 disaster put paid to the vision of airship services from Britain to Africa. The streets adjoining the City Market, such as Biashara Street, have many Asian shops selling everything from silk saris and silverwork to cheap suitcases, as well as African printed cloth lengths, called Kitenge, Kanga and Kikoi. The two former make up well into dresses. If you want to find a cheaper market, go to the hurly burly of the colourful Kariokor Market, a short taxi ride from the downtown area. Or try River Road – but guard your handbag or wallet.

Something different from mass-produced curios are genuine tribal crafts. Two places to find them are African Heritage in Kenyatta Avenue and Studio Arts in Standard Street. The most celebrated East African carvings come from the Makonde people of southern Tanzania. These, like first edition books on Africana, are likely to be expensive, if they are old. Gallery Watatu in Standard Street stocks paintings, sculpture, prints and batiks, as does the Africa Cultural Gallery in Mama Ngina Street, while the East African Wildlife Society on the mezzanine floor of the Hilton Hotel has prints, drawings, beadwork and books, and Kumbu Kumbu, also in the Hilton, has sculptures.

A quite different local speciality is semi-precious stones and jewellery. As well as rubies, you will find tsavorite (a type of green garnet mined near the Tsavo National Park), tanzanite (a sapphire-like blue stone from Tanzania), aquamarines, tourmalines, opals, amethysts and jade. These are sold both as cut stones and mounted. Amber beads from Somalia can be a good buy as well, but make sure they do not have seams – if they do then they are plastic. Two reliable jewellery shops are Treasures and Crafts in Kaunda Street and Al-Safa Jewellers in the New Stanley Hotel. It is also worth visiting Rowland Ward Ltd, close to the New Stanley Hotel, to see the glass goblets which they engrave with wildlife scenes.

For safari clothing, either made to measure or off the peg, go to Colpro Ltd in Kimathi Street.

Changing money

Banking hours are from 0900 to 1400 Mondays to Fridays and 0900 to 1100 on the first and last Saturdays of the month. Outside these hours Barclays branch in Kenyatta Avenue is open for currency exchange in the afternoons and hotels will change money at any time, though at less favourable rates and sometimes only if you are staying in them. The American Express office, which will cash cheques for card holders, is in the Express Travel Bureau, Standard Street. Do not forget that you must produce your passport and currency declaration form when changing either notes or cheques.

Hairdressers

There are hairdressers in the city centre hotels, with ladies' salons in the Hilton, Norfolk, Intercontinental, Pan Afric, Serena and Six Eighty. The Hilton's 'Elegance' and the Six Eighty have good men's barbers, as does Schoutens in the New Stanley Hotel's ground floor arcade.

Hotels

There are few hotels in the city centre and they include the five-star ones below, while almost all the cheaper ones are in the suburbs. The most famous, and the oldest established, is the Norfolk (PO Box 40064, telephone 335422), once a pioneer's hotel. The Norfolk opened on Christmas Day 1904 and is part of Kenya's history. Though it has been almost completely rebuilt since, it still has a countrified atmosphere, with old up-country wagons on the courtyard lawns. The Ibis grill room and the Lord Delamere dining room both serve à la carte meals. The terrace outside is a pleasant place for snacks or a drink and there is a pool-side bar. The Norfolk is situated opposite the university, about a kilometre from the city centre. It is hard to believe that its view was originally of a swamp and residents could hear lions roaring at night.

The equally famous New Stanley (PO Box 30680, telephone 333233) has shops, an excellent restaurant which serves Scandinavian smörgåsbord on Fridays, and the open air Thorn Tree Cafe, which is a famous social rendez-vous. The Hilton International Hotel (PO Box 30624, telephone 334000), also very central, was refurbished in 1982,

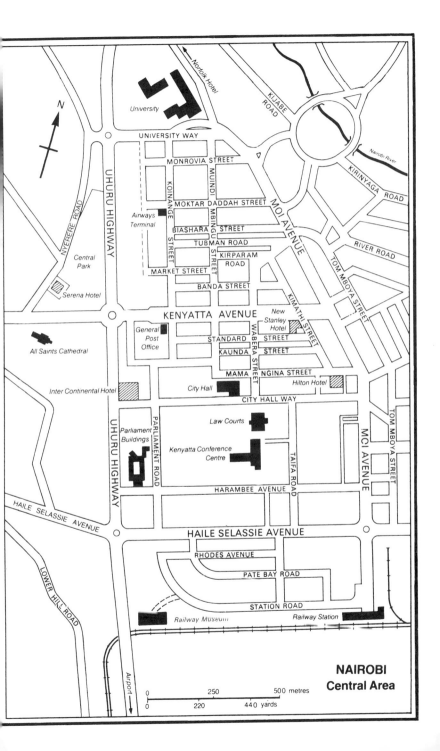

NAIROBI
Central Area

has a good grill room in the Amboseli Restaurant upstairs but, like the Intercontinental Nairobi (PO Box 30667, telephone 335550) with its Le Chateau Restaurant, has more of an international character than an African one. Both have pools. Finally the Nairobi Serena (PO Box 46302, telephone 337978), set overlooking the Central Park on Kenyatta Avenue, beyond Uhuru Highway, has admirably large and well furnished rooms and a pool, but undistinguished food. Although close to the centre, it is inadvisable to walk to the Serena after dark.

The prestigious and expensive Nairobi Safari Club (PO Box 43564, Nairobi, telephone 330621) is on University Way, near the Norfolk. It functions like an hotel but requires membership, so you cannot walk in casually for a drink or meal and it is not classified. Nairobi's fifth five-star hotel, the Utalii (PO Box 31067, telephone 802540) is some 11 kilometres (seven miles) out on the Thika Road. It has a high reputation for its food, a pool and tennis courts, although its location is a disadvantage.

The large PanAfric (Four star. PO Box 30486, telephone 720822), also at the far end of the Kenyatta Avenue extension, has a pool and a pleasant restaurant. The Ambassadeur Hotel (Three star. PO Box 30399, telephone 336803) is well placed on Moi Avenue and has one of the best Indian restaurants in town, the Safeer. The Six Eighty Hotel (Four star. PO Box 43436, telephone 332680) is large and centrally located, with a Japanese restaurant, but is very much a businessman's hotel. Probably the best value for money within safe walking distance of the centre is the smaller Boulevard Hotel (Three star. PO Box 42831, telephone 27567) on Harry Thuku Road just beyond the Norfolk Hotel. It has an agreeable outlook and a swimming pool. Among the smaller hotels with moderate prices one of the best is the Fair View (Three star. PO Box 40842, telephone 723210) in Bishops Road, about one and a half kilometres (one mile) from the centre and set in its own attractive gardens. About half the rooms have a bath or shower. Three other three-star hotels that can be recommended and which all have swimming pools are the Jacaranda (PO Box 14287, telephone 742272) one and a half kilometres (one mile) from the centre, out in Westlands; the Milimani (PO Box 30715, telephone 720760) a similar distance away in Milimani Road and the Safari Park (PO Box 45038, telephone 802493) 11 kilometres (seven miles) on the Thika Road which has a pool, tennis, a disco, and the Casino de Paradise.

Eating Out

There is now such a profusion of restaurants in Nairobi that we have had to restrict our recommendations to one or two of each cuisine.

For a lunchtime snack one of the most popular places is the Thorn

Tree open-air cafe at the New Stanley Hotel. Or you can try the poolside restaurants in the other main hotels, the restaurant upstairs in Jax fashion store on Kimathi Street, or the excellent Trattoria on the corner of Wabera Street and Standard Street.

For more serious meals, either lunch or dinner, try Marino's in Aga Khan Walk, near the American Embassy, the Red Bull Paddock in the ICEA building on Kenyatta Avenue, or the original Red Bull in Silopark House on Mama Ngina Street. Two first class French restaurants are Alan Bobbe's Bistro on Koinange Street and the French Cultural Centre's restaurant, off Koinange Street. In the evening you must book at either. In Koinange Street, too, is the Hong Kong Restaurant, with good Chinese food but uninspiring decor. The Pagoda Restaurant by the Kenya cinema on Moi Avenue also serves appealing Chinese food. For sophisticated Indian dishes there is the excellent Minar Restaurant on Banda Street and the Safeer in the Ambassadeur Hotel, while you can get a reasonable curry at the Three Bells Restaurant in Utalii House, off Loita Street. The Rasoi restaurant in Cannon House on Parliament Road serves first class Indian and Schezwan food. All the five-star hotels have good restaurants, though they are hardly cheap. Among these the Ibis Grill at the Norfolk is pre-eminent. Finally, if you want a panoramic view of the city at night go to the revolving restaurant on top of the Kenyatta Conference Centre. For a good meal expect to pay at least Shs 250/- a head without drinks, and in a top restaurant Shs 400/-. Out of town there are two establishments worth a taxi ride. First, 15 minutes drive up the Langata road is the Carnivore, specialising in every kind of meat from beef to venison and with a pleasant garden bar. Further on, in Karen, is the Horseman, one of Nairobi's best restaurants. It is only open in the evening and essential to reserve a table in advance as it is a favourite with local residents.

If you want to eat really cheaply — and have quite an experience at the same time — an alternative is to try one of the many local establishments serving African food (see Food in the General Information section). The best guide is Kathy Eldon's detailed, informative and readable book Eating Out on sale at all bookshops. Or ask your hotel for advice. But do not expect glamorous surroundings, except in the African Heritage on Banda Street, which serves Ethiopian food in the evenings at normal city prices.

Entertainment and Nightlife

Nairobi has two casinos offering blackjack, chemin de fer, craps, roulette and other gambling, as well as evening floorshows and dancing. The International Casino is on Westlands Road near the Museum, and the Casino de Paradise is at the Safari Park hotel, 11 kilometres (seven miles) out along the Thika Road. Neither is particularly sophisticated.

Kenya

About the best place to dance in a European night club atmosphere is at the Le Chateau restaurant on the top floor of the Intercontinental Hotel. A new night club named 'Luke's Place' was due to open as we went to press. There are a number of discos: at the International Casino; at a new club on Moi Avenue called Annabel's (no relation to the London club); at the New Florida in Koinange Street; at the Carnivore on the Langata road on Wednesdays, Fridays and Saturdays, where there is also a live African band. African nightclubs may be musically raucous, but they are friendly and surprisingly respectable: except that is for the inevitable clip joints.

There are 15 cinemas, showing new American, English and Indian films. The Professional Centre in Parliament Road is a small theatre with a resident company playing modern European and American dramas in repertory. Day membership, meals and drinks are available. The National Theatre has productions and concerts at irregular intervals, while the French Cultural Centre organises special film shows, concerts and talks. The World Wildlife Fund has regular showing of wildlife films there; details are posted in the lobbies of leading hotels.

Entertainments of all kinds, including cinema and theatre programmes, are listed in What's On, published monthly free, and also in the Saturday edition of the Daily Nation newspaper. Tourist's Kenya is a free fortnightly.

Sport

Racing and polo have long been favourite Kenyan sports. There are regular Sunday meetings at Nairobi racecourse, in a perfect setting, close to the city. Hurdle and flat races are sometimes run at the Limuru Country Club 27 kilometres (17 miles) out. This club has a first-rate 18-hole golf course too, and offers temporary membership to visitors, as do the Sigona Golf Club, the Muthaiga Golf Club (separate from Muthaiga Country Club), and the Royal Nairobi Golf Club. The Polo Club, where visitors are welcome, meets at Jamhuri Park on Wednesdays, Saturdays and Sundays, near where the Agricultural Society holds a tremendous five-day show every September. Parklands Sports Club (PO Box 40116, telephone 745164) welcomes temporary members to its swimming pool, tennis and squash courts. Finally, there is the toughest motor rally in the world, the three-day Marlboro Safari Rally 4,117 kilometres (2,610 miles), held every Easter. The city goes crazy over the Safari, the streets are hung with flags and all else is forgotten. The Rally is divided into 66 sections and the overall running time – without rest halts – is only 38 hours 9 minutes.

Places of Worship

The Roman Catholic cathedral, completed in 1963, is of strikingly modern design. It is built on the site of an earlier church which was the first stone building in Nairobi, and three of the bells from the old church now hang in the 200-foot campanile. The Protestant cathedral in Kenyatta Avenue is an older stone building set in an attractive garden. The Jamia mosque, off Banda Street, has an arresting silver dome. There is a Jewish synagogue on University Way. Time of services are given in What's On.

Museums and Libraries
The National Museum is well worth a visit for its exhibits of wildlife and tribal ornaments. It has one of the largest collections of African butterflies in the world and over 1,000 species of birds. The butterflies can only be viewed on request, because their wings fade from constant exposure to light. Of special interest is the display dealing with prehistoric man in Kenya. The museum carries out a great deal of research and is particularly known for its discoveries on early man begun by the late Dr Louis Leakey, of world fame, whose son, Richard Leakey, has carried on his work and is the Museum's Director. Next door to the museum is an aquarium and the Snake Park, which houses many species of snakes, with a fine collection of cobras, pythons and other rare varieties. There is also a crocodile pool and a tortoise pit. Incidentally, unless you actually tread on a snake, or corner it, you are most unlikely to be bitten. Snakes try to avoid meeting humans.

The Kenya Railway Museum, tucked away down a dirt turn-off from Station Road, is in fact far more than just an attraction for steam-age enthusiasts. Inside there are superb ship and locomotive models, detailing the whole history of railways in East Africa since 1891, as well as the lake steamer services associated with them. There is even the captain's table from the famous German cruiser Konigsberg, salvaged along with the guns after it was scuttled by Captain Looff in the Rufiji river delta in July 1915 (See also opening section of Tanzania chapter). A small entrance fee is charged.

Outside, the Museum has a collection of retired locomotives, from the smallest tank engine brought from India in 1896 to the huge Garratts which were the largest ever designed for metre-gauge railways. The rolling stock displayed in the carriage shed includes the coach from which Police Inspector Charles Ryall was seized by a man eating lion at Kima in July 1900 during the building of the railway (see under Tsavo National Park).

The Karen Blixen Museum is described below.

The city's public library, the McMillan Memorial Library, is housed in a dignified stone building on Banda Street. Naturally it is best on Africana. There are also English language libraries, with newspapers, at the American Cultural Centre in the National Bank Building, and at the British Council in the ICEA Building on Kenyatta Avenue.

Kenya

The Arboretum and Parks

There is a magnificent arboretum some two kilometres (1½ miles) from the city centre near State House. It covers 80 acres and has many beautiful trees, both native and exotic. City Park three kilometres (two miles) from town on the Limuru Road, has extensive gardens and includes some of the indigenous forest, long since cut down elsewhere in the vicinity. If you're observant, you might see a troupe of vervet monkeys feeding and grooming themselves.

Taxi and Local Tours

It is not normal to hail taxis on the street, but there are taxi-ranks at the main hotels and at the top of Kenyatta Avenue. Taxis are licensed by the City Council and in theory have meters. In practice you should always agree the fare in advance. Some taxis are in poor condition, to put it mildly.

The largest and most reliable taxi firm is Kenatco (telephone 21561). The fare to Wilson airport should be around Shs 75/- and to Jomo Kenyatta airport Shs 170/- to Shs 200/-.

Tour operators have already been listed. Among the short local tours offered one is to the Bomas of Kenya on the Langata Road, 10 kilometres (6 miles) from the city centre. Here a company of 80 performers maintain a repertoire of traditional dances from all parts of Kenya and there is an interesting permanent exhibition of traditional huts and implements. The Nairobi National Park, Langata, and Karen are dealt with in a moment. Longer range half-day excursions go to see tribal dancing at Mayer's farm Lake Naivasha and Lake Nakuru. Frankly, visiting the two lakes and back in a day is inescapably rushed and superficial, if better than never seeing them at all.

Langata and the Rothschild Giraffe Centre

Driving out to the horsey and countrified semi-suburb of Langata you pass Wilson airport and the Langata entrance to the National Park and the animal orphanage, described below. The Bomas of Kenya is at the junction with the Magadi Road. Another kilometre takes you to the Langata South Road which is the turn off for Giraffe Manor, also called the Rothschild Giraffe Centre about 16 kilometres (10 miles) from the city centre.

Giraffe Manor is an English country house in Africa, orginally built by an up-country settler as a place for his wife to hold bridge parties when in town. Neglected after their deaths, it was acquired by the late Jock Leslie Melville and his American wife Betty, who wrote two books about their efforts to save the rare Rothschild's giraffe from extinction and who established a small protected herd here. She has donated the estate to the African Fund for Endangered Wildlife and you can either pay a fee to watch the giraffe being fed

– they are very tame – as various tour operators arrange, or pay a great deal more to stay the night in luxury, which actor Robert Redford and other celebrities have done. Bookings through Abercrombie and Kent (PO Box 59749, Nairobi; telephone 334955). Giraffe Manor is located at the end of Gogo Lane, off Koitobos Road, itself a turning off Langata South Road.

Karen and the Ngong Hills

The Langata Road continues to Karen, named after Karen Blixen whose coffee farm here in the 1920s was so lovingly described in her book 'Out of Africa'. To find her house go left at Karen Road, past the Karen Country Club (members only) and you will find the sign just past the Karen College, which has been built in her former gardens. The film 'Out of Africa' has caused the house to be run properly as a Museum – though donated by the Danish Government to Kenya years ago as a memorial it was not open to the public – and it is very well kept. The guided tour shows you some of the original furniture, most of which was given by Karen Blixen to the McMillan Library in the city, and various pieces used in the film. The house itself is a modest stone building with a columned verandah around its front and a view of the Ngong Hills.

These hills, which hold an unique place in the affections of Nairobi residents, rise to 8,000 feet, resembling the knuckles of a clenched fist. The Masai story is that they were formed by a giant clutching the range with his fingers. Once thickly forested and full of game, they still shelter a few buffalo, giraffe and zebra. To reach them take the Ngong Road which joins the Karen Road at a roundabout by the Karen dukas and goes to Ngong township which is effectively where Masailand begins. You can quite easily find the dirt road up the hills if you turn right on reaching the township. This road, which is easily negotiable by ordinary cars in dry weather, leads to one of the peaks, near some radio masts. The view up here over the Rift Valley is magnificent, the air often being so clear that you can see a hundred miles or more and identify the great volcanoes in the Rift. This is a pleasant spot to picnic and now features on many tour itineraries. Unfortunately, because of thieves, it is safer to go with others, not by yourself.

Two alternative, though longer, drives are to turn left in Ngong and work your way along dirt roads at the foot of the Ngongs, passing among African farms, until you join the tarmac Magadi Road, which leads over the shoulder of the hills and provides magnificent views before it goes down into the Rift. Or you can turn left much sooner after leaving Nairobi, skirting the Nairobi National Park, and follow the Magadi Road the whole way. Magadi itself is dealt with in the next chapter.

Kenya

Nairobi National Park
For the live entertainment that most people come to see, the 115 sq. kilometre (40 sq. mile) Nairobi National Park ranks first, and is so close to the city one could call it a suburb inhabited by animals. The main gate is on the Langata Road, some 10 kilometres (six miles) from the city. At this gate are the Wildlife and Conservation Department's offices, a well laid out Wildlife Education Centre and an animal orphanage sponsored by the World Wildlife Fund, which takes in abandoned and sick animals from all over Kenya, rearing them and later releasing those which are able to fend for themselves. The orphanage allows children to watch at feeding times.

Elongated in shape, and some 22 kilometres long (14 miles), the Park's north eastern boundary is close to the Mombasa Road and it adjoins the Athi Plains, from which game come into it through the Kitengela corridor, the numbers building up at the end of the dry season in March. It contains a surprising variety of landscape and one continually flowing river, the Mbagathi. Entering through the main gate, you find yourself on a tarmac road alongside thickly wooded, hilly terrain. One possibility is to drive up — using the park map available at the gate — to Impala Point, where there is an observation hut with a panoramic view of the plains below. From here, preferably with the aid of binoculars, you will be able to see where herds of kongoni, zebra and wildebeest are grazing. You are quite likely to meet buffalo and occasional cheetah up in the wooded area behind this observation post, while on the plains there are lion, more often than not lying up in the shade of a thorn tree, or among some rocks. The early evening is the time to see them, when they are waking up from their afternoon siesta. Other wildlife include gazelle, giraffe, impala, baboons, crocodile and hippos in the river pools, leopard, cheetah, hyena, eland, warthog and ostrich while a small number of rhino have been rehabilitated and are often visible. Remember not to get out of your car except at the signposted picnic places, and that this is still at your own risk. The Park is open all the year.

It is surprisingly easy to drive much further than you think you have done and have problems getting back to the main gate before it closes at 1900. Don't forget there are other gates out on to the Mombasa Road, out to Langata among the woods, and out to the Magadi Road past the Masai Lodge which at the time of writing had been closed for several years.

The Great Rift Valley: Lakes Naivasha, Nakuru

An excursion to see the Rift Valley, either from the Ngong Hills or via the old Naivasha Road, is one of the most popular tours from Nairobi. Yet the valley itself deserves a great deal more explanation than it sometimes gets. The Rift is one of the major features of the world's land-mass, a scar as clearly visible from 150,000 kilometres out in space as the moon's continents are to us. Like the San Andreas fault in California, the rift marks the boundary between two of the plates of which the earth's crust is composed. More than 20 million years ago, before the great mountain ranges of the Himalayas and the Andes had been created by the buckling of the surface, the land subsided along the fault lines which mark the boundaries of these two plates. The resultant valley, which is roughly 50 kilometres (31 miles) wide and 2,000 ft deep in Kenya, stretches from Lake Baikal in Russia, down through the Red Sea, Ethiopia and Kenya to Tanzania and is dotted with lakes and volcanoes. A lesser rift valley associated with it runs down the present day borders of Uganda and Zaire, forming Lake Tanganyika — the second deepest lake in the world — and continuing through southern Tanzania into Mozambique.

Tremendous forces were needed to form this 3,200 kilometres (2,000 miles) long valley and the subsidence left the crust of the earth thinner along its floor. In consequence hundreds of volcanoes erupted in the Rift, the largest of them being Kilimanjaro. Although so old, this volcanic activity is not extinct. The Shetani lava-flow on the borders of Tsavo occurred only 200 years ago. Ol Donyo Lengai, the Masai 'Mountain of God' in Tanzania erupted in 1966, and the volcanoes south of Lake Turkana, where there are recent volcanic scarps, give forth jets of carbon dioxide from deep in the earth. The most powerful evidence of these releases is in Ethiopia, where the Danakil depression is vividly coloured by soda and salts and many of the string of Rift Valley lakes in Kenya and Tanzania are alkaline, both Magadi and Natron being covered in soda, or trona as it is called.

While the sections of the Rift which are most accessible are wild and impressive enough, others are still changing and the constant minor shifting in the surface has revealed important evidence about man's origin. Indeed the Rift in Kenya and Tanzania is virtually the territory of the Leakey family, since the famous palaeontologist, Dr Louis Leakey and his wife Mary, made their discoveries of the 1.8 million-year-old Homo Habilis, or handy man, at Olduvai (see Tanzania chapter) while their son, Richard Leakey, has unearthed even older fossil skeletons at Koobi Fora on the eastern shore of Lake Turkana (see Northern Kenya section).

From whichever way you approach the Rift, your first sight of it is likely to remain with you forever. Whether seen from the Ngong Hills, from the road to Magadi, from the old Naivasha Road — still the most dramatic view — or from the air as you fly to the Masai Mara, the Rift is one of the natural wonders of the world. Its floor is tawny red in times of drought, or dusty green after the rains. Its escarpment descends in a breathtaking series of terraces and its far off further wall rises dark purple against the blue sky, a procession of white clouds drifting across the volcanic peaks.

Olorgesaillie and Magadi

The road from Nairobi to Magadi is now tarmacked for its whole length of 110 kilometres (68 miles). It branches left off the Langata Road not far beyond the main Nairobi National Park gate, skirts the Park fence and then passes through the rapidly growing township of Ongata Rongai and a few villages until it rises to cross the southern shoulder of the Ngong Hills at about 6,500 ft above sea level. From here, as already mentioned, there are panoramic views towards the lake, more than 4,500 ft below, with Tanzania and Lake Natron beyond and the Nguruman escarpment and the Loita Hills rising dramatically to the south west. It is a truly primeval landscape. You will notice many circular thorn-fenced manyattas (encampments) of the Masai, whose country this is for as far as the eye can see. (The Masai people are described in the chapter on Amboseli and Tsavo.) Their cattle share the valley floor with the game. Descending rapidly, the road takes you past Olorgesaillie, 64 kilometres (40 miles) from Nairobi. Here Dr Louis Leakey excavated a prehistoric living site of the Pleistocene period, about 200,000 years old, originally discovered in 1893 by the man who gave the Great Rift Valley its name, the geologist, John Gregory. There is a field museum and a simple rest camp, where you have to bring your own food, bedding and crockery. Enquiries and bookings should be made to the Curator, the National Museum (PO Box 40658 Nairobi).

Lake Magadi, 1,900 ft, has a dirty white skin of trona on its surface, veined almost like marble, which is pumped out and converted commercially into soda ash and used for making glass. There is a small town, an airstrip and even a golf course which has 'browns' instead of greens and might just as well be on the surface of the moon, except for the heat. It is extremely hot, but the real attraction is the birdlife. Flamingoes, avocets and other waterbirds congregate around the lake, feeding off algae and apparently regarding the soda as a valuable protection from predators. This is a fact you can easily appreciate if you walk — or worse if you drive — too close. The lake-shore crust will collapse and leave you floundering, so binoculars or telephoto lenses are essential equipment for watching the birds.

Further south Lake Natron, in Tanzania, is another soda lake that has become the greatest breeding ground for flamingoes in East Africa because it offers them similar protection and is inaccessible to man.

The Nguruman escarpment, west of Lake Magadi, can be reached over very rough tracks. It is a magnificently unexplored area for foot safaris, varying from lowland plains to mountain forest, with fine views and an abundance of wildlife. However you need a fully self-contained camping expedition to tackle it.

Limuru, the Kedong Valley and Mayer's Ranch
The most scenically spectacular road to the Rift from Nairobi is not the recently constructed A104, but a turn off from it signed 'B3 Narok'. The A104 from Nairobi passes through Westlands, a major shopping centre, then climbs 2,000 feet up to Limuru, with the railway pursuing its more serpentine course close by. Limuru is delightfully wooded and green, having a much higher rainfall than Nairobi and indeed a totally different climate and landscape to the Langata side of the city. The Limuru Country Club has an excellent golf course and you can get a good meal at the Kentmere Club (telephone 0154-41053) on the Tigoni Road, which has residential accommodation and delightful gardens. Temporary membership is available.

Whereas the A104 road to Nakuru runs for some way along the top of the escarpment, giving occasional splendid panoramas of the Rift Valley, the old B3 road — which is liable to be potholed — reaches the Rift sooner. Suddenly you come out of a thin belt of forest, round a corner and there, 2,000 feet below you down an almost sheer escarpment, is the greatest valley in the world. Far ahead in its centre stands the clear cut cone of Mount Longonot, 9,111 ft high, hiding Lake Naivasha from sight. Euphorbia trees, candelabra-shaped succulents like giant cactuses, sprout on the steep slopes. Along the escarpment African boys sell a variety of souvenirs including attractive woven baskets and sheepskin hats, though unhappily there have been attacks on tourists here and it is wiser not to stop. Approximately half way down a dirt road to the left leads to Mayer's Ranch, in the Kedong Valley, a favourite place for excursions, where you can watch traditional Masai dancing every afternoon in a man-yatta, take as many photographs as you want without charge, and get tea. This ranch, along with the Bomas of Kenya in Langata, is the best place to see traditional dancing. The great white space-age aerial dish on the plains not far away transmits telephone calls by satellite to Europe and the United States, an extreme contrast to the life of the Masai, though it would be wrong to assume the Masai are backward. Many of their children now go to universities.

Continuing on the main road, at the bottom of the escarpment is a tiny chapel built by the Italian prisoners of war who made this road in 1942 to 1944. They had been captured during the campaign in Ethiopia. It is easy, driving along either here or on the new road above, to take for granted the engineering problems which the descent of the escarpment posed, especially for the railway, which has also had its alignment improved over the years. The problem of finding a safe gradient down from Limuru to the valley floor seriously held up construction of the line at the end of the last century. Both road and rail run through the Kedong valley towards the shoulder of Mount Longonot, before which is the turn off to Narok, the Loita Plains and the Masai Mara Game Reserve (see later chapter). The road is tarmacked as far as Narok.

Longonot can be climbed without undue difficulty: a dirt road leads from the Naivasha Road near Longonot Station, and there is a track up to and around the precipitous crater edge, from which you can look down the mile-wide crater, with eddies of steam rising among the trees on its floor. Needless to say, the view of the Rift is magnificent. The mountain's 52 sq. kilometres constitute a national reserve, but there is no security for vehicles parked at the designated viewing places. Further west, on the far side of Hell's Gate National Park, there are geysers and deep drilling is harnassing the natural steam jets to make electricity in geo-thermal plants, the residue of water being used for irrigation.

Naivasha

Irrigation for farming and tourism have brought about a considerable increase in activity around Lake Naivasha in the past decade. Much of the open grassland has been divided into smallholdings and the gazelle that used to crop it have largely gone. The township itself, only 97 kilometres (60 miles) from Nairobi, is expanding rapidly, though it still has only ordinary dukas and the atmosphere of a frontier settlement, as so many up-country places do. It used to be famous, not for its tourist facilities round the lake, which now make it a popular weekend retreat, but for the magnificent yellow-barked acacia thorn trees that grow in the neighbourhood — nicknamed 'fever trees' because it used to be believed the trees caused malaria. Actually, the trees grow along watercourses where mosquitoes can breed.

The township itself has two small tourist hotels. The New Bell Inn (unclassified) is on the main road through the town and has been revived by French management. The meals are good and patisserie is sold from a counter. The more recently built Malaika Hotel (unclassified) is situated on a hill overlooking the town and the lake. It offers full board accommodation. The town has banks, filling station and fairly basic shops, as well as a railway station on the Nairobi to Kisumu line. Buses ply constantly to Nairobi and Nakuru.

Hotels around Lake Naivasha

The better known hotels and lodges are all around the south side of Lake Naivasha itself (6,187 feet above sea level) and are reached by a turn-off a couple of miles along the old A104 road to Nairobi, called Moi South Lake Road. This is tarmacked as far as the Lake Naivasha Hotel (Three stars. Bookings through Block Hotels, PO Box 40075, Nairobi; telephone 335807). Thereafter the road, which makes a complete circuit of the Lake back to the other side of Naivasha, is appalling and very dusty. The Lake Naivasha Hotel is better than its

Above: Rare albino zebra on a game ranch below Mt Kenya. By Richard Cox
Below: Lion

Above left: Malachite kingfisher. By John Karmali
Above right: Young Fish Eagle. By Richard Cox
Below: Flamingos on Lake Nakuru. By Richard Cox

Above: Samburu moran of northern Kenya
Below: Herding goats and camels on the Tana River near Garissa. By Richard Cox

SERENA
. . .simply the best

Our unique world starts in Nairobi with the beautifully landscaped Nairobi Serena Hotel.

Then out for thrilling safaris and game drives from our lodges, Mara Serena, Amboseli Serena and the Samburu Serena.

Climax your Kenya safari with a stay at the Serena Beach Hotel, one of Kenya's premier coast hotels.

A wonderful welcome is yours in our special Serena world!

SERENA LODGES & HOTELS
P.O. Box 48690, Nairobi, Kenya. Tel: 339800 Telex 22878

classification. All rooms have a private bathroom. There is a swimming pool, and punts and motor boats for fishing and bird watching can be hired, along with fishing tackle. Six kilometres (four miles) further along the South Lake Road is the independently owned and less expensive Safariland Lodge (PO Box 72, Naivasha; telephone 0311-20241), which offers extensive facilities including riding and a camping site, with a golf course planned. Around the lake are a number of small marinas which offer facilities for boating, fishing, camping, water skiing, including Fisherman's Camp 17 kilometres (10 miles) from the lake road turn-off near Hippo Point (Class B. Bookings PO Box 14982, Nairobi; telephone 720382). This offers self-help accommodation in cottages or bandas in two camps, one by the lake and the other overlooking it, and the possibility of staying in the owners' house by special arrangement. They take their guests birdwatching and to Hell's Gate gorge.

Crescent Island and the Lake

From any of these places you can arrange a trip to Crescent Island, a bird and wildlife sanctuary where over 350 bird species have been recorded and Thomson's gazelle, waterbuck, monkeys and other wildlife live. A stroll with a pair of binoculars makes a very pleasant few hours. The lake shore is fringed by papyrus swamps inhabited by Goliath heron, storks, warblers, coot, purple gallinules and lily trotters, while cormorants, pelicans and others are often seen.

Crescent Island is in fact part of the rim of an ancient volcano and when the lake level is low the water it encloses forms a separate lake, with greater salinity than the main lake, which is one of the few freshwater lakes in the Rift. The reason remains mysterious. The water in the Sonachi Crater lake close by to the south west, for example, is highly saline. Farmers have taken advantage of the fresh water for extensive irrigation schemes. The Sulmac Flower Farm is the largest producer of carnations in the world, which like other flowers grown here are air-freighted to Europe. One of the lake's other features, and a less believable one when you see it on a calm day, is that even though its average depth is only 5 metres, storms blow up on it with great rapidity in the afternoons. Many people have drowned in its waters.

The Lake also suffers from a free-floating aquatic fern called *salvinia molesta,* which clogs the shores, and from coypu, which have destroyed the lilies. Nonctholess it remains uniquely beautiful, set against a back-drop of mountains, which is why the late Joy Adamson, authoress of 'Born Free' made her home here. In the Pleistocene period, the lake was part of a vast area of water which included Lakes Elementeita and Nakuru, the outlet for which was the Njorowa Gorge, now generally known as Hell's Gate.

Kenya

Hell's Gate National Park
This gorge, a mecca for rock climbers and ornithologists, shelters large herds of game and is a small 28 kilometre (17 mile) long national park. It is reached by a turn-off through the Sulmac Ranch some five kilometres (three miles) beyond the Lake Hotel. At the entrance the Park road passes a lone rock pinnacle known as Fischer's Tower, which was once the plug of a volcano. The cliffs are the breeding ground of vultures, Verreaux's eagles, augur buzzard and thousands of swifts. The star attraction, if it can be found, is the lammergeyer, a bearded vulture rare in East Africa. Gazelle, and sometimes eland and buffalo, graze in the open valley beyond the gorge while there can be lion around. If you penetrate far enough down here you will find natural steam jets and great clefts in the earth full of red volcanic rock, a reminder of the thinness of the earth's crust in the Rift. Hell's Gate indeed! It is possible to go through on foot or horseback, aided by some steps cut in the rock for the making of a film, passing down into another gorge and eventually out on to the plains north of the Narok road.

Elsamere
Near Safariland is Joy Adamson's former home, Elsamere, where she and George Adamson lived with the lioness made famous in her books. Now run by a Trust, the house is open to members of any genuine wildlife society and to conservationists, who may stay there for a small fee. There is a library of Africana and a collection of papers relevant to Lake Naivasha. For information write to Elsa Ltd, c/o Livingstone Registrars, PO Box 30029, Nairobi; telephone 74221. Casual visitors can be given escorted walks and tea from 1500 to 1700 daily.

Round Lake Naivasha
Among the attractions, some not visitable by tourists, are the Naivasha Vineyards bordering the road between the Lake Naivasha Hotel and Safariland, where both red and white wine are produced; the Moorish style house called the Djinn Palace (private) which was central to the 1930 'Happy Valley' life depicted in James Fox's book 'White Mischief'; and on the north side of the lake various large farms. One of these, the 15,000 acre Kongoni Farm, will be taking private guests through Abercrombie and Kent (PO Box 59749, Nairobi; telephone 334955). It has superb views across the lake.

From Naivasha to the Aberdares
East from Naivasha the road to the Kinangop Plateau leads on up to the Park Road across the Aberdare National Park to Nyeri (see page 90). The road reaches 10,000 ft above sea level and can be impassable in the rains. A board at the turn-off in Naivasha states whether this road is open.

From Naivasha to Nakuru

At the small township of Gilgil a tarmac road branches off up the side of the valley to Nyahururu. Following the Nakuru Road you pass Lake Elementeita, a soda lake that is a nesting place for pelicans, greater flamingoes and sacred ibis but which is on private land. Though it is hard to imagine now, this route is close to the old caravan trail down which Arab traders took slaves and ivory from the interior to the coast and which the early European explorers followed inland, both suffering from attacks by the warlike Masai. Mythically, this was the road to 'King Solomon's Mines' in Rider Haggard's famous novel. But it was the railway which opened the country up to European settlers and farming early this century.

Prehistoric Sites

There are many remains of early man here. Gamble's Cave near Nakuru was occupied by Stone Age man from about 30,000 BC. There are other prehistoric sites at Hyrax Hill, just outside Nakuru, and at Kariandusi, near Gilgil. They are well signed and at Kariandusi there is a small site museum, with fossils of straight-tusked elephant — a species which once ranged from Britain to South Africa — and an interesting display of hand axes and other primitive tools. These and the fossils were buried and preserved by movements of earth and volcanic ash during the later faulting phases of the Rift Valley. The Museum opens from 0800 to 1800. Next door to the site is a diatomite mine; the white product is used in making toothpaste, fertilisers and soaps.

Nakuru and Lake Nakuru National Park

Continuing along the new road which, the signs tell you, is part of a Trans-African Highway from Mombasa to Lagos and which already carries a large volume of traffic to Uganda, the southern Sudan and eastern Zaire, you pass turn-offs to the Nakuru National Park. The first, shortly after the Gilgil turn-off, has a board for the Park and the Lake Nakuru Lodge. Avoid this road. It is rough and passes circuitously behind Lake Elementeita without any views of the lake, though you would see some plains game on the ranches it passes through. It is far quicker to continue on the main road and take the Lanet Gate turn-off, from which the Lodge is signed via the Nderit Gate.

The Park is world-famous for its fantastic agglomeration of lesser flamingoes which, when they are here, literally turn the shores pink. Nakuru is the first and only National Park in Africa to have been created for their protection. At the end of the 1960s they were estimated to number between 1½ and 2 million, while 389 species of other waterbirds have been recorded. In the mid-1970s the flamingoes appeared to desert the lake, possibly because the algae on which they feed had declined, and many went to Lake Bogoria further north. More recently they have returned. But in any case the 202 sq. kilometre Park is notable for other wildlife too, particularly pelicans, Defassa's waterbuck — there are some 3,000 here — Bohors reedbuck, found in the grasslands west of the lake, impala and Rothschild's giraffe, of which a small herd was introduced in 1977. Coke's hartebeest has disappeared from the area between here and Elementeita and so, very nearly, had the rhino. By 1984 there were only two left. In 1987 construction of a rhino sanctuary began with a holding-pen near the Naivasha sub-headquarters south of the lake. Black rhino will be brought from Solio ranch in Laikipia and it is hoped to establish a herd of 30 to 40.

The Park is centred on the lake, though it has taken in former ranch-land to the south, so it includes grassland and acacia woodland, with four seasonal rivers flowing into the lake. Access roads are reasonable to most of the area and there is a good recently produced map available for sale at the entrance gate offices for Shs 50/-. Although many visitors come only on a day trip, there is ample accommodation. The Lake Nakuru Lodge (Three star. Bookings PO Box 70559, Nairobi; telephone 20225) is built around a stone farm house on a hillside south east of the Lake and is signed from the Gilgil to Nakuru road. The Sarova Lion Hill Hotel, formerly a camp, (Class B. Bookings PO Box 30680, Nairobi; telephone 333233) offers full service. There are several campsites around the lake (camping fees Shs 30/- a night, payable at the gates) and self-help bandas near Sarova Lion Hill. The Lanet Gate is 15 minutes drive from Nakuru.

Nakuru

Nakuru itself is a thriving trading centre for a large farming area and the administrative headquarters of the Rift Valley Province. The telephone code for Nakuru is 037. There are banks, filling stations, shops and two hotels. The Midland (One star. PO Box 908, Nakuru; telephone 037-41277) and the Stag's Head (Unclassified. PO Box 143, Nakuru; telephone 037-42216) are both in the town centre and fairly basic. Both have restaurants. One good buy locally is a sheep skin jacket, made to measure if you want. But apart from the National Park, the town is best known for its annual Agricultural Show, held in late June and usually opened by the President.

From Nakuru the main road leads on to Lake Victoria and to the upland towns of western Kenya, dealt with in a later chapter. You can also cross the 10,000 ft Mau summit to Narok and the Masai Mara, if the weather is dry. Or you can take advantage of the excellent tarmac road to Lake Baringo and explore the Rift Valley further, including Lake Bogoria, only recently made easily accessible. Between this road and the new tarmac road to Nyahururu lies the Menengai Crater.

Menengai Crater
Menengai, the second largest volcanic crater in the world, is 90 sq kilometres in extent, with a partly forested floor 485 metres (1,592 ft) below what remains of its rim. The slope up is so gradual that one is hardly aware of it from the town. To reach the summit viewing point take the main Nairobi road and turn left immediately after the long white wall of Nakuru State House — easily recognisable because it bears the national colours and the gates are guarded. Then go past houses up Menengai Drive and into Forest Drive, which is a rutted dirt road. After a further 13 rough kilometres you pass some woodland and reach a viewing point with a much photographed signpost, showing distances to the rest of the world: New York 12,560 kilometres, London 6,924 kilometres, Tokyo 10,988 kilometres and so on. The height here is 2,272 metres (7,459 ft) above sea level. There are magnificent views both of the crater itself and towards the Aberdare mountains to the east.

Lakes Bogoria and Baringo

From Nakuru town take the well-signed B4 road for Marigat, which passes through a changing landscape as it descends into the drier country further north. Beyond Mogotio the country becomes drier and more reddish brown, with farmland and greenery giving way to thorn scrub. Access to Lake Bogoria has been greatly improved. There is a graded dirt road from Mogotio to the southern entrance gate at the village of Maji ya Moto, near the lake, which passes through only one potentially tricky drift and which is allegedly due to be tarmacked. It is a distance of 43 kilometres (27 miles), about 45 minutes dusty drive through sisal estates. From Maji ya Moto you can either take a short rough road across to the hot springs by the lake itself or continue the long way parallel to the lake. You reach a road junction where a luxurious hotel was built in 1986 (it has not yet opened). There turn right to the Loboi gate to the Reserve. In the other direction the road at this junction goes past papyrus swamps 16 kilometres (10 miles) to Marigat on the main road to Lake Baringo.

Lake Bogoria National Reserve
The 107 sq kilometre Reserve encompasses the whole of this soda lake, lying up against the eastern wall of the Rift, which here is thickly wooded and the haunt of both greater and lesser kudu. Leaving the entrance gate you drive down to the flat shore, the lake reflecting the sky in a way Lake Baringo's muddy waters do not, despite its being coloured green from the algae. It is a much more beautiful lake. Flocks of flamingoes are usually feeding close in and you can walk almost to the water. In colonial days the lake was called Hannington, after a missionary bishop who was murdered here.

Kenya

At the lake side beyond the Loboi Gate the road divides. The route around the east is rough, but the escarpment above is dramatic. The better road along the west leads to the hot springs, which belch sulphurous fumes. They are 13 kilometres (8 miles) from Loboi, though there is access from Kampi ya Moto, described above.

As well as birds and animals, the vegetation round Bogoria is interesting. The desert rose, a stumpy grey succulent bush with bright pink flowers, grows in many places. However, be warned that the lake is only 3,160 ft up and the area becomes very hot in the middle of the day. There are four campsites, the coolest being at Fig Tree. Enquire about them at the office at the Loboi Gate. Opening hours of the Reserve are 0700 to 1800.

Lake Baringo

Driving direct from Nakuru to Lake Baringo takes about 1½ hours and the lake first comes into sight some 25 kilometres (15 miles) before Marigat, lying dully in the centre of the distant valley and giving no impression of its attractions. Marigat itself is a small dusty township near a river. The Marigat Inn, signed at the main road, is half African eating place, half tourist oriented, with a shaded outdoor bar and a limited menu of cheap but perfectly edible dishes. At Marigat a road heads west to Kabarnet and the Kerio valley, dealt with below. Around here, incidentally, you may notice small dark trunked trees with yellow blossom. These are *Albizia* used by the locals to treat malaria. Continuing straight on the lake is little more than 15 minutes drive, though the road here has several concrete drifts through river beds which could hold you up in the rainy seasons. It terminates at a cluster of tin-roofed huts, rapidly growing to the size of a village. Before this there is a turn off to the Lake Baringo Club.

Although not a national park, Lake Baringo has great attractions. Hippo and crocodile are easily seen despite its muddy waters, and the birdlife is astonishing: 448 species have been identified here, from goliath herons and fish eagles to tiny Madagascar bee-eaters and sparrow weavers, one mating pair of which may build as many as 15 nests in order to deceive snakes as to the nest they actually use. The lake was full of fish until the Luo from Lake Victoria moved in to capitalise on this asset. You can still see the local Njemps fishermen, sitting with knees bent on fragile rafts which they paddle far out into the lake. The Njemps are related to the Masai and their rafts are made from ambatch wood, which has similar properties to balsa, being extremely light and pliable. You can watch them being made if you visit a fishing village. The Tugen fish from more conventional boats, and are also pastoralists, though the land here is becoming sadly eroded from over-grazing.

There are two excellent places to stay at the lake as well as self-help accommodation and a cheaper lodging house. The Lake Baringo Club, situated on the lake shore is very well run by Block Hotels (Three Star. Bookings PO Box 47557, Nairobi; telephone 335807). It has a swimming pool, a games room, organises boat trips and has a resident ornithologist who leads early morning and late afternoon bird-walks. A boat taking eight people costs Shs 400/- per hour and you are bound to see hippo: indeed you can hear them grunting at night and may find them feeding on the Club's lawns in the dark. They are known as the 'night gardeners'.

The other lodge is the Island Camp, delightfully situated on an island in the centre and reached from a jetty roughly one and a half kilometres (one mile) beyond the Club. A boat takes you across. The Island Camp (Class A, Bookings through Thorn Tree Safaris, PO Box 42475 Nairobi; telephone 25941) has good food, a pool and 50 beds in double tents. Water skiing, boat trips, bird watching and other excursions can be arranged. Boats cost Shs 400/- an hour. Both the Island Camp and the Lake Baringo Club will meet visitors at the airstrip by the main road.

A few hundred yards from the Club is the home of Mrs David Roberts, who has both a campsite with toilets and showers and self-catering rondavels available at Shs 60/- per night. Further along, before the T junction in the village, there is a small African hotel which charges only Shs 30/- per night.

Excursions which both lodges arrange include visits to Njemps fishing villages; visits to the Snake Park run by Jonathan Leakey, brother of the Director of the National Museum; half-day trips to Lake Bogoria; boat trips to Ol Kokwe island in the centre of Lake Baringo, where there are hot springs; a three-hour boat trip to the Molo River to see crocodiles and water birds; and trips to the Mukutan swamp on the eastern shore, again to watch bird life. If you have your own transport it would be well worth while going on a drive through the Tugen hills. The Lake Baringo Club has produced a detailed itinerary for a four-hour expedition, obtainable from the reception, and this author found it very useful in writing the next few paragraphs.

North from Baringo the tarmac ceases, but the dirt road round the north end of the lake and up to the Laikipia Plateau and Maralal is kept graded. There is now a tourist circuit from Baringo right across to the Samburu National Reserve (and vice versa), which is a full seven hours' dusty drive. If you are organising your own safari it is better to break the journey at Maralal, described in the Northern Kenya chapter, as is Lake Turkana.

The Tugen Hills, Kabarnet and the Kerio Valley
The line of basalt cliffs that bound the valley to the west of Lake

Baringo are backed by the Tugen hills. To climb up into them return to Marigat and take the C51 road signed to Kabarnet. You very soon come into magnificent scenery and some 20 kilometres (12 miles) from Marigat will have the first of a succession of views back towards Lake Baringo, especially after passing the village of Sesia. You are now at 1,830 metres (6,000 ft), having climbed 3,000 ft, and will soon come into much lusher country, with coffee-growing among its occupations.

The inhabitants of this area are the Kalenjin, whose combination of bravery and acclimatisation to high-altitude living has produced a number of world-class athletes, including world record-holder Henry Rono and the famous long distance runner Kipchoge Keino. The President of Kenya, the Hon Daniel arap Moi, is a member of the Tugen, a sub-tribe of the Kalenjin, who live around Lake Baringo.

Kabarnet, perched on the hills and with fine views across the Kerio valley to the great western wall of the Rift, is the administrative centre for the Baringo district. The Kabarnet Hotel (Bookings PO Box 30471, Nairobi; telephone 336858) deserves at least two stars. It is a pleasant place to stop for a meal or a drink and is one of a number of good small hotels recently built in western Kenya. The Kerio valley is outstandingly lovely. Part of it, around the Kerio river gorge, has been designated a national reserve. At the time of writing, the road on from Kabarnet into the valley and up the Elgeyo escarpment through Tambach on the other side of the Rift was very bad. However it is being tarmacked to provide a link to Eldoret and the farming land of the Uasin Gishu, described in the next chapter.

The Masai Mara

Although theoretically Western Kenya can be conveniently summarised as everything west of the Rift Valley, in practice road and rail communications towards Lake Victoria are forced northwards in a huge arc by the massif of the Mau Summit and its forests. Only a single road heads directly west to Narok and the magnificent game country of the Masai Mara, and few visitors continue from there to the tea-growing districts of Kericho and the shores of Lake Victoria, not least because of the roads. Tours normally either return to the capital or rejoin the Rift Valley route described in the previous chapter. Consequently we will deal first with the Masai Mara and then with the bulk of western Kenya.

The route to Narok and the Masai Mara
As mentioned earlier, the B3 road to Narok is signed off the A104 from Nairobi. Shortly after you reach the bottom of the Rift Valley escarpment you turn left again. From here on the surface is much better and you can reach Narok from Nairobi in two hours. On the

way you pass the great volcano Suswa, which rears up on your left to 7,734 ft, and then climb steadily to cross the southern end of the Mau and enter one of the major wheat and barley growing areas of Kenya, where the Masai have turned to cash crop farming and the fields seem to stretch as wide as the Canadian prairies. Narok itself is both an important trading centre for the Masai and the last watering hole for tourists en route to the Mara. There are several petrol stations, dukas and two cafe/restaurants, neither of star quality, as well as a horde of souvenir sellers, principally offering traditional Masai beadwork, often at asking prices which can be higher than they are in Nairobi.

Beyond Narok the roads are murram, and sometimes poor. After the first 18 kilometres (11 miles) you come to two junctions, where you need to keep your eyes open for lodge signs as conventional direction signs are very few. After crossing the Uaso Ngiro River (not to be confused with the Uaso Nyiro in the Samburu country) you reach a junction by some houses. The left turn here heads south to the Loita Hills, among which is the Masai settlement of Morijo, some 70 kilometres (44 miles) from this turn-off. The Masai in these hills are among the most traditional and unchanged in Kenya. From Morijo a rough road swings round the western side of the hills to join the main Keekorok Road across the Loita Plains. Another rough road goes on to Entasekera (the Survey of Kenya map does not record this area accurately), from where a hunter's trail goes through to the spectacular Nguruman escarpment. There are many colobus monkeys and leopard among the forests here. You must have four-wheel drive to negotiate the Loita Hills.

Returning to the road from Narok to the Mara, the second junction is a couple of kilometres beyond the first. Signs for Keekorok Lodge, Cottar's Camp and others show that the left fork leads south west across the Loita Plains to Keekorok and the southern Mara. You should manage Narok to Keekorok in three to four hours. But the road straight ahead to the Mara River bridge, Governor's Camp, Kichwa Tembo and the northern Mara is less good. It can take five hours to the bridge. This is why many visitors use the scheduled air services from Nairobi. The road to the bridge starts off as the road to Sotik and western Kenya. For the Mara you branch left after the tiny settlement of Ngorengore. If you were going to Sotik and Kericho, you would find the road between Ngorengore and Kapkimolwa bad, but good thereafter. This point marks the boundary between the Masai and Kipsigis peoples.

Masai Mara Game Reserve
As can be seen from the map, the Masai Mara Game Reserve has only one natural boundary, which is the Esoit Oloololo escarpment to the west. This line of hills is an unmistakeable feature when you are there, cutting off the horizon behind Governor's Camp and the

Kenya

Mara River. The other boundaries of this 1,690 sq kilometre (640 sq miles) reserve are arbitrary: The Tanzanian frontier to the south and an unmarked line across the Loita Plains to the north and east. The animals take no notice of any boundary except the escarpment and whether you are travelling to Keekorok or the Mara Bridge you will see plenty of game as you cross the plains, though the greatest concentration is in the magnificent country of the Reserve because the waters of the Mara River play a vital part in the ecology of the area. In wildlife terms, the Mara is the extreme northern end of the Serengeti in Tanzania.

Every year a massive migration of game takes place across the Serengeti and up towards the Mara as the animals move in search of green grass. This migration and its importance to the survival of one of Africa's largest populations of wildebeeste and other ungulates was turned into a matter of world-wide concern in the 1960s by the book 'Serengeti Shall not Die' written by the Director of the Frankfurt Zoo, Dr Bernard Grzimek and his son Michael, who was killed flying in the Serengeti before it was even published. Expert research on the migration has continued ever since: and as experts seldom agree the explanations have changed. It used to be thought that the animals moved along ancestral routes that they followed by instinct. Now they are considered to be more intelligent in seeking fresh grazing. The numbers involved have altered too. Since the 1960s the wildebeeste population has exploded, apparently as a result of rinderpest vaccination of cattle removing it from them as well. Aerial photography puts their total at around 1.4 million, together with 200,000 zebra and eland and perhaps 250,000 Grant's and Thomson's gazelles. Following them are the predators: nomadic lions, cheetah and hyenas.

The migration starts from the southern Serengeti in May, with the herds trailing west in long columns. They move into the Serengeti's western corridor, then turn north — largely outside the National Park itself — and up to the woodlands and the permanent water of the Mara, where they start to arrive in late June. The Mara River, draining off the Mau Summit, nourishes the grazing that has dried out further south. The wildebeeste cows have calved in January to March and they bring their young with them, a frequent prey to the predators; while the bulls are rutting on the way, in preparation for the next season. Within Kenya they cross first the Sand River, then the Talek and the Mara, usually at the same points, charging through the waters in a tumbling cascade of bodies, uncaring how many drown. For a couple of months they graze here and around September they re-group and return. As on the way up, the lions and other predators follow, preying on the stragglers.

The migrations are one of the greatest wildlife spectacles anywhere and they depend to a great extent on the rains. It normally rains in

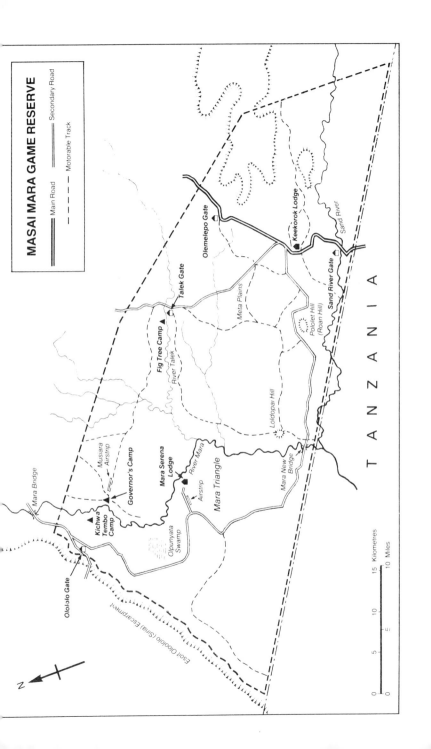

MASAI MARA GAME RESERVE

Main Road
Secondary Road
— — — Motorable Track

N

Mara Bridge

Ololoolo Gate

Esoit Oloololo (Sira) Escarpment

Kichwa
Tembo Camp

Musiara
Airstrip

Governor's Camp

Mara Serena
Lodge

Olpunyata
Swamp

River Mara

Airstrip

Mara Triangle

Mara New
Bridge

Fig Tree Camp

River Talek

Talek Gate

Loldopai Hill

Meta Plains

Olemelepo Gate

Pololet Hill
(Roan Hill)

Keekorok Lodge

Sand River Gate

Sand River

TANZANIA

0   5   10   15 Kilometres
0   5   10 Miles

E

Kenya

October/November, which the wildebeeste know will bring new grass in the Serengeti, so they move again. That's the new theory. The old one was that the gathering storms drove them.

This does not mean that there is no game in the Mara at other times. It includes a wide variety of country, from riverine forest to the open plains, and supports a correspondingly wide range of wildlife, from lion and the rest of the Big Five to hippo, crocodiles, roan antelope, topi — an antelope you will see standing on top of anthills to get a better view and to mark its territory — countless gazelle, hyenas, silver-backed jackals and many smaller animals. It has always been a splendid area for game viewing, but only opened up when the Tanzanian frontier was closed and Kenyan visitors could not go to the Serengeti. Nor, of course, is the wildlife confined to the Reserve. There is a permanent population of wildebeeste on the Loita plains, which moves in and out of the Mara; while there is cheetah, leopard, wild dogs and gazelle on both sides of the Narok road, as at Aitong. The Mara Reserve and its surrounding country are also one of a declining number of areas in Kenya where you can explore freely without being confined to park roads, provided you have four-wheel drive, though whether the growth of tourism will permit this much longer is another question. Some animals, like lion, seem unbothered by the vehicles. Others, particularly cheetah and leopard, are inhibited in their hunting and fail to breed.

There is only one good road around the Reserve and it goes from the Mara River Bridge round in the lee of the escarpment, past Kichwa Tembo Camp, across the Mara Triangle — a great game area between the river and the escarpment — then heads near one of the many hippo pools to the Mara New Bridge and on to Keekorok. There is also a road which traverses part of the Reserve on the way from Keekorok, north to Narok via the Talek Gate. Otherwise all the routes are glorified game trails. There is a route directly across from the Musiara airstrip near Governor's Camp to Keekorok, which crosses drifts in several streams and rivers and is not at all easy to follow. In general, therefore, game runs tend to be done in the vicinity of the lodge or camp you are staying at.

Lodges and Camps in the Mara

Several new lodges have been built or are under construction both inside and outside the Reserve. The oldest established, though completely modernised, is Keekorok (Five star. Bookings PO Box 47557 Nairobi; telephone 335807) situated where hunters used to bring their clients to shoot lion in the old days. It has a pool and a tarmac airstrip, served by all the scheduled air services. Keekorok is near the centre of the Reserve. On the western side is the Mara Serena (Five star. Bookings PO Box 48690 Nairobi; telephone 338656), set on a hill in the Mara triangle, overlooking the Mara River. Inspired architecturally by Masai huts, the lodge has a pool, its own airstrip and a hippo-viewing platform by the river. You may notice rock hyraxes running around below the lodge verandah in the evening. Unbelievably these small furry creatures share a common ancestor with the elephant and have similar reproductive organs and toe nails on their feet. The only other lodge, not yet classified at the time of writing, is the Mara Sopa (Bookings PO Box 72630, Nairobi; telephone 336088), which has a growing reputation and is situated between Keekorok and the Tanzanian border. A further lodge is planned on top of the Esoit Oloololo or Siria escarpment: the line of hills that are the backdrop to the western Mara.

In practice many people prefer to stay under canvas in the wild and there are some excellent tented camps. The best known — and the most expensive until the Mara Intrepids Club was set up recently — is Governor's Camp (Class A. Bookings PO Box 48217, Nairobi; telephone 331871). This is a site on the Mara River where colonial governors used to pitch camp in the old days, close to the Musiara airstrip and to very good game viewing. Governor's is usually heavily booked with German one-night tours from the coast and another, slightly less expensive camp, called Little Governor's (Class B) has been put up on the other side of the river, which has less of a package tour atmosphere. Governor's is strongly rivalled by the nearby Kichwa Tembo Camp (Class A, Bookings PO Box 59749, Nairobi; telephone 335900). This has very comfortable tents, each with its own shower and lavatory, a permanent dining-room and bar and a swimming-pool. None the less it retains a camp-fire atmosphere.

Expeditions organised from Kichwa Tembo include ballooning (see below); nature walks in the riverine forest to see blue and copper-tailed monkeys and birds including kingfishers, trogon and turacos; a flying safari to Rusinga Island in Lake Victoria to fish for Nile perch; visits to Masai manyattas; and trips up on to the escarpment, described below. Game drives cost Shs 1,000/- per vehicle. Further north, on the other side of the Mara bridge, 30 minutes from the Reserve, is the Mara River Camp (Class B, Bookings PO Box 45456 Nairobi; telephone 21992). Reached by a turn-off from the Narok road about 2 kilometres before the bridge, it has been improved lately. This was the base from which the artist and naturalist Jonathan Scott worked on the drawings and photographs in his book about the Mara, 'The Marsh Lions'. He is currently at Kichwa Tembo.

On the eastern side of the Reserve are two quite different and worth-while tented camps. Fig Tree Camp (Class A, PO Box 67868 Nairobi; telephone 21439) is well situated overlooking the Talek River, just outside the Reserve. It is reached most easily via Keekorok. Also inside the Reserve 17 kilometres (10 miles) from the Olmelepo gate, among hills to the east of the Keekorok Road, is Cottar's Camp

Kenya

(Class A, Bookings PO Box 44191 Nairobi; telephone 27930). Here accommodation is partly in bandas (thatched bungalows) partly in tents, situated by a large stand of fig trees, and with its own airstrip. Run by a former hunter, Glen Cottar, it specialises in night drives and in game walks, neither of which can be done within the Reserve. There are elephants, buffalo, lion and leopard in the immediate area, while giraffe, impala and waterbuck are attracted to the oasis which the stream running near the camp creates. From a specially built 'blind', shaped like a miniature pagoda, and with beds for seven people, you can watch leopard come to a bait and other animals at a salt lick.

There are other camps, including the Mara Serova (Bookings PO Box 30680, Nairobi; telephone 333233), but the last word has to go to the Mara Intrepids Club (bookings through Archer's Tours, PO Box 40097, Nairobi; telephone 24069): if, that is, your idea of being intrepid centres on four-poster beds and Persian rugs. It clearly does to the Saudi Arabian financier Adnan Kashoggi, who is part owner. American friends who have stayed there report that it's expensive, luxurious, excellently run, and as if a New York designer had been told 'make it like Africa'.

Lodges and camps provide vehicles for game drives, with a driver guide, at around Shs. 200/- per person or Shs 1,200/- per vehicle. If you are staying on the western side of the Reserve and not rushed, it is worth going up the Siria escarpment. There are zebra, lion and quite a lot of other game in the orchard bush up here. In fact the great migration ends here, though the animals are less easy to spot because of the trees. Various scenes in 'Out of Africa' were shot on this escarpment. In the film the spectacular panorama across the Mara towards the Serengeti doubled for the view from the Ngong Hills and it is one of the finest anywhere in the continent; unless you argue that the vantage point of a balloon is unbeatable.

Ballooning in the Mara

Around 0715 each morning the multicoloured shapes of several hot air balloons rise gracefully from Keekorok, the Mara Serena and Governor's Camp to drift with the light breeze across the plains. From the baskets slung beneath them four or five passengers watch the game for a couple of hours before descending, albeit sometimes bumpily, to the grass some 15 to 20 kilometres from where they started. The experience is unique, certainly in Kenya, probably anywhere. Furthermore the wildlife seems not disturbed by the monster above. The balloons themselves are made in Bristol, England, by the same firm who have created American millionaire Malcolm Forbes' fantasy balloons in the shapes of his chateau, his Harley Davidson motorbike, Beethoven's head and others. The idea was originated by the wildlife photographer, Alan Root. Vehicles follow the balloons to serve champagne breakfast in the bush after landing and bring the passengers back. The cost is Shs 3,600/- or US$270, per person. You can book on arrival at any lodge or camp or through a travel agent beforehand.

Western Kenya

From the Masai Mara to Western Kenya
It is possible, with four wheel drive, to reach Kisii, Kericho and Kisumu by driving up the escarpment, along to Lolgorien, then north to Kilgoris, from where the road is tarmacked to Kisii. But the 30 kilometres (18 miles) to Lolgorien can be all but impassable in the rains, and even on the better Kilgoris stretch matatus prefer driving through the bush to staying on the road. A preferable, if longer route, is to drive back on the Narok road to Ngorengore and take the B3 to Sotik, already mentioned. However, until these routes are improved most people will travel to Western Kenya via Nakuru.

Nakuru to Mau Summit
We have already described Nakuru. From the town — the fourth largest in Kenya — the railway and the A104 road continue north west to Eldoret and the Uasin Gishu Plateau and Uganda, while both road and rail branch off to Kericho and Kisumu on Lake Victoria at the Mau Summit. What is at first a gentle climb becomes gradually more arduous, as you ascend to nearly 2,740 metres (9,000 ft) with the great long line of the Mau escarpment to your left and Mount Londiani ahead. In the Mau Forest live a few of the extremely shy Wanderobo tribe, diminutive honey-hunters, who dress in skins and are Kenya's oldest inhabitants. On the way you pass turn-offs to Njoro, the home of Kenya's principal agricultural college, Egerton College, founded many years ago by the settler Lord Egerton, and to Molo. At Molo the Highlands Hotel (One Star. PO Box 142, Molo; telephone 50) maintains quite a good standard, while the 9-hole golf course adjoining it has been rehabilitated. Riding and trout fishing are also available.

This is some of Kenya's most productive farming country and trad-itionally Molo lamb has been to Kenya what Canterbury lamb is to New Zealand. Up here you will also notice fields of white flowers, like large daisies. These are pyrethrum plants, from which a natural — and very potent — insecticide is made. 'Kills all dudus (insects) dead' proclaims the label on one local brand called 'IT'. And it does. At Mau Summit the B1 road branches left to Kericho (59 kilometres) and Kisumu (147 kilometres), while a shorter, more twisting route to Kisumu is through Londiani and Fort Ternan. The A104 road con-tinues to Eldoret and via the B2 to Kitale and Mt Elgon.

Kericho
This western side of the Mau watershed is Ceylon in Africa, Kenya's great tea-growing area, where the combination of morning sun and

Kenya

rain 335 days a year, together with the altitude, create ideal conditions. The fresh green bushes, as close-planted across the fields as a green carpet, are a fine sight and the product is among the world's best. Kericho is the centre of the tea cultivation and the Tea Hotel (Three stars. PO Box 75, Kericho; Bookings: telephone Nairobi 21855) is one of the better up-country hotels. Tennis, golf and trout-fishing are available and visits to a tea estate can be arranged. The hotel has a list of trout streams compiled by the Kericho/Sotik Fishing Association (PO Box 281, Kericho) and holds the keys to a picturesque wood and stone built fishing hut on the Kipteget River (Shs 15/- a night, self-help). The Kipteget is one of many attractive streams flowing down through the Mau Forests. Remember that you are 7,000 ft up here and it is cold at night.

Kericho is effectively the gateway to South Nyanza, where roads have been greatly improved. Indeed Kenya is one of the few countries in Africa where communications become better instead of worse. The B6 road out of the town leads to Sotik and Kisii, described below. The B1, which turns off just outside Kericho, winds gently down the hills to the plain surrounding Kisumu (88 kilometres), the traffic becoming heavier as you approach the town which lies on the Winam Gulf (formerly the Kavirondo Gulf).

Kisumu and Lake Victoria
Kenya's third largest town is a busy commercial centre served by scheduled flights from Nairobi, by trains and by long-distance buses. Most banks operating in Kenya have branches here, there are good shops and hairdressers, but a shortage of car rental facilities.

The best centrally placed hotel is the Imperial (PO Box 1866, Kisumu; telephone 41485) on Jomo Kenyatta Highway. For some reason un-classified, it is air-conditioned and has an excellent restaurant, the Florence, where a set dinner costs Shs 85/- or you could eat a-la-carte for about Shs 175/-. The hotel's main disadvantage is a rather gloomy pool, compared to the lakeside pool and splendid views of its rival the fully air-conditioned Sunset Hotel (Three Star. PO Box 215, Kisumu; telephone 41100) on the southern edge of the town near Hippo Point, appropriately named. The Sunset has open air barbecue lunches on Sundays: a good idea, since at 1,162 metres (3,718 ft) above sea level, the climate can be humid as well as hot. Local fish features on all menus. The Luo people of this area are Kenya's pre-eminent fishermen, and further along the lake shore from the Sunset Hotel, is the village of Dunga, where every morning scores of fishing boats set out at dawn to fish in the lake and canoe races are traditional events.

From a visitor's point of view there are a number of attractions, the first of which is the lake itself. Lake Victoria is the largest freshwater lake in the world, the size of Ireland and one source of the Nile, which made it an endless source of speculation among 19th century explorers. Kisumu used to be the starting point for steamer services around the lake and maybe one day they will be resumed. In the meantime you can take a four-hour trip on the M.V. Alestes or its companion vessel to see Mount Homa and the Winam Gulf. The boats leave daily at 0900 except on Thursdays and return every day except Fridays. Some stop en route at Kendu Bay and take longer. The first class fare to Homa Bay, described below, is Shs 55/-, and the booking office is at the harbour where steamers dating back to the early years of the century lie tied up, out of service. One, the Nyanza, was launched here in 1908, having been brought in sections from Mombasa, as all the ships had to be.

Kisumu has a recently created wildlife reserve, basically a zoo park, to the south of the town; a pleasant golf course laid out on the lake shore, reached by the road to the airport. Visiting players are welcome but there are no sets of clubs for hire. The green fee is Shs 30/-. Tennis and sailing are among other sporting facilities.

South of Kisumu, Kisii, Homa Bay, Lambwe Valley
The A1 road south from Kisumu, which goes eventually to Tanzania, is a good tarmac highway. The immediate area around the Winam Gulf is alternately stricken by floods and drought and considerable international aid has gone into helping its people. However further inland the villages of South Nyanza are more prosperous. On the way to Kisii you pass a pelicanry at Oyugis, some 96 kilometres (60 miles) from Kisumu, best visited between August and March.

Kisii is a hill town which is the home base of Kenya's most renowned stone carvers. They work in the locally quarried soapstone, soft and almost rose coloured, making all sorts of objects from statuettes to tankards. A major statue by the Kisii sculptor Elkana Ong'esa stands outside the offices of UNESCO in Paris. The town has shops, a branch of Barclays Bank, and the Kisii Hotel (One star. PO Box 1385, Kisii; telephone 20691), signed at the main road, which is an adequate place to stop for a drink or a meal.

From the A1 past Kisii a good road leads down again to Homa Bay, on the lake with the hump of Mt Homa beyond. There are many pre-historic remains in this area, especially on Rusinga Island at the entrance to the Gulf of Winam. The fishing camp there, which has an airstrip, has seen notable catches of giant Nile perch. The island was the birthplace of the politician Tom Mboya, to whom there is a memorial. It can be reached by ferry from the town of Homa Bay where there is a small landing stage at which the ships from Kisumu dock, and you will see the traditional long-prowed Luo fishing boats, see colour illustration. The Homa Bay Hotel (Two star. PO Box 521, Homa Bay.) is modern, clean and very pleasantly situated overlooking the lake, within walking distance of the jetty. It charges Shs

175/- single or Shs 260/- double per night and Shs 60/- for a meal. This hotel is the place to stay for the little visited Lambwe Valley National Reserve, 25 kilometres (15 miles) from Homa Bay at the foot of the Gwasi hills. Only 119 sq kilometres in extent, this is an area of grassland and bush where tsetse fly have prevented cattle-raising in the past and so protected rare colonies of roan antelope and Jackson's hartebeeste. It is due to be renamed the Ruma National Park.

North of Kisumu, Kakamega, the Nandi Hills
Less than an hour's drive from Kisumu is the under-appreciated hill country of Kakamega, dotted with rock outcrops like castles and adorned with flame trees and with its own unique National Park. In the 1930s it enjoyed a real old-style gold rush. Prospectors poured in from the USA, Canada and South Africa, as if it were another Yukon. Hotels and nightclubs sprang up. But the dream collapsed as extraction costs rose and the mines were flooded, though there is still some gold in them. However, the area's tourist potential has created a new hotel, the Kakamega Golf (Three star. PO Box 118, Kakamega; telephone 0331-20460), well situated with a swimming-pool. Lunch is Shs 60/-, dinner Shs 70/- and the 9-hole golf course is free to residents. 15 kilometres (9 miles) away is the only forest in Kenya that is West African in character. It was separated from the rest of the West African forest when the climate dried up, resulting in trees being replaced by grasslands. Now a National Park, the forest has many types of birds, butterflies, insects, trees and shrubs not found elsewhere in Kenya. There is an unfurnished do-it-yourself rest house which can be booked through the District Forest Officer (PO Box 1233, Kakamega), and the Kakamega Hotel can provide a map of the forest paths.

From Kakamega you can either drive on up the A1 road to Kitale, with the option of branching right on the A104 to Eldoret, or skirt the National Park and make your way east to Kapsabet and go to Eldoret via the Nandi Hills. On the whole the roads here are of high standard and gratifyingly well signed. If you are going to Uganda there is the Bungoma Tourist Hotel on the road to Tororo at Bungoma (Two star. PO Box 972, Bungoma; telephone 126).

Kapsabet is another hill town, less interesting than Kakamega though with the Kapsabet Hotel (One star. PO Box 449, Kapsabet; telephone 96), banks, filling stations and a few shops. It is the administrative headquarters for the Nandi District, an area of rolling hills and tea estates, home of the renowned Nandi warriors and of a mythical Nandi bear, as well as the real aardvark or ant bear. If you make the circuit of the hills and want to rejoin the Eldoret to Nakuru road, follow the sign for Nabkoi, a village close to it. Equally you can take the B11 direct from Kapsabet to Eldoret.

Eldoret
Eldoret itself is a major farming centre and home of the Moi University, Kenya's second. It has a new hotel, the Sirikwa (Four star. PO Box 3361. Telephone 31655) which is the obvious place to base oneself. There is very fine country to the east, especially the Kerio Valley, and the climate up here on the plateau is close to ideal, with warm days and cool nights.

Kitale and Mount Elgon
Kitale, at the foot of Mount Elgon, is a farming township rather similar to Eldoret with one hotel, the Kitale on Luthuli Avenue (Unclassified. Bookings PO Box 60342, Nairobi; telephone 34033 or 20054.) and from a visitor's viewpoint is the stepping-off point for a visit to the Mount Elgon National Park 48 kilometres (30 miles) away. Alternatively, if you want to stay on a private estate, you could go to the Lokitela Guest House run by the Mills family on their 874-acre farm, which includes 70 acres of forest where some 250 species of birds have been recorded. Lokitela (PO Box 122, Kitale or telephone Nairobi 882253) is 19 kilometres (12 miles) west of Kitale and costs Shs 1,500/- double, full board, per day. Ask for directions when you book. Excursions can be arranged to Mt Elgon and the Saiwa Swamp National Park.

The Mount Elgon National Park lies between 8,000 and 14,000 ft, being a strip of 65 square miles running up the side of the mountain, the 14,178 ft summit of which is in Uganda. The Park has herds of buffalo, elephant and eland, inhabiting the forests and moorland slopes, splendid bird life and caves filled with bats, into which you can venture if you have the nerve. Two of these caves, called Kitum and Makingeny, both within reach of the Park Road, have been largely gouged out over thousands of years by the small forest elephants; apparently to get at the sodium sulphate in the walls.

Mount Elgon can be climbed: for information contact the Mountain Club of Kenya or read Peter Robson's book 'Mountains of Kenya.' You will pass through three main vegetation zones: montane rain forest, where you will see black and white colobus monkeys leaping among the tall trees; bamboo thickets; and finally alpine moorlands, where the same giant groundsels and lobelia grow as are found on Mount Kenya. This curious vegetation is described in the Mount Kenya chapter. You can reach the moorlands and return in a single day's strenuous climb. The nearest accommodation is at the Mount Elgon Lodge (One star. Bookings PO Box 30471 Nairobi; telephone 29751). The lodge is a converted farm house with beautiful views and is 25 kilometres (15 miles) from Kitale.

Pokot and the Saiwa Swamp
The country north of Kitale is home to the Pokot tribe whose men wear conical ivory lip plugs and decorate their hair with ostrich

feathers. While here you should stop 25 kilometres (16 miles) north of Kitale at the Saiwa Swamp Park, a tiny tract of swampland created as a reserve for the sitatunga, a rare antelope with spiral horns and stripes on the flanks that stays up to its knees in water most of the time and feeds on swamp vegetation. The Park, which is only 1.9 sq kilometres in area, has no entrance fee and no roads; you walk to the swamp and climb tree platforms for game viewing.

The dirt road past Saiwa goes to Kapenguria, principally famous for the trial of the late Mzee Jomo Kenyatta, Kenya's first President, ten years before Independence. The main tarmac A1 from Kitale continues through Kapenguria to skirt the Cherangani Hills into West Pokot and link with the new tarmac road to Lodwar and the west side of Lake Turkana (see later chapter). The Cheranganis themselves are some 80 kilometres (50 miles) long, rise to 10,832 ft and offer lovely, if rugged, scenery and abundant birdlife, especially along the dramatic Kongelai escarpment.

Nyeri and the Aberdares

From Nairobi to Nyeri is all Kikuyuland, densely populated and so almost devoid of animal wildlife, though not of birds. The steep ridges that rise towards the Aberdares force the road to twist and climb even though the A2's re-routing to sweep east of Murang'a avoids the worst, and the 155 kilometres (96 miles), though all tarmac, is a two to two-and-a-half hour drive, while the train puffs along for seven hours and five minutes.

Near Kiambu and Thika there are coffee, pineapple and sisal estates, easily visited by arrangement. Although better known for fine arabica coffee, Kenya is also the world's third largest producer of pineapples. Greater interest lies in the Kikuyu villages. The Kikuyu are Kenya's largest ethnic group (3.2 million in 1979) and originated as agriculturalists. A family may occupy three or more of the traditional round thatched huts, though increasingly they are being replaced by more modern rectangular houses. Both land and firewood are in short supply, which is why cattle graze on the road verges and you may see women pass by carrying loads of wood bought from traders, held up on their backs by a traditional leather thong passing round the forehead. Kikuyu women do much of the work on the family plots of land (*shambas* in Swahili), and some men have several wives, since polygamy is legal. However, the Kikuyu are one of the most forward looking tribes in Africa and female emancipation has progressed rapidly since Independence, particularly through a nationwide organisation called *Maendeleo ya Wanawake*.

The road by-passes Thika but it does pass the New Blue Posts Hotel, (Unclassified. PO Box 42, Thika; telephone 22241) a favourite stopping place since before Winston Churchill shot a lion nearby in

1908; it has recently been modernized. The hotel has an attractive garden overlooking the Chania Falls and a swimming pool. There is a lot of tall papyrus grass about like that from which the ancient Egyptians made paper. Elspeth Huxley wrote enchantingly about this neighbourhood in 'The Flame Trees of Thika'. The town has developed industrially beyond recognition since, but the flame trees, which one sees in many other places too, still grow high and thick, with dark green foliage in which blossom dozens of reddish orange flowers, as vivid as shellbursts.

Ol Doinyo Sapuk National Park
To the east of Thika rises a great humped hill, visible from far away. This is Ol Doinyo Sapuk, the name being Masai for 'The mountain of the buffalo', and there are buffalo, impala and bushbuck among its densely forested slopes as well as many birds, including the African harrier hawk. The mountain is a miniature national park of 18.4 sq kilometres (7 sq miles). A road, negotiable by cars in dry weather, leads to the 7,041 ft summit. There is no admission charge. Just outside the Park boundary, close to the Thika Road, are the Fourteen Falls on the Mbagathi, spectacular particularly during the rains and a haunt of crocodiles. This river is better known as the Athi and flows all the way to the Indian Ocean, changing its name to the Galana in Tsavo East and to the Sabaki before it debouches north of Malindi.

Close to the Ol Doinyo Sapuk Park road, in the bush, are the graves of two American pioneers, ennobled by the British. Before the Great War Sir Northrup and Lady McMillan owned Juja Farm near the mountain, where President Roosevelt stayed during his great safari in an Edwardian wooden house shipped from India and re-assembled. Roosevelt described it as being "of one storey, a broad vine-shaded verandah running round it". The house still stands and has often been used as a film set. Sir Northrup is commemorated by the McMillan Library in Nairobi.

The A2 also by-passes Murang'a, formerly Fort Hall, where there is a church decorated with remarkable Goya-like mural paintings by a Chagga artist called Elimo Njau. They show the life and crucifixion of an African Christ in local landscape. Otherwise there is little more than Kikuyu villages and markets until you reach Nyeri, save that you may see the glaciered peak of Mount Kenya rising out of the clouds ahead of you. According to Kikuyu tradition it is the dwelling place of the god Ngai, and, like Mount Olympus in Greece, It is shy of revealing itself, except in the early morning and the evening. Many of Kenya's Africans are animists, believing God resides in natural objects, like trees and hills. However about 25 per cent are reckoned to be Christians.

Kenya

Nyeri and Treetops

Nyeri, 5,750 ft up, is a well-laid-out township, with a 9-hole golf course and many excellent trout streams. It has an airfield with scheduled airline services. The best tourist shop is in the Outspan Hotel (Three star. PO Box 24 Nyeri; bookings telephone Nairobi 22860) which is one of the best up-country hotels in East Africa, and stands one kilometre from the centre of Nyeri in its own delightful grounds. It has extensive facilities including squash, tennis, trout fishing, swimming, car hire and riding. The hotel hires out all sporting equipment and fishing licences are cheap. Lord Baden Powell, founder of the Boy Scout movement, spent his last years at the Outspan — and very enjoyable they must have been. His cottage, Paxtu, is preserved. Nyeri's other three star hotel is the Green Hills (PO Box 313 Nyeri; telephone 2017).

Trips to the world famous game-viewing hotel, Treetops, start with the excellent buffet lunch at the Outspan, after which a hunting car with a hunter escort takes you up into the forest, bringing you back next morning for breakfast. This is the only way of going to Treetops; you cannot simply drive there yourself, even if you could find the track. Book through Block Hotels (PO Box 47557 Nairobi; telephone 335807). The 1987/88 high season tariff was Shs 1800/- per person including transfer from Nairobi but not including the Shs 80/- national park entrance fee.

Treetops stands by a pool on a low spur of the Aberdare Forest known as the Treetops salient. When it's raining in the bamboo higher up, which it often is because the rainfall is 80-100 inches a year, the game come down to drier ground in the salient and are attracted to Treetops itself by the adjacent salt licks and the pool. Buffalo, rhino, elephant, giant forest hog and antelope are common visitors. The Aberdare Park Warden says he has counted 500 elephant in the area at one time. They are kept off the farms below the forest by a ditch more than five miles long, six ft deep and six ft wide, the maintenance of which occupies at least 40 men all the year. Daytime gamedrives into the salient are available from the Outspan.

The original hotel was literally built in a tree in 1932, and the present Queen of England was staying there in 1952 when her father died and she acceded to the British throne. The Visitor's book records that she and Prince Philip saw 50 elephants. The present hotel is larger, built 40 ft high on stilts among the trees and has a dining room, bar, bedrooms and verandahs, from which you get a grand circle view of the forest wildlife beneath, aided after dark by an artificial moon.

Leaving Nyeri you can either follow round the side of the Aberdares through Mweiga to Nyahururu (Thomson's Falls) and then strike north to Rumuruti on what is a much improved route to Maralal, being tarmac to Rumuruti and well graded murram to Saguta. Or you can go directly north to Naromoru, Nanyuki and Mount Kenya. We deal with the Rumuruti direction first.

Aberdare National Park, the Ark and Mweiga

The Park Road from Nyeri to the Aberdare National Park (the highest game park in the world) and Naivasha climbs 4,000 ft in 22 kilometres (14 miles); it is closed in wet weather. It passes first through forest reserve, mainly planted with fast-growing exotic trees like gums; then into the alpine bamboo, feathery-leaved but impenetrably dense, with occasional bars of sunlight slanting down through it like rays from the windows of a great cathedral. Not far past the Park gate you suddenly emerge on to open moorland, 10,000 ft above sea level, and consisting of huge tussocks of grass. Up here you are allowed to leave your car and go up to 100 yds from the roads and rivers. There are two spectacular waterfalls on either side of a wide ravine. Karura dropping 894 ft in three stages, and Gura 791 ft, also in three stages. Especially near the water, there is fantastic growth of moss and giant vegetation, peculiar to the East African mountains. Groundsel and lobelias, small plants in Europe, reach 15 ft high here. It is as though one had suddenly been transported to Brobdingnag, the giants' country of 'Gulliver's Travels'. In good weather the Park Road leads to superb views of the Rift as it descends on the other side of the Aberdares to the Kinangop Plateau and Naivasha. The road is partly tarmacked on the Naivasha side.

The wildlife in the Park is mostly shy, like the bongo. There are elephant, buffalo, rhino, eland, waterbuck, reedbuck, colobus monkey, serval cats, mountain buzzard, crowned hawk eagle, green parrots and Jackson's francolin. The author saw a melanistic black leopard on one trip. There are a few lion and hyenas too. You may also come across patrols of game scouts, clad in green uniforms, and armed with rifles. Their job is checking on trespassers and poachers. Camping is not permitted.

Near the Park and the township of Mweiga is the Aberdare Country Club, a delightful former farmhouse, where riding and fishing are available. The Club is the starting-point for trips to The Ark, a 'tree hotel' rivalling Treetops for night game-viewing high in the forests of the Aberdares, where the animals you may see are similar, not forgetting the elusive bongo. The Ark is very well designed with several terraces both open and glass enclosed. The King and Queen of Sweden are among notables who have stayed there. A visit starts with lunch at the Aberdare Country Club, followed by an 18 kilometres (11 mile) drive up the forest road in the company of a professional hunter. You have dinner and spend the night at the lodge, returning after breakfast the following morning. The Club is classified three star (bookings through Signet, Box 59749 Nairobi;

telephone 335900). Charges for one night at the Ark including transfer from Nairobi, are similar to those for Treetops. The Club can also arrange day time game-drives in the Aberdare salient.

Across the valley from the Aberdare Country Club is one of the few private ranches in Kenya where visitors can stay, the 6,500 acre Sangare ranch, owned by the Prettejohn family. Their own farmhouse has now featured in a number of films, while the estate has become an unofficial wildlife sanctuary: herds of elephant, buffalo and a few rhino, as well as impala, eland and gazelle share the land with cattle and horses. The guests stay in a private cedarwood lodge, sleeping four, by a lake, with their own cook and servants. Charges are Shs 950/- per person, with game-drives, the use of a leopard blind and other expeditions extra. Sangare is a base for riding safaris using zebroids — a cross between a zebra and a horse — as pack animals. Bookings through Sangare Ranch, PO Box 24 Mweiga; telephone 20. Or Safari Consultants Ltd, 83 Gloucester Place, London W1H 3PG, England. The next ranch along, as it were, is the American-owned Solio Ranch, which also doubles as a private game reserve. Solio can be visited by arrangement with the Aberdare Country Club for a Shs 100/- fee per person, plus vehicle charges. The ranch is beyond Mweiga on the Nyahururu Road and you are more certain to see rhino there than anywhere else in Kenya. Rhino from Solio have been transferred to the Nairobi and Nakuru National Parks. Driving on past here you will catch sight of the Aberdare peaks on your left, notably Satima (13,120 ft). The Ngobit River is a fine trout stream.

Nyeri to Nyahururu and Rumuruti
This fast tarmac road from Nyeri through Mweiga to Nyahururu, a distance of 115 kilometres (74 miles) takes you across the glorious plains of Laikipia which is ranching land dotted with umbrella thorns and spiritually akin to Texas. Here Santa Gertudis is as much a household word as Hereford or Boran, these last being the African humped cattle with which imported stock are often crossed to combine yield with resistance to local conditions.

Cattle have a tough life out here, what with tropical fevers and ticks, which they catch all too easily from the buffalo, buck, giraffe and other game that also wander over Laikipia. However there is no tsetse fly, so many farmers keep horses. Among the largest ranches are one belonging to the Paris art dealer Wildenstein; the Ol Pegeta Ranch owned by Lonrho, where game is preserved alongside 16,000 head of cattle; and the two already mentioned. A smaller ranch where you can stay is El Karama (PO Box 172, Nanyuki), which has a self-service camp on the Uaso Nyiro river, 42 kilometres (26 miles) from Nanyuki, off the Maralal road. Riding, bird-watching and game walks are available. More details from Let's Go Travel in Standard Street, Nairobi (PO Box 60342, Nairobi; telephone 29539).

Nyahururu, a township originally called Thomson's Falls after the same explorer who gave the elegant 'Tommy' gazelle its name, stands 2,377 metres (7,800 ft) above sea level, so can be chilly at night and the Thomson's Falls Lodge bar has a log fire in the evenings. The Lodge (One star. PO Box 38, Nyahururu; telephone 0365 - 22006) is on the outskirts of the town, by the 243 ft falls and overlooking the dramatic forested gorge into which they plunge. Unhappily the view is partly spoilt by souvenir sellers' stalls. The rooms are comfortable, if simple, and have private baths. The menu is modest. About one kilometre from the Lodge, up-river, there is a hippo pool. The town has grown in recent years and now has banks, shops and other facilities.

The explorer Joseph Thomson, a Scotsman, began his East African journeys in 1880 when he was only 21 and achieved great fame for his exploits: among them calming down a tense situation with a band of Masai warriors by removing his false teeth. He named the Aberdare mountains after the then President of the Royal Geographical Society and was the first European to see the waterfall here. He died at the age of 37.

From Nyahururu a new tarmac road runs direct to Nakuru through Subukia, where the stone Norman style church was in fact built in 1951, while a branch railway line and a road run south to Gilgil via Ol Kalou, through the farming country known before World War II as the 'Happy Valley'. Here the more riotous of the British settlers lived, people whose extraordinary life style has been brought alive again by James Fox's book 'White Mischief' about the murder in 1940 of Lord Errol. Using either of these roads you can complete a circuit of the Aberdares and return to Nairobi along the Rift Valley.

North from Nyahururu a much improved dirt road goes the 34 kilometres (21 miles) to Rumuruti, where there is an airstrip but only very basic shops, no filling station and no hotel. Surprisingly a non-residential club survives from the days of the white settlers. Nearby you will find hippo and a multitude of birds along the Ewaso Narok river, where there are papyrus swamps.

Beyond Rumuruti the road becomes decidedly rougher and hotter on the way to Maralal, a distance of 112 kilometres (70 miles), one of the gateways to northern Kenya and described in the next chapter.

Mount Kenya, Meru and Embu, Isiolo

Nyeri to Nanyuki
The tarmac road from Nyeri to Nanyuki, a distance of 51 kilometres (32 miles) is good. Before Naro Moru is the signpost to the Mountain Lodge (Five star. Bookings PO Box 30471 Nairobi; telephone 336858) the third of the 'tree hotels' and for game viewing possibly the

best. Certainly it is one of the best high-altitude bird watching spots as well as attracting large numbers of big game. You must arrive between 1600 and 1830 hours. The lodge can also be reached from the Karatina-Nyeri road, if you are coming direct from Nairobi. The fourth tree hotel, Secret Valley, was burnt down.

Naro Moru

The trading post of Naro Moru, once the centre of a European farming district, is now farmed by Africans. Lying on the lower slopes of Mount Kenya, it is attractive country and many of the scenes in 'Born Free' the film of Joy Adamson's book about her tame lions, were shot around here.

About half a mile from the main road is the comfortable Naro Moru River Lodge (Three star. PO Box 18 Naro Moru; telephone 23). Set on the river, which is stocked with rainbow and brown trout, the lodge has pleasant cedar log cabins, each with its own bathroom. Cheaper self-service chalets for two or more people are also available. As well as riding, walking, fishing and bird watching (Jackson's Francolin and Lanner Falcon are among local species), the lodge offers foot safaris up Mount Kenya by the Teleki route. These involve no rock climbing, though you need to be reasonably healthy. They last either one or three days and cost from Shs 1,000/- to Shs 2,500/- per person. A one-day trip is also possible, as is a full-scale mountaineering ascent. Clothing and equipment can be hired.

Mount Kenya and the Aberdares also have several fishing camps for the ardent trout fisherman, including Thiba, Thego, Kimakia and Kiandongoro. At these places you must bring your own food, bedding and equipment, but there are hot and cold water, beds and cooking equipment. Further information from the Fisheries Dept (PO Box 58187 Nairobi.) Some trips to Mountain Lodge include a luncheon stop at Thego Fishing Camp.

Nanyuki

Nanyuki, a railhead and shopping town with banks, chemists and a hospital, is mainly dedicated to farming and to the Kenya Army and the Air Force 82, so named since a brief and abortive coup attempt by some of its junior ranks in 1982. The town is the real stepping-off point for Northern Kenya and a place to climb Mount Kenya from. It lies 6,400 ft up at the foot of the mountain and smack on the Equator. In fact the Silverbeck Hotel used to claim the Line ran across its bar floor, so that you could be in the northern hemisphere while your drinking companion was in the southern. Unhappily the bar was burnt down and awaits rebuilding. A couple of miles out is the renowned Mount Kenya Safari Club (Five star. Bookings, Box 54546, Nairobi). Calmly luxurious, it has its own golf, airstrip, bowls, swimming pool, sauna baths, riding, fishing, displays of traditional dancing — the lot in fact. Peacocks wander on the terrace and the 200 staff have looked after many of the world's famous people. Temporary membership is available. Adjoining the club is the Mount Kenya Game Ranch, founded by the late William Holden, the film star, who was part owner of the club. Recently several film stars have paid $150,000 apiece for house sites nearby. The neighbouring game ranch provides a haven for animals whose habitat is threatened.

Nanyuki used to be a safari centre, and safaris still start from here. However one of the organisers, John Alexander, is now based in Nairobi, (PO Box 20127; telephone 891487) as is David Allen (PO Box 40132; telephone 60365) and Julian McKeand is running his notable camel safaris from Lewa Downs (Private Bag, Isiolo), while the Prettejohns operate from Mweiga (PO Box 24, Mweiga; telephone 20) with riding safaris, as already mentioned.

Mount Kenya National Park
When the German missionary Ludwig Krapf sent home reports that he had observed a snow-capped mountain on the Equator, no-one in Europe believed him. Eminent authorities declared such a thing to be impossible. Today mountaineers come from all over the world to tackle the difficult ascent as a training ground for the Himalayas. In practice, how much of a challenge you make of climbing Mount Kenya depends largely on you. By merely walking to the top hut you are getting higher than Mont Blanc in the Alps, and the trek up through the forests of bamboo and podo and across the moorland is rewarding, though not for anyone who gets short of breath at normal altitudes. There are the same animals as on the Aberdares, plus some of the most lovely birds in Africa — malachite sunbirds, golden-winged sunbirds, yellow francolin and the Abyssinian long-eared owl — and the same curious 'old man's beard' hanging ghost-like from the trees. In four days you can 'conquer' the easiest peak, Lenana, 16,355 ft, and see the glaciers, the 32 lakes and tarns and the giant vegetation of the mountain slopes.

This vegetation is unique to the East African mountains. It includes blue-flowering lobelias which grow to 10ft high and giant groundsel which reach 19ft. They have apparently developed in response to the extremes of freezing cold at night and hot tropical sun by day, a variation made greater by the altitude. Their long stems are insulated by layers of dead leaves, helping protect them from the particularly cold air lying on the surface at night.

Walking to the moorland and the tarns is easy. However reaching the twin summits of Batian (17,058ft) and Nelion (17,022ft) is a different matter. There are very high winds, tricky rock, shifting ice and the risk of contracting fatal pulmonary oedema from prolonged effort at this altitude. The peaks have claimed many lives and the

Kenya

Austrian mountain rescue service has been training Kenyans for rescue work. Because the mountain is on the Equator the south side is in sunshine during the first six months of the year and the north in the second, thus the time of year dictates which face you climb. The best seasons are the driest periods of mid-January to late February, late August and September. Batian and Nelion, joined by a ridge called the Gate of Mists, are actually hard cores of rock exposed by erosion of the crater rim, for Mount Kenya, like Kilimanjaro, is an extinct volcano. More information can be had from the safari firms, or the national parks or the Mountain Club of Kenya (Box 45741, Nairobi).

The Mountain Club publishes the excellent 'Guide Book to Mount Kenya and Kilimanjaro' with full details of climbing routes and sections on the geology, flora and fauna of the mountain. There is accommodaton in chalets at the Meteorological Station on the Naro Moru track, which can be booked either through the Naro Moru River Lodge or through the Park Warden (PO Box 69, Naro Moru). The Mountain Club's huts further up can also be booked through the River Lodge, but their facilities — anyway very basic — have been sadly abused by tourists who are not true climbers.

Of the various tracks up the mountain, the best known are the Naro Meru track which enters the Park through the main gate at 8,000 ft and continues to 10,000 ft, and the Sirimon track from the north west which reaches 11,000 ft. The Carr track from the Mero side reaches 14,000 ft. Obviously, all demand four-wheel drive and dry weather. The Park itself starts around the 10,000 ft contour, enclosing only part of the forest in its 600 sq kilometres (231 sq miles). You can get some idea of the huge scale of the mountain by comparing it to Britain. If its 56 kilometre (35 miles) base was superimposed on the Home Counties, it would stretch from central London to Aldershot.

Towards Isiolo and Meru
From Nanyuki the main tarmac road climbs steadily north east through Timau, where a sign to the right indicates the Kentrout Trout Farm (Telephone Timau 14), which has a restaurant and is a pleasant, shady spot to break a long journey. You can, of course, buy trout to take home. Here you are coming to another of Kenya's wheat-growing areas, with huge fields which suddenly end as the road descends over the escarpment to the north revealing a truly magnificent panorama towards the Samburu country. The escarpment drops almost 5,000 ft in under 30 kilometres (19 miles), described in the next chapter. A short way down the road divides, the A2 continuing to Isiolo, while the right hand fork leads around the contours of Mount Kenya to Meru, with the Meru Hills on the left.

If you continue some 2 kilometres past this junction on the Isiolo

Road you pass a sign on a rock indicating Wilderness Trails. This is the entrance to a private 40,000-acre ranch where Ker and Downey have rights to camp: see the Safaris chapter. Private guests are sometimes accepted. Game on the ranch runs from elephant down to bush babies and bat-eared foxes, including the long necked gerenuk, leopard and cheetah. The ranch is the base for Julian McKeand's camel safaris in the Samburu country further north, described in the next chapter.

Embu and Meru
Both the road to Meru town around the north of Mount Kenya and the direct road from Nairobi are tarmacked. The direct road forks right off the Nairobi to Nyeri road at Sagana and goes through Embu, 131 kilometres (82 miles) from the capital.

At Embu there is a pleasant small hotel set in well kept gardens called the Izaak Walton Inn (One star. PO Box 1, Embu; telephone bookings Nairobi 27828). It is named after the famous English angler on account of the fine fishing in the mountain streams here and the Inn can arrange fishing for guests.

The old murram road from Embu to Meru looped east to avoid the mountain foothills and its tortuous bends form a notorious stretch of the Safari Rally. Happily for other drivers it has been made obsolete by a £25 million British aid project providing tarmac road which cuts through hills and bridges ravines, halving the distance between the two towns.

Meru Mount Kenya Lodge
Approximately half way along this new road is a turn off left to Chogoria and the self-catering Meru Mount Kenya Lodge (Bookings Let's Go Travel, PO Box 60342, Nairobi; telephone 29539). Situated 27 kilometres (17 miles) from Chogoria, the Lodge is well placed where the forest and bamboo ends and the high altitude moorland begins. The altitude is 3,000 metres (9,700 ft).

Game is attracted to two dams and the lodge is a good base for climbing or walking. Accommodation is not particularly beautiful but practical bandas, each with fireplaces, electric light, beds and bedding, crockery and utensils. Families we know have enjoyed it. Rates are Shs 160/- per adult per night, Shs 50/- per child, plus taxes. Lets Go Travel provides a useful leaflet about the lodge with a route map for finding it.

The Meru district is densely populated and mainly known for fishing, rare butterflies and Meru oak, one of Kenya's most beautiful indigenous woods. Plus, of course, the Meru National Park. There is a small museum in Meru town, with displays of traditional dress and ornaments.

Meru National Park

From Meru town to Meru National Park is 78 kilometres (49 miles). The road, tarmacked as far as Maua, can be negotiated by any kind of vehicle. Meru National Park's 821 sq kilometres (317 sq miles) contain an excellent system of roads and tracks, plus several airstrips. By the Meru National Park runs the Tana River, 704 kilometres (440 miles) long, which winds through the Northern Frontier down to the Indian Ocean near Lamu. Up here its banks attract wildlife like jam pies flies, and a motorboat is available for river exploration. There is plenty of game in the reserve, including reticulated giraffe and Grevy's zebra, lion, leopard, black rhino, elephant, buck and a great variety of birds. A herd of white rhino, previously extinct in the area, was introduced here from South Africa. Unhappily they have to be kept in semi-captivity and are breeding poorly. They can be seen at their compound near Park headquarters or else feeding in the vicinity, escorted by a ranger. The altitude of the Park varies from about 1,000 ft along the Tana to 3,400 ft in the Nyambeni foothills. East of Leopard's Rock there is a wilderness area with no roads, while the site of Elsa's camp, used by the late Joy Adamson, is on the Ura River in the south of the Park.

There are several kinds of accommodation available in or adjacent to the Park. The Meru Mulika Lodge (Three star, Bookings PO Box 30471, Nairobi; telephone 336858) has comfortable rooms in rondavels, a water-hole where game comes to drink and a swimming pool. A few miles away is Leopard Rock Self-help Lodge, a self-service lodge with ten bandas (huts), each with private bathroom. The only thing you need take is your own food, although there is a shop. Bookings can be made through AA Travel (PO Box 14982, Nairobi; telephone 339700). There are several campsites and also the Bwatherongi Bandas, (self-help), near the Park HQ, all of which can be booked through the Park Warden (PO Box 162, Meru).

Kora National Reserve

Adjacent to Meru National Park, on the south of the Tana River, is the Kora National Reserve, created largely through the effort of George Adamson; he still lives here, rehabilitating tame lions for release though he is now in his 80s. Kora is 1,787 sq kilometres (about 500 sq miles) of remote, dry bush country with game similar to that found in Meru National Park. Unhappily the area is being invaded by Somali nomads from further north, together with their goats and camels, to the great detriment of the wildlife. There are tracks negotiable by ordinary cars, but no accommodation as yet. Camping is permitted.

Isiolo: Gateway to Northern Kenya

The Great North Road is tarmac as far as Isiolo, descending a total of over 4,000 ft from Timau. Isiolo is very much a frontier trading centre, attracting nomadic tribes-people from all over the north, as well as being an administrative centre with a large army base nearby. There are shops, filling stations and a colourful open air market, plus a hospital being constructed with British aid. There are no tourist hotels. In an emergency it may be possible to find a bed at the Italian Mission — the Fathers speak little English — but it would be easier, if you have transport, to go on to one of the lodges in the Samburu Reserve. There are also a number of fairly rough African lodging houses.

Leaving the town you have to state your destination at a checkpoint. If it is not the Samburu Reserve or the Maralal road through Wamba you will have to wait until a convoy with an armed guard departs. This is normally every two days. The northbound convoys leave on Mondays, Wednesdays and Fridays at around 1100 — in theory — and return from Marsabit on Tuesdays, Thursdays and Sundays. The road is liable to be attacked by *shifta,* or brigands, which nowadays effectively means Somalis.

Northern Kenya: Maralal, The Samburu

The vast semi-desert that stretches north of the Highlands and the Tana River to the frontiers of the Sudan, Ethiopia and Somalia is more than half of Kenya. In colonial days it was known as the Northern Frontier District, or NFD, which had a mystique all of its own. Today it is split between the Rift Valley Province in the west, and the Eastern and North Eastern Provinces (the latter being dealt with in the next chapter). But the 'jade sea' of Lake Turkana continues to be a magnet to the adventurous and it is impossible not to be moved by one's first sight of the north. There are three main routes. Via Baringo or Kitale through West Pokot to Lodwar, west of the lake. Via Maralal to the eastern shore. Or by the Great North Road via Nanyuki and Isiolo to Marsabit and Moyale. Approaching from Nanyuki on the main road through Timau to Isiolo you find yourself abruptly at the top of a sloping 4,000 ft escarpment. Spreading away below is a reddish landscape out of which occasional mountains rise, hot and barren, save for scrub — and fiercely exciting. In it, rivers mysteriously disappear, as the Uaso Nyiro does into the Lorian Swamp, or run for miles beneath the sand. Elephant are coated with red dust. The nomads herding their goats and camels and fat-tailed sheep to water holes remind one of Biblical scenes, though most of them are Moslems.

The nearer part of the north has become a minor tourist circuit taking in Nanyuki, the Samburu National Reserve, swinging round north west through Wamba to Maralal, and returning to Nairobi via Lake Baringo. The roads on this circuit have been improved. But further north they are difficult if not impassable in ordinary cars and the north remains inaccessible except to those who make special plans. Only well organised safaris survive. One firm which specialises in arranging them is Ker Downey Safaris (PO Box 41822 Nairobi; telephone 556466) who have taken Britain's Prince Charles there. Julian McKeand, as well as doing the short camel safaris described further on, undertakes longer ones as far as Lake Turkana.

The start of the route north via Kitale has already been described. The road is tarmac as far as Lodwar, from which a road is being constructed to the southern Sudan, a major enterprise. From Lodwar you have access to both Ferguson's Gulf and Eliye Springs on Lake Turkana, where there are fishing lodges, described under Lake Turkana below.

Maralal and the Samburu

The Maralal route, either from Lake Baringo or Rumuruti, has also been improved. Totalling 348 kilometres (217 miles) from Nairobi via Rumuruti, the last 112 kilometres (70 miles) run across the Lorochi Plateau and the Karisia Hills, which used to be a favourite hunting area in the old days and still has a fair amount of game. Maralal itself is a centre for the Samburu and has the atmosphere of a frontier town, the dusty main street crowded with tribes-people, the market place loaded with bangles, necklaces and beadwork. The renowned travel writer, Wilfred Thesiger, has a house here. Note that petrol supplies are erratic.

The Samburu are a tall, handsome people. The women adorn themselves with coil upon coil of heavy bead necklaces and the *moran* decorate themselves with red ochre and are every inch noblemen. They customarily wear loincloths of a vivid red and stand, spear in hand, on one leg, the other foot raised behind. The *moran* have to serve as warriors for at least ten years before they are allowed to marry. Like the Masai they are nomadic cattle owners and construct very similar *manyattas,* with low huts roofed with mud and dung. They inhabit a large tract, stretching east beyond the Isiolo to Marsabit Road and north to the Ndoto Hills and are associated with the Rendille beyond. The Maralal Safari Lodge (Three star. Bookings Thorn Tree Safaris PO Box 42475; telephone 25641) is very well situated within the area of the Maralal National Sanctuary. It has a waterhole which attracts game in the evening and a hide up on the hill where bait is put out for leopard. The lodge has comfortable cedar log cottages, reminiscent of Swiss chalets, each with its own bathroom.

About 24 kilometres (15 miles) out of Maralal on the progressively rougher road to Lake Turkana (formerly Rudolf) you come upon one of the most spectacular views in Africa: the Losiolo escarpment, overlooking the Rift Valley and its volcanic moonscape. If in doubt about finding this escarpment, engage the services of a local guide at Maralal. The main road north from Maralal continues a bruising 304 kilometres (190 miles) to Loiyangalani (see below). The journey by road should be undertaken only by well-equipped expeditions with four-wheel drive. This is the route taken by the Turkana bus and other overland expeditions to the lake. Passengers normally camp at Maralal and at South Horr en route.

Samburu National Reserve, Buffalo Springs Reserve

The Samburu National Reserve is one of the best known game viewing areas in northern Kenya. Its 225 sq kilometres (87 sq miles) lie along the north bank of the wide Uaso Nyiro River, west of the main road, while the Buffalo Springs National Reserve of 339 sq kilometres (130 sq miles) partially adjoins it on the south bank. The major, central, part of both reserves is fairly open thorn bush, extremely dry much of the year, thick with grass after the rains. The big attraction for game is the river, lined with a thick belt of trees including picturesque doum palms, though the water itself is muddy brown. Crocodiles sun themselves on the sandbanks — and also move a lot faster to snap at prey than one would think possible. As well as elephant, buffalo, waterbuck and other frequently seen game, there are several northern specialities such as the long necked gerenuk, a gazelle which reaches up to feed off thorn bushes, reticulated giraffe, Grevy's zebra and oryx, with long straight horns and distinctive dark markings. The most rewarding game runs are along the roads and tracks near the river and particularly at the swamp and famous clear pools of Buffalo Springs, where unhappily the large pool has been enclosed with a stone wall to keep out crocodiles. The roads away from the river to the hills in the north are particularly poor.

There are four entrances to these two reserves. Coming from Nairobi the most convenient entrance if you are going to the lodges is the Ngare Mara gate. You turn off the main road 20 kilometres (12 miles) beyond Isiolo to the Buffalo Springs Reserve. Another gate is three kilometres (two miles) short of Archer's Post, and is called the Buffalo Springs Gate. The Archer's Post Gate into the Samburu Reserve is reached from the township on a bad road. However you pass several Samburu *manyattas* en route. Finally the West Gate Road leads eventually to Wamba.

The two lodges are close to the bridge which crosses the Uaso Nyiro in the centre of the area. The Samburu Game Lodge (Five star. Bookings PO Box 47557 Nairobi; telephone 335807) is run by Block Hotels and is on the north bank of the river with an aptly named Crocodile Bar close to the water. The rooms are unusually spacious for a lodge and each has a proper bathroom. The food is excellent. There is a swimming-pool and game drives are organised by UTC at Shs 200/- per person in shared vehicles. The shop sells maps of the reserves and you can get petrol — a point worth noting up here. The newer River Lodge (Three star. Bookings PO Box 48690 Nairobi; telephone 338656) is on a more open stretch of the river, outside the Reserve on the south bank. As at Samburu Lodge, lights illuminate the game at night. There is a large swimming-pool and at the time of writing substantial improvements were being made. Both lodges are 15 minutes drive from the new airstrip. Additionally there is the Buffalo Springs Tented Lodge (First class. Bookings PO Box 30471 Nairobi; telephone 336858) and several campsites, which can be booked through the Park Warden. Security cannot be guaranteed at these campsites.

Shaba National Reserve

On the other side of the Great North Road, protecting a more scenically beautiful and much less opened-up area along the south bank of the Uaso Nyiro, is the Shaba National Reserve of 362 sq kilometres (140 sq miles). It was here that Joy Adamson re-introduced her leopard Penny to the wild and here that she was mysteriously murdered in 1980. Shaba takes its name from the copper colour of the sandstone hills, especially Mount Shaba (5,322 ft) which is partly inside the Reserve. Access is by a turn-off two kilometres south of Archer's Post. You pass a new Game Department anti-poaching unit HQ, then traverse a long lava flow before reaching the Natorbe Gate, seven kilometres (four miles) from the road. The Gate is open 0630 to 1830. Straight ahead is the main Reserve road running east, which is usable by ordinary cars, though the river tracks off it definitely are not. Initially the country is savannah, dotted with thorn bushes, becoming acacia woodland as you approach Mount Shaba, beyond which is wide grassy plain. Joy Adamson's camp was by Turkana hill in the centre of this plain. She christened the 40 ft waterfall at the extreme north east corner of the Reserve 'Penny's Drop'. The spring, one of many in Shaba, cascades down on to a sandbank of the river. This and the central river gorge are the two places where visitors are allowed to walk, but beware of crocodiles, which take more human lives in Kenya than any other predator.

Shaba is characterised by areas of lava flow, which came from the Nyambeni hills some 5,000 years ago, and are the reason for needing four-wheel drive in much of the Reserve. Although Shaba has a poor reputation for game viewing (because the animals are completely wild and suffer from poaching), in one morning the author saw several herds of elephant, buffalo and oryx, gerenuk, baboons, waterbuck, Grant's gazelle and many of the 280 species of birds on record, such as lilac-breasted rollers. There are also leopard, lion, cheetah and hippo. After the rains in November and April the hillsides bloom with thousands of tiny flowers.

The Shaba Tented Camp, which was at an idyllic spot on the river with a natural rock swimming-pool, is indefinitely closed. There are campsites which can be booked through the Park Warden for the Isiolo/Buffalo/Samburu Complex in Isiolo (PO Box 29 Isiolo;

telephone 21Y2 — note that some of the old telephone numbers combine letters and digits).

Shaba to Meru via Magado
At the north-east corner of the Reserve is an unmanned entrance via which you can drive in about four and a half hours to the Meru National Park, passing Chanler's Falls and the curious Magado Crater Lake. There are soda deposits in its centre, mined by the local Meru people, while the sweet water at the edges attracts nomadic Boran to bring their camels and stock to drink.

Camel Safaris
The Samburu country has long been the scene for camel safaris. Julian McKeand, a former game warden, runs first class ones from Lewa Downs near Isiolo, going up to the Uaso Nyiro west of the reserves. On average 12 clients are attended by 19 camp staff, including trackers, and 26 camels. It is a magnificent way of seeing the wild, though it involves a lot of dusty walking. McKeand also arranges much longer safaris, as far as Lake Turkana if required. He can be contacted either care of Lewa Downs (Private Bag, Isiolo) or care of Flamingo Tours (PO Box 44899, Nairobi; telephone 28961).

Lolokwe and Wamba
On safari anywhere near the Uaso Nyiro you will notice the precipitiously steep, flat-topped shape of Lolokwe Mountain in the distance, with the Mathews Range behind it. Lolokwe stands between the Great North Road and the fork left to Wamba. You can walk up Lolokwe's sloping northern side to find game on the top, superb views and specimens of the three most ancient trees in Africa: *cycads,* and the conifers *juniper* and *podocarpus.* It is beyond Archer's Post, a police post with a few *dukas,* which is the place you could hope to get petrol between Isiolo and Marsabit. Wamba itself is a colourful Samburu trading centre. The C78 dirt road past it to Maralal has been greatly improved recently. Petrol supplies at Wamba are erratic. The distance to Maralal is 164 kilometres (102 miles) via Kisima.

Northern Kenya: Marsabit, Lake Turkana
The Route to Marsabit
On the way to Marsabit from Isiolo you cross the corner of the Losai National Reserve 1,806 sq kilometres (697 sq miles), largely forest abutting on the Ndoto Hills. At the edge of the Reserve is Laisamis, on a stream, which is a pleasant spot to camp — given the savagely inhospitable nature of the lava-strewn Kaisut desert beyond.

Marsabit
Marsabit is completely different from the other northern outposts,

not in the tin-roofed dukas of the town, but in its setting. Marsabit is a 5,593 ft volcanic mountain rising green and forested out of a black lava-strewn semi-desert. The area is a national reserve of 2,208 sq kilometres (852 sq miles) noted for its large tusked elephant, reticulated giraffe and leopard. In the early evening the game comes down to drink at the crater lakes. Ahmed, once the 'king of elephants' is long dead — his replica stands at the National Museum in Nairobi. His successor, Mohammed, is reckoned to have tusks weighing more than 100 lbs each. Marsabit Lodge (One star. Bookings, PO Box 30471 Nairobi; telephone 336858) is by one of the craters. The township has an airstrip and is about one and a half hours' flying time from Nairobi. At the time of writing it was difficult to obtain transport locally.

It is interesting to see how the tribes up here adapt to the harsh environment. Camel trains are a common sight and it's worth having a guide take you to one of the 'singing wells', the most colourful ones being at Sagante. The wells are deep so the Boran stand on scaffolds one above the other, chanting rhythmically while they pass up giraffe hide water buckets: easier to grip than metal. Cows, goats and donkeys crowd around, anxious to drink.

Lake Turkana
From Marsabit an extremely rough road loops north to Lake Turkana while the more conventional route and approach is from Maralal via South Horr. The lake (formerly Rudolf)) makes you feel you have walked into a 'National Geographic Magazine' story. The lake itself, is savagely beautiful. In the middle of a near desert, it is shimmering blue in some lights, jade green in others. Migrating wildfowl from Europe, cormorants, sacred ibis, egrets and other waterbirds flock along its shores, while pelicans fly ponderously above like flying boats on patrol. The lake is also curious. Three rivers flow into it, and none out. In fact 11 feet of water a year are taken off its 3,000 square miles by evaporation. Less explicable is why Nile perch grow to such a giant size here or indeed what geological upheaval separated the lake from the Nile aeons ago. The record perch is 170 kilograms (375 lbs) and there are also tiger fish and tilapia, but the lake is in danger of being over-fished commercially.

There is an oasis with two lodges and an airstrip on the lake's eastern shore at Loiyangalani, where hot springs from Mount Kulal run in a stream down to the lake. Both lodges arrange fishing trips. The Oasis Club (One star. Bookings through Bookings Ltd, PO Box 56707 Nairobi; telephone 25255) is on the site of a fishing camp where Prince Philip has stayed and the hot springs feed a small swimming-pool. The stone-built huts become rather hot. The newer Lake Turkana El Molo Lodge (Bookings PO Box 34710, Nairobi; telephone 28384) has thatched roof cottages. It is possible to camp nearby, as the more adventurous travellers on Safari Camp Services seven-day 'bus' trip do when they arrive. There is a Catholic Mission near the oasis.

Close to Loiyangalani lives one of Africa's most curious tribes, the El Molo. They exist on fish, harpooned from log rafts, and the occasional hippo, and are thought to be related to the Bushmen of the Kalahari Desert in southern Africa. They number around 100, as they did when Count Teleki discovered the lake in 1888.

South Island
South Island in the centre of the lake opposite Loiyangalani, is now a tiny national park, of 39 sq kilometres (15 sq miles) for the benefit of ornithologists, though it can be a dangerous one to visit by boat on account of the sudden storms which blow up on the lake.

Sibiloi National Park
Some 145 kilometres (90 miles) north of Loiyangalani lies the Sibiloi National Park; 1,570 sq kilometres (606 sq miles) bordering the eastern shore of the lake. Besides a profusion of birds, there are herds of oryx, topi, waterbuck and other antelopes. The road from Loiyangalani to the Park is still rough, although negotiable by four-wheel drive vehicles. Camping is possible with the permission of the Warden whose office is at Alia Bay. In the park at Koobi Fora is a site explored by Richard Leakey, director of Kenya's National Museum and the son of the late Dr Louis Leakey and Mary Leakey. The site has yielded important finds, including part of a skull about 2.8 million years old that may have belonged to the first known ancestors of modern man; so this site, fertile and wooded in that long distant past, may be 'the cradle of mankind'. The skull is known by its catalogue number, '1470'. Visitors can see some of the other fossil finds in the area, including those of other hominids and of a three-toed horse, at a small museum 12 kilometres (seven miles) from Alia Bay.

Across the western side of the lake is a magnificent natural bird sanctuary at Ferguson's Gulf. You can stay comfortably at the Lake Turkana Fishing Lodge (One star. Bookings PO Box 41078, Nairobi; telephone 26808) which provides facilities for fishing, Eliye Springs, formerly a lodge, is now only a campsite. There is an airstrip at Ferguson's Gulf, and the Fishing Lodge office can arrange flying safaris, while there is a scheduled air service to the government post of Lodwar, with its battlemented headquarters. By land it's a two-day journey.

The Turkana themselves are as impressive as the Samburu or the Masai. Their men have their hair elaborately plaited and set with white feathers, like a coxcomb, while their necks are chokered with bead necklaces and their upper arms bound in rings of shining wire. They are nomads and almost worship their cattle. To them cattle are a man's intermediaries with his ancestors' souls; they are depended on for milk, for buying wives and for security in old age. One of the government's problems is persuading the Turkana to take them to market and exchange them for mere money. Another more serious one, is that the Sahel drought of 1984/85 affected this area badly and some Turkana are still dependent on food aid, while many international organisations are involved in assisting their future development.

Eastern Kenya and the Tana River

Kenya's eastern border is with the Somali Republic and its north eastern with Ethiopia. Most of the country up here is wild, semi-desert, populated by a number of nomadic tribes such as the Rendille, and including a substantial population of Somalis. The Somali government's long-standing claim to part of the North East has helped undermine security up here since well before Independence, as have the activities of shifta, or nomad bandits. In consequence it requires police permission to travel north-east; effectively beyond the curving line of the Tana River. So Moyale on the Ethiopian border; Wajir, a Foreign legion type of outpost with white-washed and castellated buildings; and Mandera, where the three countries' frontiers meet, are all out of the question for normal tourists, although proper expeditions are allowed up to Ethiopia, via Moyale. The Northern Kenya chapters cover what can be visited in that direction. Confusingly, administrative boundaries define most of northern Kenya as the Eastern Province, while this part is more logically the North Eastern.

However the Tana River is the setting for a number of wildlife sanctuaries, some of which have accommodation. The Tana itself rises from sources on Mount Kenya and the Aberdares and flows some 600 kilometres (375 miles) to the Indian Ocean, providing the water for the Seven Forks Power Station in Embu, then passing through untouched bush until reaching the Indian Ocean north of Malindi. In the 19th century, until the railway was constructed, the Tana was a route to the interior for traders and missionaries, who believed they could reach the Highlands up it, but were always defeated by rapids. Being a permanent river, its banks are lined with tall trees and other vegetation and it attracts myriad game animals and birds as well as harbouring hippos and crocodiles, while some of the country's more interesting peoples depend upon it for their agriculture. Only in 1976 was the first complete navigation of the river made.

The Meru National Park and Kora National Reserve have already been described. To the north of the Tana, adjoining Kora, is the Rahole National Reserve, 1,270 sq kilometres (490 sq miles) of thorn scrub around 1,000 ft above sea level, sheltering a variety of plains game, but with no tourist facilities. Down river from Rahole some 80 kilometres (50 miles) is the trading post of Garissa where 20 years ago a remarkable American missionary, Brother Mario, a one-time Detroit nightclub owner, began the Garissa Boys' Town for local Somali orphans. By irrigation they have made a fruit farm in the desert round the school and their Garissa melons are famous in Kenya. The photograph of camels and goats in this guide was taken on the Tana River near Garissa and shows the thickness of the vegetation close to the banks.

A main road (dirt) runs from Thika to Garissa and on to Somalia. Another principal road branching from it goes south all the way down to Garsen and Malindi, while a more primitive road on the eastern side eventually reaches Lamu 268 kilometres (167 miles), passing the Arawale National Reserve on the way. This recently gazetted reserve of 533 sq kilometres (206 sq miles) is dedicated to preserving the rare Hunter's Antelope, a hartebeest with lyre-shaped horns.

The Tana River is a major barrier, crossed by few ferries, most notably at Garissa and Garsen. By taking the main Garissa to Garsen road (238 kilometres or 148 miles) you pass close to Hola, the only important settlement on the way and gradually come into more fertile, greener country, though it is still only sparsely inhabited. A little more than half way between Hola and Garsen is the interesting Tana River Primate National Reserve.

Tana River Primate National Reserve
This 169 sq kilometre (65 sq miles) reserve lies both sides of the Tana River near the village of Wenje and is bounded to the west by the Hola to Garsen road. It centres on a 60 kilometre (37 mile) stretch of what little West African gallery forest remains in East Africa and preserves its inhabitants.

There is some gallery forest in Kakamega and probably the Tana strip is the end of a forest chain which used to run across the continent from present-day Zaire and through Uganda. Certainly the Mangabey monkeys here, which are a West African species, have their nearest relatives in Zaire. The Mangabey and the Red Colobus are the two small primates which the Reserve protects. They needed protecting because of the intrusion of riverine cultivation on the forest by the local Pokomo people. Both the Mangabey and the Red Colobus are very sensitive to their environment. The highest troop in the 'gallery' are the 100ft pale barked Tana poplars. Both trees and the dense riverine bush are alive with birds, while the river attracts game from elephant down to Red Duiker and is the home of numerous crocodiles and hippo.

The few roads in the reserve are rough and the former Baomo Lodge on the river is closed. The entrance to the reserve is approximately 158 kilometres (99 miles) from Malindi. At the time of writing security in the area was threatened by Somali *shifta.*

Garsen and the Tana Delta
The township of Garsen is an administrative and trading centre, mainly of tin-roofed buildings, for the Pokomo, Somalis and Orma of the area. Its ferry provides a vital link for road traffic to Lamu, but is liable to extensive flooding after the rains up country. The delta itself is wild country, sparsely populated by the Watta tribe who were moved out of Tsavo when the park there was created. The river debouches in Ungwana (Formosa) Bay and it is nothing odd to see elephant as you fly from Malindi to Lamu, or off the road from Garsen to Lamu.

Finally, north east of Lamu, close to the frontier with the Somali Republic, are two reserves of wilderness. The Dodori National Reserve of 877 sq kilometres (338 sq miles) can be reached by a track. Elephant and greater kudu are among the species there, while hippo can be seen at Kibukoni. The Boni National Reserve of 1,339 sq kilometres (517 sq miles) is more easily reached by boat, though it also has an airstrip.

At the time of writing both these reserves were considered dangerous to visit on account of the *shifta,* although the beach resorts at Kiwaiyu Island, described in the North Coast chapter were perfectly safe.

Southern Kenya: Masailand, Amboseli, Tsavo
All of the Mombasa Road's 485 kilometres (301 miles) are tarmac. From Nairobi it leads out south-east past Nairobi National Park and on to the Athi Plains. It then skirts Kitui passing close to Machakos District, where the Kamba of Wamunyu practise their traditional wood carving. These craftsmen work sitting on the ground, with legs outstretched, whittling the wood with a hoe-shaped blade called an *ngomo.* The Kamba are Kenya's third largest tribe and are also noted for being fine soldiers, and for spectacular dancing, spiced with fantastic gyrating leaps in the air and double somersaults.

The Masai
Broadly speaking the Kamba live north of the Mombasa Road, and the Masai south. The Masai's ancestral territory stretched north up the Rift and round to Laikipia and today they still herd their cattle as far west as the Mara and way down into Tanzania: the colonially established frontier divides the tribe. Within this broad ethnic grouping, there are distinct Masai communities, for instance those in the Mara are different to those centred on Loitokitok. However they all share the same legendary warrior tradition. The young

moran, or warrior, athletic, aquiline-featured, his hair braided and thickened with red ochre, looks like a figure from a classical Greek vase as he stands leaning on his spear. His traditional stories are folk epics of lion hunts and he grows up believing that they are told only at night because if you waste time telling stories during the day you will go blind. Like the Turkana *moran,* he lives by and for his cattle. The traditional Masai food is blood mixed with milk and curdled, the blood itself being expertly taken from the jugular vein in a cow's neck without injuring the beast. Most Masai still live nomadically, building their *manyattas* wherever there is grazing. A *manyatta* is a group of low huts made of dung and surrounded by a thorn fence, inside which the cattle are brought at night for protection. You see them everywhere in Masailand, often abandoned because the herdsmen have moved on to new pastures.

The 1979 census recorded 240,000 Masai in Kenya, while numerous books detail their lives and the important ceremonies which punctuate their existence, such as the *Emorata,* or circumcision and the traumatic *Eunoto,* when the warrior's mothers shave off their long, plaited hair in token of their progressing to elderhood and marriage. A magnificent pictorial account of the tribe, written by a Masai, is 'Maasai' by Tepilit Ole Saitoti, with photographs by Carol Beckwith (Purists sometimes spell the word with two 'a's.) The traditionally noble Masai is a far cry from the opportunist men and women who today besiege tourist buses outside Amboseli.

Amboseli National Park
Amboseli, lying almost in the shadow of Mount Kilimanjaro, is part of an important Masai district. To reach it by road you turn off the Nairobi to Mombasa A109 at Athi River on to the A104 to Kajiado, Namanga and Arusha in Tanzania, which is a good fast tarmac road. Kajiado is a small township of tin-roofed *dukas.* Nearby are the quarries producing Kenya's marble. Namanga is the frontier post, 135 kilometres (84 miles) from Nairobi on the Tanzanian border. From Namanga a reasonable road runs through the Namanga Gate of Amboseli into the Reserve and so to the Park. The Namanga Hotel (unclassified; telephone Namanga 4) is like a game lodge in appearance but not in quality.

The Namanga entrance to Amboseli is the most popular. The alternative is to drive down the Mombasa Road to Sultan Hamud, from where a straight well-graded dirt road runs south and passes Amboseli going on to Loitokitok. You can either turn off at Makutano for the Lemi Boti Gate or go further and enter the Park at the Kimana Gate.

Before the 3,199 sq kilometres (1,235 sq miles) of the Amboseli Game Reserve had their most vital 378 sq kilometres (146 sq miles) designated as a national park, the Masai shared the area with the game which they seldom kill for meat, being preoccupied with their cattle. But there was not pasture for both and under an agreement with the government the Masai moved out after a pipeline had been constructed to bring water from outside the Park. However the Park's boundaries have had to be further reduced, particularly to the east, and in times of drought you will still see Masai herding cattle and goats within the Park. Amboseli's landscape is dominated by Mount Kilimanjaro to the south, though its snowcapped summit is often shrouded by cloud and it is most likely to be seen either early or late in the day. People commonly look too low down on the horizon for it. Remember it is 19,340 ft high. Seen from Amboseli the main summit, Kibo (Uhuru Peak), is on the right while the sharper peak of Mawenzi (16,900 ft) is on the left.

Although there is game to be seen in most parts of the Reserve, organised tours concentrate on the Park, almost at the centre of which are the airfield, the Park Headquarters at Ol Tukai and the main lodges (see below). To the west is Lake Amboseli, optimistically marked blue on maps, but in practice a dry bed of soda most of the year, which produced mirages like a desert. There are tracks across it, though if it has rained your vehicle will sink through the surface. Kongoni and eland are among animals that frequent the lake area.

However most of Amboseli's game is drawn to the swamps and permanent water in the centre and south of the Park. The Loginye swamp east and north of Ol Tukai is fed by natural springs, is green all the year and attracts a lot of game in dry weather. The zebra and wildebeest congregate here, pursued by lion; elephant move in and there are a number of rhino. Loginye is uncrossable in the rains. The other swamp is the Enkongo Narok to the south, where you will find waterbuck, buffalo, elephant and a multitude of birds. Between the two swamps is the Empash area, once forested but now losing its trees due to the depredations of elephants and the rising salinity in the earth.

A causeway road crosses one arm of the Enkongo Narok swamp and leads round to Observation Hill, or Enamishera Hill, a knoll perhaps 100 ft high on which there is a viewing hut. Elephant often congregate in the swamp below and you can get an idea of the whole Park, since it is almost completely flat.

Other animals which can be seen, though you need a guide, include caracal, cheetah, civet cat and serval cat; gerenuk up near Lemi Boti, oryx, impala and giraffe. Leopard like the trees along the southern boundary towards Kitirua. Pelicans, herons and jacanas are among the many waterbirds.

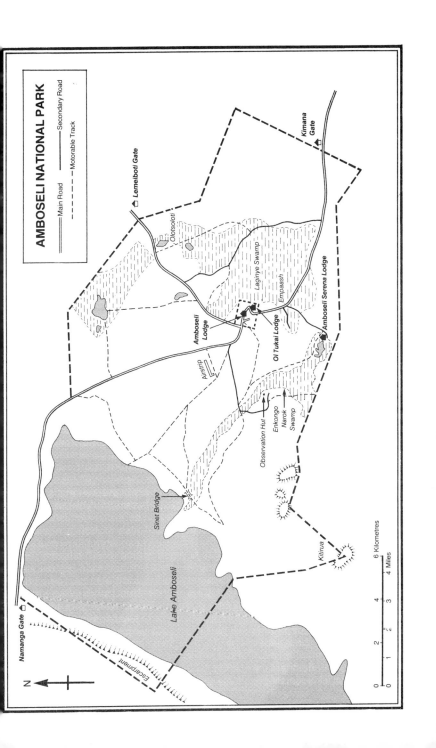

AMBOSELI NATIONAL PARK

Main Road — Secondary Road — — — Motorable Track

N

Namanga Gate

Escarpment

Lake Amboseli

Sinet Bridge

Airstrip

Amboseli Lodge

Olotsoloti

Lemelboti Gate

Laginye Swamp

Empaash

Ol Tukai Lodge

Amboseli Serena Lodge

Observation Hut

Enkongo Narok Swamp

Kilirua

Kimana Gate

0   1   2   3   4   6 Kilometres
0   1   2   3   4 Miles

Kenya

Amboseli's accommodation

Accommodation at Amboseli has steadily been increased. There are now six lodges or camps in or near the Park. The best situated is the very comfortable Amboseli Serena Lodge (Five star. Bookings PO Box 48690, Nairobi; telephone 338656). It stands alongside the Enkongo Narok swamp so that you get good game viewing both from the verandahs and from the rooms and is built in a style derived from the traditional Masai manyattas.

Close to Ol Tukai is the Amboseli Lodge, recently enlarged and renovated, with a swimming-pool. Near it, under the same management, the former tented camp has been reconstructed as the Kilimanjaro Safari Lodge with accommodation in bandas. A fleet of vehicles transports visitors arriving by air to either lodge. Transfer from the airstrip costs Shs 400/- per 7-seat vehicle and a half-day game drive Shs 1,050/-. Bookings for both through the Kilimanjaro Safari Club (PO Box 30139, Nairobi; telephone 27136). The same firm also owns the Kimana Lodge (One star), outside the Park to the east some 45 kilometres (28 miles) from Ol Tukai. Kimana is comfortable, has a pool, is cheaper than the Amboseli Lodge, but has no game drive vehicles available. Bait is put out for leopards at night for guests to watch from the verandah. Also outside the Park to the east is the Kilimanjaro Buffalo Lodge (Five star. Bookings PO Box 72630, Nairobi; telephone 336088). Accommodation is in luxurious rondavels, there is a pool and conference facilities.

Finally, the cheapest accommodation is in the self-service bandas at Ol Tukai, which have good facilities including gas cooking and a shop. Bookings through Let's Go Travel (PO Box 60342, Nairobi; telephone 29539). The campsite has been moved outside the southern boundary of the Park some three kilometres (two miles) from Observation Hill and it is well signed. It is run by the Masai Group Ranch and you book on arrival at an office near the southern boundary, which is equally well signed.

Amboseli to Tsavo National Park and the Chyulu Hills

From Amboseli it is possible to drive direct to the western part of the Tsavo National Park, a distance of approximately 80 kilometres (50 miles), though the dirt road is extremely rough in places. You leave Amboseli by the Kimana Gate, go briefly down the C102 road to Loitokitok, then turn left again. Loitokitok itself is a Masai township, 8,000 ft up on the slopes of Kilimanjaro. It is along the road to Tsavo that the local Masai can be so obstructive. We have experienced them physically blocking the road in order to demand money for *piksha* (photographing them). The only answer is to drive firmly on, unless you want to be completely besieged. Within Tsavo Park, before reaching the gate, you drive across the edge of the Shetani lava flow at the foot of the Chyulu Hills. The road surface is appropriately bad. The lava itself, still black and almost untouched by vegetation, is worth stopping to see. It derived from an eruption some 200 years ago which is vividly remembered in Masai folk tales.

The Chyulu hills rise to 7,248 ft and a substantial part of them has been designated a National Park. Its 560 sq kilometres adjoin Tsavo National Park West and its own western boundary is the summit of the hills, so it takes in the slopes on the Mombasa road side, but not on the Amboseli side, which is a Masai group ranch. The Chyulus have long been a favourite place for Kenya residents to camp.

The views are splendid and there is a lot of wildlife, plus a network of caves. The only snag — and the reason they have been relatively undisturbed by man — is the lack of water. So take plenty. The normal approach to the hills is taking the C102 from Sultan Hamud on the Mombasa Road and turning left at Makutano, though there are ways in to the range from the Amboseli to Kilaguni road and from Mtito Andei, which brings us back to the Mombasa Road and the better known entrances to Tsavo.

Nairobi direct to the Tsavo National Park
The Mombasa Road is a fast one. You should reach the Mtito Andei entrance to Tsavo West National Park (236 kilometres or 148 miles) in two and a half hours. You will notice small distance signs every two kilometres, which are marked with abbreviations of place names. Thus 'Msa' stands for Mombasa and 'Nbi' for Nairobi. There are several places to stop the night or eat en route to the coast. At Makindu, 145 kilometres (90 miles) where there is a petrol station, is the Hunter's Lodge (Two star. Bookings PO Box 67868 Nairobi; telephone 21439) more attractive than its classification suggests as it is set by a small lake and is well furnished. Snacks are served on the terrace. This used to be a base for hunting in the Chyulu and there are some interesting caves not far off. Further on at Kibwezi is the left turn-off to reach a self-service lodge, the Bushwhackers Camp (address PO Kibwezi) on the border of Tsavo East. Mtito Andei is the recognised half way house to the coast, with several service stations and snack bars, as well as the Tsavo Inn (Two star. Bookings Kilimanjaro Safari Club, Box 30139 Nairobi; telephone 27136) which has a restaurant and a swimming pool. The Inn is opposite the main gate to the Park and if you stay there you often hear the lions roaring at night.

Tsavo National Park
The Tsavo National Park is roughly kidney shaped and its 21,000 sq kilometres (8,100 sq miles) are bisected in the middle by the Mombasa Road. For administrative convenience the part north-east of the road is called Tsavo East, with a headquarters near Voi and the part south-west of the road is Tsavo West, with Wardens' offices near Mtito Andei. Overall this famous national park covers a vast section of the 200 miles of thorn scrub, spiked with the bulbous

trunks of baobab trees, that separate the tropical vegetation of the coast from the great central plateau of the African continent.

It was the endless thorn scrub here that kept the peoples of the interior remote from western civilisation for so many centuries. Try walking through it as the early missionaries did and you will soon understand. It has various names — the Nyika, which means thorn country, the Nyiri Desert, the Taru Desert. Much of the year it is burnt dry and dusty by the sun. Then overnight the rains transform it. Convolvulus flowers burst out white and purple, grass seed germinates, the bushes are suddenly green. Explorers hated it for the very reason that makes it a major attraction today — the game. 'Full of wild beasts, such as rhinoceros, buffaloes and elephants', the German missionary, Rebmann, noted in his diary on May 11, 1848. Indeed it is full, though over-grazing has depleted the vegetation in parts and the elephant have suffered both from drought and a rise in the price of ivory in 1973. Park wardens estimate that from 15,000 to 20,000 in the 1960s the numbers dropped to 8,000 by 1978 and in 1987 were possibly up again to 10,000. Rhino have been hugely worse hit by poachers. In the early 1970s there were 5,000. Now only some 200 remain and they are being moved into a fenced sanctuary near the Ngulia Lodge in Tsavo West.

Tsavo's lions are noted for their ferocity. J. H. Paterson's book, 'The Man Eaters of Tsavo', describes how they obstructed the building of the railway in the 1900s by the simple expedient of eating the linesmen. The railway carriage from which a lion dragged a man is displayed in the Railway Museum in Nairobi. Nowadays they seem to prefer the eland, kongoni, impala, klipspringer, kudu, reedbuck, waterbuck and zebra which also inhabit the Park. Humans are apparently an acquired taste.

Tsavo West National Park

In Tsavo West, which is rather hilly, the volcanic area where the Mzima Springs and other waters rise attracts most species of game. The Springs, 40 kilometres (25 miles) from Mtito Andei, form a series of clear pools fed by a flow estimated at 97 million gallons a day, coming underground from the Chyulus. Of this, seven million gallons are piped down to Mombasa and the bulk flows into the Tsavo and Galana rivers. This oasis attracts many animals and an observation tank in the top pool enables you to watch hippo and crocodile from underwater. Other major viewing places are at the Kangethwa Dam, the Kilaguni waterhole and an artificial spring right in front of the Kilaguni Lodge verandah, where a sign reads 'Animals are requested to be quiet whilst guests are drinking, and vice versa.'

There are three lodges in the northern part of Tsavo West, all near Mzima Springs. The long established Kilaguni Lodge (Five star. Bookings PO Box 30471 Nairobi; telephone 336858) is justifiably renowned. It has its own airstrip, swimming-pool and reasonably priced game park tours. A short drive east of the Springs is the Ngulia Safari Lodge built on the edge of the Ndawe escarpment with a magnificent view over vast plains and the rhino sanctuary below. There is a swimming-pool in the grounds, and an airstrip a short distance away. It is classed five star, bookings as for Kilaguni. Nearby is Ngulia Safari Camp, on a site 'haunted' by lions which leave no footprints, according to local legend. You must bring your own food and bedding. It can be booked through Let's Go Travel (PO Box 60342, Nairobi; telephone 29539), as can Kitani Lodge, west of Mzima Springs. Kitani is also self-service, but bedding can be hired. Both are cheap. There are also camp sites near the Mtito Andei and Tsavo gates to the Park.

As the map shows, the area these lodges are in is only a small part of Tsavo West's expanse. The Park stretches much further south into a part known as the Serengeti Plains, or the Little Serengeti, which is being increasingly opened up. The name is confusing. These plains have nothing to do with the Serengeti National Park far away in Tanzania, though it is similar country. It is crossed by the meandering road and railway from Voi to Taveta, in the shadow of Mount Kilimanjaro, both of which continue across the frontier to Moshi. Halfway across is the abandoned ghost town of Murka, while both along here and up in the shallow valley of the Tsavo River there are reminders of a curious piece of history. The railway line was built by the British during World War 1 to bring supplies to the front against the Germans, who had colonised Tanganyika. The British chased the German Commander, General Paul von Lettow-Vorbeck, and his troops all the way through what are today Tanzania, Mozambique, Zambia and back into Tanzania without capturing them; they finally surrendered in 1918 on hearing of the Kaiser's capitulation in Europe. The story is well told in Charles Miller's 'Battle for the Bundu'. The high ground north of the Tsavo River was one British defensive line against the initial German attack and astonishingly traces of the war are still to be found there, including empty whisky bottles! For the benefit of military enthusiasts the map on the next page indicates three of the more significant military positions within the National Park (1) is General Mallinson's HQ at Maktau, (2) is the German command post at Umbuyuni, captured by General Smuts, and (3) is General von Lettow-Vorbeck's fortified post on Salaita hill. The heaviest fighting took place west of Taveta.

Walking safaris along the Tsavo River, usually taking four days and covering 80 kilomotres (50 miles), are conducted by Tropical Ice of Mama Ngina Street, Nairobi (PO Box 57341, Nairobi; telephone 23649).

Two excellent lodges serving the central part of Tsavo West, outside the Park, are situated close to the Voi-Taveta road south of the

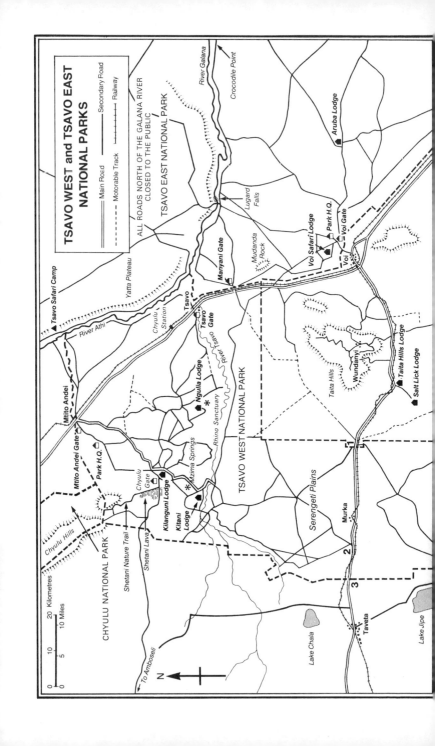

Taita Hills. They adjoin each other in a 28,000-acre private game reserve while a further 60,000 acres are leased by the lodges. Both rate five stars and are run by Hilton Hotels (PO Box 30624, Nairobi; telephone 334000). The Taita Hills Lodge supposedly resembles a World War 1 fort, though this curious idea does not detract from its comfort. Salt Lick Lodge has rooms like African thatched huts set on stilts to give a view over a large waterhole, which attracts many animals in the evenings, including herds of buffalo. The trees beyond make this a natural amphitheatre, lit by an artificial moon.

Other game seen are lion, cheetah, elephant, lesser kudu, fringe-eared oryx and gerenuk. One welcome — and cheap — alternative to normal game drives is that you can go out with the scout who leaves early to locate the game. A variety of birds can also be seen, 385 species have been recorded, among them migrants from Europe which arrive in late November on their way south and return at the end of January. Trips organised from the lodges include excursions into the Taita Hills, where there is a mysterious 'cave of skulls', and to lakes Chala and Jipe.

Lake Chala and Jipe
These two lakes are just outside the western boundary of the Tsavo Park, and easily reached by the main A23 road to Taveta. Both are bisected by the Tanzanian frontier, which for a long stretch south east from Lake Jipe becomes the Park boundary, with the Mkomazi Game Reserve on the other side. However, the two lakes are completely different in character.

Lake Chala, north of the road, is reached by a turnoff before Taveta. It is a circular crater lake, coloured a surprising green by the minerals in the water and with a large population of crocodiles. There are no facilities for humans.

Lake Jipe, by contrast, is being opened up and makes a good day-excursion from Salt Lick Lodge. It lies south of the main road and is about 800 ft lower than Salt Lick, which is at 1,000 metres (3,280 ft). You can either drive via Taveta or cut across the Serengeti plains on a murram road which descends straight towards the lake, with the Pare Mountains in Tanzania in the far distance. This will take at least one-and-a-half hours and you are bound to see game on the way. The lake is fringed by tall reeds which, unless you hire a boat, sometimes obstruct one's watching the waterbirds for which the lake is famous. Among the rare species here is the pygmy goose. During 1987 a new lodge was built on a hill two miles from the lake, designed as clusters of rondavels raised on stilts. It has a swimming-pool. At the time of writing it had not opened or been classified, but it will be bookable through Let's Go Travel in Nairobi, and have the advantage that if you approach via Taveta you will be able to arrive after dark without breaking any regulations since it is outside the Park. At the lakeshore there is a campsite which has fly-screened rooms, with canvas beds, in a thatched cabin, running water and a shower, and a brick barbecue. Returning to the Taita area, the other totally different part to explore is the Taita Hills themselves.

The Taita Hills and Voi

These hills, rising steeply to 2,210 metres (7,248 ft) at their highest, are like a Switzerland in Africa, though without the snow. Three roads climb up to the town of Wundanyi and with the aid of a map you could make your own circuit. Houses are perched on the hillsides, there are dramatic rock pinnacles and above Wundanyi a pearl-like face of smooth grey rock shines in the sun. Bananas, beans, potatoes, sugar cane and coffee grow in profusion: and there are frequent splendid views over the contrastingly arid plains below. Up here people even dress differently, the women resplendent in gaily printed kangas. They are very friendly and if you have any curiosity about Africans and how they live you should enjoy looking around the villages and markets. The hills also have one less visible product: gemstones. There are at least 20 green garnet mines, though the average weight is only two grammes and three grammes is a large stone. Occasionally there are rubies. The more serious of Kenya's ruby mines are in a corner of the Tsavo West Park, 60 kilometres (38 miles) south of here. The rubies were discovered by accident, when the Game Department workers were digging a water catchment.

Voi, a township just off the main Nairobi to Mombasa road, has the usual *dukas* and filling stations, but is hardly a tourist shopping centre. Its chief interest is that you pass through to enter the Tsavo Park East and reach the Voi Safari Lodge. The Park also has entrances further north at Manyani.

Tsavo East National Park

Tsavo East is less hilly than Tsavo West, apart from the dramatic line of the Yatta Plateau escarpment which rises almost parallel to the Mombasa Road and in origin is a lava flow. Beyond this escarpment, to the east, is a seemingly endless expanse of low lying semi-desert, spiked with thorn bushes, most of which you can only visit by special permission of the Park Warden. All roads north of the Galana River, which cuts across Tsavo East, are closed to the public, except with special permission from the Park Warden. The spectacular Lugard Falls, populated at the foot by giant crocodiles, and Crocodile Point on the river are worth a visit, though the best places to see animals are unquestionably Mudanda Rock and Aruba. The former is a great hump of rusty coloured rock overlooking a huge waterhole making a natural amphitheatre. It is signed off the park road between the Manyani gate and the Voi gate and you can leave your car to climb up.

Lodges and Camps

The Voi Safari Lodge, along this road, is ingeniously set on the Worsessa look-out hill above the plain and a small waterhole. (Five star. Bookings Box 30471 Nairobi; telephone 336858). The Aruba Dam, pretty well in the centre of this part of the park, is a successful man-made watering place for game. Nearby is the self-help Aruba Lodge (Bookings AA Travel, PO Box 14982 Nairobi; telephone 339700). Finally, five kilometres (three miles) outside the Sala gate on the Galana River, is the Crocodile Tented Camp (Three star), haunt of the reptiles. It is on the road to Malindi and is owned by the Eden Roc Hotel (PO Box 350 Malindi; telephone 20480). Set under thorn trees by the river, this is a good place to stop if you are driving direct from the Park to Malindi, which is 95 kilometres (60 miles) further on (see below). Remember you must be into your lodge by 1900 which means being at the park gates considerably earlier. Also note that midday temperatures down here reach (32° C to 38° C) (90° F. to 100° F), which is too hot for both animals and sightseers — so early morning and early evening are the times for game viewing. Further up in Tsavo East on the east bank of the Athi River — which becomes the Galana at the southern end of the Yatta escarpment, where the Tsavo River joins it — is the excellent Tsavo Safari Camp (First class. Bookings PO Box 30139, Nairobi; telephone 27136). A dirt road from Mtito Andei runs to the west bank of the river, opposite the camp and you are then taken across by boat. Camp vehicles are kept there and a guard is always in attendance. (You must have a pass or accommodation voucher before making this drive). Once across, you are in one of the best equipped camps in Kenya, each tent having its own bathroom, in a beautiful setting. The Camp has its own airstrip, a new swimming-pool, good food, and operates its own hunting cars for expeditions both in Tsavo West and up on the Yatta Plateau.

Among the trips are ones to Lugard's Falls, further down the Athi river, and to an exclusive area of 7,770 sq kilometres (3,000 square miles) in Tsavo East, to which no other lodge or camp has access. The views from the Yatta escarpment, above the Camp, where you can go for a sundowner, are magnificent. In origin this escarpment is an immensely long lava flow, deriving from Ol Donyo Sapuk east of Nairobi. Up on the plateau beyond is an unique 'blind' for watching leopard and other nocturnal game. Constructed by the founder Warden of Tsavo East, David Sheldrick, and named after him, the 'blind' is by a natural spring. It has five comfortably equipped sleeping-rooms and a dining-room overlooking the Spring. You drive there in the late afternoon and return next day after breakfast. In several visits to the Tsavo Camp we have seen elephant, rhino, buffalo, waterbuck, giraffe, warthog, various antelope, the inevitable crocodiles — and very few other vehicles.

Tsavo to Malindi and the Galana Game Ranch

Although the vast eastern side of Tsavo is bleak, bordering on the Taru Desert, and has been heavily poached by ivory hunters, the dirt road from Manyani to Malindi along the south bank of the Galana is well worth taking if you are not in a hurry. You need four-wheel drive in the rains, the driving time from Sala to Malindi being two hours or so. After leaving the Sala gate the road takes a reasonably direct route, sometimes close to the river. Seven kilometres (four miles) from the gate and two kilometres from Crocodile Camp is the left turn-off to the largest ranch in Kenya, the 1½-million-acre Galana Game Ranch, which is reached by a three kilometre road to the river, crossing a causeway and checking-in at the guarded barrier. The ranch has a private lodge, each banda style room having its own shower and lavatory, and is pleasantly set on a bluff above the river. Overall it is a completely self-contained safari area, 1,500 ft above sea level, with tree game-viewing platforms and many species of plains game sharing its immense territory with 21,000 head of cattle. Night game drives, camel safaris and bird watching are amongst the activities that can be organised. Some imaginative experiments in ranching game have been tried here, and there is a herd of domesticated oryx. It is associated with Sangare Ranch near Mweiga and with the Indian Ocean Lodge at Malindi (see North Coast chapter) from which it is 30 minutes flying time. Enquiries to Galana Game and Ranching Ltd. (Bookings PO Box 76 Malindi; telephone 20394. Or through Safari Consultants, 83 Gloucester Place, London W1H 3PG; telephone 01-486 4774).

Continuing along the Malindi Road, the bush gradually becomes thicker until some 40 kilometres (25 miles) from the town you enter the completely different vegetation of the coastal strip, including palm trees and mango and cashew nut trees. The road cuts through a corner of the Jilore Forest and past the airfield to Malindi, described later.

The Coast

The Kenya coast is a series of long bays between coral headlands, punctuated by occasional river creeks running for 480 kilometres (300 miles) from Somalia to Tanzania, though the northern extremity is little visited because it is so inaccessible. It is lined with waving palm trees, mangoes, casuarinas and gorgeously flowering hibiscus, oleander, frangipani and bougainvillaea. The beaches are great sweeps of white coral sand, while about a kilometre out in the Indian Ocean runs a coral reef protecting almost the whole length of the shore from sharks and creating a series of lagoons where the water is crystal clear and an enormous variety of tropical fish feed on the coral. The skin-diving — known locally as goggling — rivals the Caribbean's and so does the big game fishing. Overall it would make a superb backdrop to a James Bond story.

This part of the country has been influenced by invaders and traders through the centuries. Most influential were the Arabs who have exported Ethiopian gold, ivory, skins and slaves from here for more than a thousand years. But they also brought their religion and cultures, colonised and intermarried, and have contributed a courteous and leisurely atmosphere to the coast.

The Reef and Marine Parks

The story behind the reef and its teeming fish is both simple and unexpected. The Continental shelf is narrow, descending sharply to considerable depths only three to eight kilometres from the beach (two to five miles), and reef building corals canot survive below 45 metres. Therefore the reef, usually several parallel reefs in fact, is close inshore. Furthermore corals like warm, clear, saline water. So there is always a break in the reef where rivers like the Sabaki bring down cooler, muddy, fresh water, for instance at Malindi, Kilifi and Mombasa. The coral itself is made up of the hard, calcareous skeletons of countless tiny polyps, growing one upon the other. What is surprising is that the fish living along the reef, feeding on the coral — angel fish, parrot fish and myriad others — originated in the South Pacific. They were brought to Africa by the South Equatorial Current, which flows continuously east to west, then carried to Kenya's coast by the East African Coastal Current running north from Mozambique. A useful reference book on them is 'A Guide to the Common Reef Fishes of the Western Indian Ocean', by K. Bock, published by Macmillan Education Ltd, London.

There are two Marine National Parks and two Marine National Reserves on the coast. The Parks are at Watamu near Malindi and Wasini Island, off Shimoni on the south coast. The Reserves are at Malindi and far up to the north east at Kiunga. They are described in the text.

Skindiving along the reef to observe the fish, sponges, anemones, crabs and starfish that live there is easy: all you need is a rubber mask or snorkel, with flippers or tennis shoes. But beware of the poisonous mottled brown stonefish and of spiny black sea urchins. Both can cause seriously infected wounds. Even worse are the depredations caused to the reef by shell collectors and coral hunters selling to tourists and threatening the life of the reef. To save it the export of shells has been banned since 1979.

Big Game Fishing

Big game fishing centres dot the coast: Malindi, Watamu, Kilifi, Shimoni and Kiwaiyu to name only the major ones. Catches often make records. One Mako shark caught off the coast weighed 325 kilograms (716lbs). Returning fishing boats sport flags to denote their successes: yellow for shark, red for sailfish, black for black marlin, blue for blue marlin, green for striped marlin, white or black and white for a mixed bag. For enthusiasts these safaris into the ocean are as exciting as any on land.

The fishing, the reef, above all the superb coral beaches and the average of ten hours sunshine a day, have made the Kenya coast into an international playground. Half of the country's best hotels are at the coast and many visitors never go up-country at all. Unhappily tourism has undermined local culture and traditions, which were particularly strong and ancient here.

Climate
The coast's climate is tropical. February and March are the warmest months, 31°c (86°F) mean maximum temperature, but really it's the relative humidity of 75 that one notices, so April and November, when the wind is slack, can seem the hottest. The cooler season from July to mid-December is when many local people think the coast climate is at its best. It's advisable to take anti-malarial pills: see also General Information.

Mombasa

Kenya's second town, the largest port on this coast north of Durban, Mombasa is strictly speaking an island, connected to the mainland by the Makupa Causeway, which carries both the famous railway and the modern road. Moi International Airport is on the mainland side of the causeway, some 20 minutes drive from the city centre. Kenya Airways operates two or more flights a day to Mombasa, the flying time being one hour from Nairobi and less than half an hour from Malindi. By road the 485 kilometres (301 miles) take five or six hours, depending whether you stop en route. The express bus fare is only Shs 100/-. Even so, hitch-hiking is common, though it presents a slight risk of being beaten up and robbed. As already explained in the Transport and Safaris section, the overnight train is good value.

Mombasa has a long and proud history. Identifiable as a port in a sailing guide to the Indian Ocean called 'The Periplus of the Erythraean Sea' published in Alexandria AD 80 even before Ptolemy gave it a name. It became one of the principal settlements of Arabs from the Oman and Muscat who colonised the East Africa coast and who gave such a hostile reception to the first European to land here, Vasco da Gama, that the renowned Portuguese explorer sailed on to Malindi. Nonetheless Portuguese warships followed in his wake and the occupation of Mombasa which resulted was only ended when the Arabs recaptured the port in the 18th century. From then on the town and port remained a key possession of the Sultan of Muscat's empire until he transferred his court to Zanzibar in 1832. The opening of the railway in 1901 revived Mombasa as the gateway to East Africa, though the Sultan of Zanzibar's plain

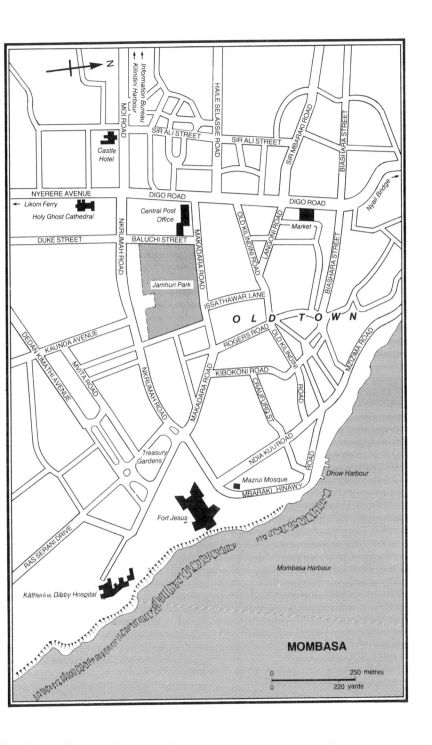

MOMBASA

red flag continued to fly in Mombasa by courtesy of the British until Independence in 1963.

The Old Town

The Arab influence at the coast is most clearly visible in Mombasa and the far smaller port of Lamu, also an island, further north. However it is more relaxed in Mombasa, because this is one of the world's great cross roads, the meeting place of traders from many nations. Easily the most fascinating part of Mombasa is the Old Town, which lies between Makadara Road and the old harbour (see map). Its narrow streets are overshadowed by high houses with elaborately carved ornamental balconies. Itinerant Arabs sell coffee from traditional long-beaked copper pots. Oriental music drifts out from the shops of moneylenders, goldsmiths, tinsmiths, tailors, makers of sweetmeats and other traders, mostly Asian. Oriental mosques and temples, like the new Jain Temple, its pillars and domes as white as icing on a gargantuan wedding cake, jostle for space with bustling African markets and stalls. Everywhere there is hustle, life and a multitude of languages. Mombasa, in fact, has the same cosmopolitan feeling as Hong Kong, Singapore and other world ports. Both old and new parts deserve a visit.

It's worth paying a few shillings for one of the Old Town's numerous self-appointed guides. Get him to show you the cliff west of Government Square, down through which a flight of steps leads to a cave with a well, where the slaving dhows used to take on water secretly. Mombasa was an important staging post in the inhuman business of taking African slaves from all over the interior of East Africa to the slave market in Zanzibar: a market which was only closed in 1873. Frere Town, outside Mombasa to the north, was created at the instigation of Sir Bartle Frere to house freed slaves (see below). Even today the horrors of the slave trade are still remembered. Your guide should take you past the stumpy white minaret of the ancient Maudhry Mosque in Mbaraki Hinawy Road.

He should point out the pure Arabs in their beaded hats and embroidered cloth gowns; the Hindus whose women wear tiny gold studs in their noses and colourful silk saris; and the Swahili men who wear a long white robe, or more often a brightly printed length of cloth wrapped round the waist like a skirt and known as a *kikoi,* while the women wear *kangas,* wrapped round beneath the armpits and falling to mid-calf length. *Kangas* are brighter and gayer than *kikois* and are a real fashion bargain. They are cheap, infinitely varied and, like the useful straw sunhats made locally, you can get them all along the coast. Women of the Moslem faith modestly drape themselves from head to toe in an all-enveloping black garment called a *buibui,* Cynics, however, claim the *buibui* remains popular because it doesn't matter what the wearer has on underneath, or if she has done her hair. You will see schoolgirls, compromising between tradition and modernity, with their *buibuis* thrown back to reveal their faces and their white school blouses, rather as if the garment was an academic gown, not a veil. Girls wear the *buibui* from puberty for the rest of their lives.

The Old Harbour
To find the old harbour go down Nkrumah Road, past the interesting old Treasury Square with its monuments, and past Fort Jesus. The street becomes Mbaraki Hinawy Road and leads past alleyways to the tiny Government Square and the Customs Landing Stage. Between January and March you can be shown round the dhows. For a few shillings a boatman will row you out to one. The *Nahoda*, the dhow captain, will usually welcome a visitor with coffee, black and bitter, from a tiny cup, and may well have fine carpets and Arab chests for sale among his cargo. Dhows and other boats sail up the coast to Lamu and with some discomfort you could take passage in one.

Fort Jesus
At the north corner of the Old Town stands the Portuguese castle, Fort Jesus, weathered and immense. Its building began in 1593. A century later the Arabs took it in 1698 after a 24-month siege, though they lost it again. The Portuguese finally left in 1729. Today its guns still command the harbour, looking out beyond English Point, but the fort itself houses a comprehensive museum dealing with the culture, architecture and history of the coast. Fort Jesus is open daily and a detailed booklet about it is on sale at the entrance. Among many interesting things there are two cycads, fern-like plants which have been in existence for 200 million years, and relics salvaged from a Portuguese warship which sank near the fort. The coats of arms, carved in stone, of Portuguese commanders are worth studying. There is also a curious room of ordinary sailors' *graffiti*, including drawings of the ships of their time, which show what the sunken warship may have looked like to her crew.

Outside the fort, guarding the main entrance, stand two relics of the First World War and the campaigns mentioned in the description of the Tsavo Park. One is a 4.1 inch gun from the German cruiser, the SMS Koenigsberg, which the Royal Navy sank in the Rufiji Delta in southern Tanganykia in 1915. Ten of these guns were salvaged at the orders of the ingenious and tireless General von Lettow Vorheck, turned into field guns, and hauled with him across the bush for many months. The other gun is a 4-inch one converted to coastal artillery use after the British cruiser HMS Pegasus was sunk by the Germans off Zanzibar in 1914.

If you take the path down to the left of the fort, it leads along beneath the battlements above the shoreline, where you can watch local fishermen casting their nets. This path is one of the best places from which to photograph the fort, which is not an easy subject. Immediately adjoining the fort is the old colonial style Mombasa Club, while on the other side there are attractive old buildings in Treasury Square. On Mvita Road, near Treasury Square, is the Wildlife Conservation and Management Department's ivory room, where elephant tusks, rhino horns and other game trophies taken from poachers or dead animals are displayed. The room is open on weekdays.

Shopping
The shops around Government Square offer carpets, Arab chests, brasswork and carvings. Nearby is Yusuf Jaffer's Perfume Shop, where exotically named scents line the walls. They are made without alcohol, which means they do not evaporate (and persist for weeks if you don't bathe!). His shop sign says it all: '. . . the right and real non-alcoholic perfumes super power natural flowers. 300 varieties with sandalwood oil . . .' At another shop the sign announces 'Dealers in carpets, bedsheets, Arab chests, toys, folding bags, non-alcoholic perfumes, pure leather slippers.' Although you might expect these back streets to be squalid and even dangerous, they are neither, and considerably more entertaining to stroll around than the curio stalls which line Moi Avenue along from its junction with Digo Road, where you will be constantly pestered to buy. While in the Old Town make a point of going to the Old Port Tourist shop in Government Square, which among many things sells batiks, amber jewellery and Ethiopian silverwork.

The rest of Mombasa is a modern, thriving city, basing its prosperity on Kilindini Harbour, to which the QE2 makes regular calls, thanks to the enlargement of the harbour entrance to enable US Navy fleet carriers to enter. One of the main shopping streets is Moi Avenue, formerly Kilindini Road, leading to the port, past the famous arch of giant elephant tusks (metal not ivory!) close to which is the Information Bureau (PO Box 85072; telephone 25428). Round here and in Digo Road and Nyerere Avenue you can buy wood carvings, curios, brass-bound Arab chests of all sizes, Indian saris, sandals, straw hats and baskets. Teadin's and Kenrocks, both in Moi Avenue, are good for gemstones. Biashara Street near the Municipal Market (itself worth a look) sells African fabrics and also Moslem caps, called *kofias* in Swahili. A visit to the African market in Mwembe Tayari, off Jomo Kenyatta Avenue, is amusing. You can buy *kikois, kangas*, colourful shirts of African design and beaded hats, not to mention all the necessary herbs and relics for witch-doctoring. Medicines and photographic goods can be bought from chemists in Moi Avenue. There are several good small shops for men's clothing, shoes and tourist curios, and a Home Industries Shop which displays locally made goods.

On Moi Avenue, near the junction with Digo Road, is one of the most lively social gathering places in the whole of Kenya: the verandah terrace of the Castle Hotel. Its patrons are an amazing mix of young 'travellers', African girls whose unabashed role is the pursuit of pleasure, sailors — especially Americans when the US Navy is in port — and holiday-makers. The *samosas* they serve here can be recommended.

Hotels
Because there are no beaches in Mombasa Island, virtually all the hotel development in the area has taken place to the north and south, which we come to in a moment. The most modern hotel on Mombasa Island, and certainly the largest, used to be the Oceanic. However it has been partly converted into apartments and has only a number of economy rooms, albeit air-conditioned, and is unclassified (PO Box 90371; telephone 311191). The Outrigger Hotel (Two star. PO Box 84231, telephone 20822) on Ras Liwatoni Road is also air-conditioned, has a pool and overlooks Kilindini Harbour. A reliable older hotel is the Manor (Two star. PO Box 84851; telephone 21821) on Nyerere Avenue. The Castle Hotel is also two star (PO Box 84231; telephone 23403). Others range down to the very cheap, where you share a room. A list is published in 'What's On in Kenya'. Except at the latter, it is desirable to book in advance in the high season, roughly August to March, although off-peak rates offer large discounts.

The closest hotels off the island are at Nyali, the well-to-do suburb immediately to the north of the new Nyali Toll Bridge. Among the best are the Nyali Beach, the Mombasa Beach and the Severin Sea Lodge, described in the next section.

Sport
Most hotels can arrange sailing and big game fishing. Otherwise a place to hire boats is the Bahari Club, near Nyali Bridge (PO Box 90413; telephone 471316). There is a golf course near the Oceanic Hotel and another in Nyali. The Mombasa showground is also in Nyali, just across the old bridge.

Restaurants and Nightlife
Mombasa has few good restaurants. About the best, both for atmosphere and food, is the Tamarind on the Nyali side of the creek looking towards the old harbour, which also offers dinner while cruising on a dhow. In the town the Capri has continental cuisine; for Chinese food try the Hongkong and for Italian the Bellavista. The Manor Hotel is reliable, while the grill-rooms of the Oceanic, Nyali Beach and Mombasa Beach hotels have a nightclub atmosphere. The International Casino is in the Oceanic. As to nightlife, it's a matter of taking the rough with the smooth. The beach hotels have bands or discos, though the New Florida in Mama Ngina Drive

is about the only nightclub *per se*. Or you could spend a sailor's night out at the Sunshine or the Casablanca.

Theatre and Cinemas
There is one theatre, the Little Theatre Club, on Mnazi Moja Road, which provides a good evening's entertainment. Temporary membership is available. The city has several cinemas, showing both English language and Indian films.

Taxis and Car Hire
The yellow banded taxis are municipally licensed, however you should always agree the fare beforehand. Trips within Mombasa Island should cost around Shs 40/- and to the Nyali hotels around Shs 100/-. Going further out, for example to Diani, would be around Shs 600/-. Most coast hotels have daily minibus trips into the City. If you want to travel up or down the coast cheaply, the Mombasa Peugeot Service operates a mini-bus service from fixed points in towns and villages. Ask your hotel where to find the stops.

Reliable car hire firms include Hertz (telephone Mombasa 316333 or any Hertz office), which has desks at the bigger coast hotels; Archers (telephone 25362); Avenue Motors (telephone 25162) Pollman's (telephone 316732); and Kenatco (telephone 433721). Rates and conditions are as described earlier. Open top mini-mokes used to be popular, but are being replaced by small Daihatsus and Fiat Unos.

Tours and Travel Agents
Bunson Travel Service in Moi Avenue (PO Box 90291; telephone 311331) is deservedly well known. Abercrombie and Kent (PO Box 90747; telephone 316539) have opened offices in Ambalal House. UTC is in Moi Avenue (PO Box 84782; telephone 316333) sharing offices with Hertz there, and at hotels and Moi International airport. The most popular tours go to Tsavo or Amboseli National Parks for two or three days; to the Shimba Hills National Reserve for half-a-day; up to Gedi, Watamu and Malindi; and out on a dhow from Mtwapa creek, north of the city.

Information
The Information Bureau is in Digo Road, near the giant tusks, as already mentioned, and the Mombasa and Coast Tourist Association (PO Box 99596; telephone 25428) is in Moi Avenue. A useful map of the city and island is published by Esso.

Hospitals
Mombasa has excellent hospitals, the one most used by Europeans being the privately run Katherine Bibby Hospital, close to the sea. Hotels can provide the names of doctors.

Consular Representation
The following countries maintain consuls in the city — Austria, Belgium, Denmark, Finland, France, German Federal Republic, Great Britain, Greece, India, Italy, Netherlands, Norway, Rwanda, Sweden, Switzerland and the USA.

The Coast north of Mombasa

Since the construction of the new Nyali Bridge, traffic normally goes north across it. The toll charge is Shs 2/- for a car. To reach the bridge from the city centre go down Digo Road, continuing into Abdul Nassir Road, then left into Tom Mboya Avenue and it is on the right. It is signed both from the centre and from the Makupa Causeway. Immediately on the other side is a right turn for the showground and the old Nyali route, while the main road continues straight ahead. At this corner the old Freretown bell hangs in a white arch, a reminder of the Church Missionary Society's settlement of freed slaves close by here. Their descendants run their own District Council and keep up their old church. Mombasa was a great centre for 19th century missionary activity and there is a handsome memorial to the German missionary Dr Krapf on English Point. Together with Rebmann, Dr Krapf founded the first Christian Mission in East Africa at Rabai, a few miles inland from Mombasa in the hills, in 1846.

Nyali to Mtwapa Creek
As well as being the most prosperous suburb of Mombasa, Nyali has several of the best beach hotels on the entire coast. They are all signed to the right of the main tarmac road. The best known is the Nyali Beach Hotel (Five star, PO Box 90581; telephone 471551) which is some six kilometres (four miles) from the bridge. It has recently been completely renovated and all the rooms are air-conditioned. It has several restaurants, golf, tennis, a windsurfing school and in the evening open-air dancing twice a week and a disco every night. Although the author admits to having a soft spot for this hotel, its rivals do offer similar facilities, trying to be resorts in themselves, though not always with similar finesse. All have pools as well as access to the beach. Thus the newer Mombasa Beach Hotel (Five star. PO Box 90414; telephone 471861), a gleaming white modern block set on a low promontory, sports its own shops and entertainment. A slightly cheaper luxury hotel is the Reef.

Beyond Nyali this immediate stretch of coast is bounded to the north by the Mtwapa Creek 18 kilometres (11 miles) from Mombasa, and there are a host of hotels between Nyali and Mtwapa along the Bamburi, Kenyatta and Shanzu beaches, principally catering for package tours. Notable at Shanzu are the Intercontinental (bookings through any Intercontinental Hotel); the Severin Sea Lodge (Four star. PO Box 82169 Mombasa; telephone 485001) which is in an

African architectural style, the rooms being thatched rondavels set among palm trees; and the five star Serena Beach Hotel, delightfully designed on the lines of the ancient Arab styles of Lamu. The rooms are air-conditioned and the food is excellent (bookings PO Box 46302 Nairobi; telephone 338656). A comfortable, less expensive, hotel is the Whitesands (Four star. PO Box 90173 Mombasa; telephone 485926) on Bamburi Beach and the Bamburi Beach Hotel (Three star. PO Box 83966 Mombasa; telephone 485611) can also be recommended. Unlike some hotels which are overwhelmingly patronised by Germans or Italians, these two keep a balance of nationalities and are popular with English-speaking people, as are the Nyali Beach and the Serena. There are also self-help cottages for rent on Bamburi Beach, but not on a centralised basis.

There are a number of minor attractions close to the coast road between Nyali and Mtwapa. Although the Bombolulu Gardens are not what they were, there is an enterprising Nature Trail at Bamburi. Here some apparently unpromising abandoned quarries have been transformed into a semi-wild environment with waterbirds, eland, buffalo and hippo. The nature walk ends at a crocodile and fish farm. Not far away is Kipepeo aquarium. For eating out there are a few worthwhile restaurants. The Sea Haven at Shanzu is noted for seafood and the Le Joli Coin pleasant. However the best restaurant near here is Le Pichet (Telephone 48248) just the other side of the toll bridge across Mtwapa Creek. Situated close to Marineland (see below), it is reached by turning right immediately after the toll bridge. The dining room is large, cool and informal and the French cooking first class. Although the hotels all have discos one night of the week or another, an entertaining night-club to visit if you want to get away from hotels is the Bora Bora on Bamburi beach.

Mtwapa to Kilifi

Mtwapa Creek is quite a centre of activity. Kenya Marineland is there, with a display of some 150 species of tropical fish such as you could see along the reef, including shark and barracuda which are fed daily by a scuba diver. Nearby is a serpentarium with African snakes and crocodiles. F. G. MacConnell and Co organise deep sea fishing, goggling (snorkelling) and water-skiing, as do the Adcock Fishing and the Aqua Sports Centre. During the day dhow excursions are run from Mombasa to Marineland.

The 40 kilometre (25 mile) length of coral sand between Mtwapa Creek and Kilifi Creek is generally known as 'the north coast'. The main road runs parallel to the shore a short distance inland, with side roads leading to hotels and other sites. While it has long been popular among Kenya residents and the beaches are near-perfect, it has not attracted international development and standards are low. There are beach houses to rent, like the Continental Beach

Cottages (PO Box 124 Kikambala). The best hotel is the Whispering Palms at Kikambala (Three star, PO Box 5, telephone 4). At Kanamai there is a Youth Hostel and campsite run by the National Christian Council of Kenya.

As everywhere up the coast, water temperatures in the sea range from 27°C to 35°C (78°F to 95°F), hardly less than the average shade temperature on land of 35°C (95°F).

Jumba Ruins
Shortly after the Mtwapa Bridge there is a signed turn-off to the Arab ruins of Jumba la Mtwana, a village dating from about AD 1,350, whose name means 'the large house of the slave'. It was abandoned a century after it was built, for reasons which are as mysterious as they are at the Gedi ruins further north. There are remains of two mosques, the one by the sea being delightfully situated; and evidence of houses and tombs. A guidebook is available and after your tour you can walk on down to the sea and swim. Like other coastal sites, Jumba is a reminder of the many centuries during which the Omani Arabs dominated the coast and there are many such remains all the way up to Lamu. If you are interested, go to the Fort Jesus Museum which has a large scale map, indicating them all, together with photographs. Equally the 'Kenya Coast' map, published by the Survey of Kenya, marks them all but without descriptions. They can be overgrown.

The Giriama
The present day native inhabitants of this part of the coast are the Giriama. In the villages you will see Giriama women wearing short, white, flouncing skirts, fluffed out from underneath by bustles made of coconut fibre. At Kikambala, on the main road, is the 'Porini Village', where you can watch traditional Giriama dancing and eat Swahili style food, such as fish cooked in coconut milk, at very reasonable prices.

Kilifi
At Kilifi, 57 kilometres (36 miles) from Mombasa, is the Mnarani Club (Three star. PO Box 81445 Kilifi; telephone 18), originally a big game fishing establishment with its own airstrip, jetty and facilities for water-skiing, sailing, goggling, scuba diving, and underwater photography, as well as fishing. The club is now a package tour hotel, strongly German oriented. It is situated on the south side of Kilifi Creek, which is safe for swimming, and which offers one of the most spectacular birdlife sights in Africa. This is the evening flight of hundreds of carmine bee eaters, tiny but splendidly coloured birds who spend the day feeding inland, then return to a small mangrove island just before sunset to roost. You can hire a motorboat from the hotel to watch this and will see herons, egrets and many other waterbirds on the way.

Kenya

On the other side of the road as you approach the ferry is a path to the Mnarani ruins, mainly distinguished by a fine Arab pillar tomb. The site overlooks the creek. Also on this side is a serpentarium. Crossing the creek involves a toll-free car-ferry, but waiting time can vary greatly. If you have a schedule to keep, allow half-an-hour to get across.

The main part of Kilifi, which is basically an administrative centre, is on the north side of the creek, where there is the Seahorse Hotel (Two star. Bookings PO Box 67868, Nairobi; telephone 20592). It is situated on the creek, not on the sea, and the creek's best friends could hardly claim that the water is clean. The Seahorse also caters mainly for German tourists. It has a pool, water-skiing and an agreeable restaurant. There is a fairly active disco bar in Kilifi village, but otherwise little entertainment.

Kilifi to Gedi

Although there are some excellent and completely deserted beaches immediately beyond Kilifi, further on the access to the sea is less easy and the 61 kilometres (38 miles) of fast road to Malindi passes close to the mangrove swamps of Mida Creek, reaching nothing of much interest until the turn-off to Watamu at Gedi, some 16 kilometres (10 miles) south of Malindi. Here there are the best preserved remains of an Arab town anywhere on the coast, a 15th century settlement which covered 45 acres and only part of which has been recovered from the jungle which rampaged through it until 1948 when it was made a national park and excavations were begun. In the course of the 17th century all the Arab settlements between Somalia and Mtwapa Creek were abandoned as the nomadic Galla tribesmen advanced south. Today you can get a good idea of what it was like in its heyday, with its Great Mosque and fine houses, while the huge trees themselves are fascinating and among the ruins live unique golden rumped elephant shrews. Adjacent to Gedi is the Jilore Forest Reserve, which protects an area of ancient forest and is the home of a great variety of birds.

Watamu

By Gedi is the turn-off to the growing resort of Watamu, which has one of Kenya's few national marine parks, part of a national reserve stretching from Mida Creek up to Malindi. You can swim or water-ski freely, but not collect any seashells. The goggling is superb, especially in the coral garden just inside the reef by Turtle Bay. For this, however, you must pay a park entrance fee of Shs 50/-. Equipment, and glass-bottomed boats can be hired from Ocean Sports Ltd (PO Box 340 Malindi; telephone Watamu 8) whose shop and informal bar and restaurant are right on the beach.

There are frequent fishing competitions, boats and tackle can be hired and enthusiasts stand with binoculars on the shore identifying

Elephant at Amboseli.
Kenway Publications.

Above: Luo fishing boat on Lake Victoria. By Richard Cox
Below: Buffalo by a waterhole

Above: Rhino and egrets
Below: Diani Beach. By Richard Cox

Fly
with pride

If you ever get the feeling that in-flight service is all pretty much the same, fly Kenya Airways.

From the moment you step into the First or Club class aboard any of our Airbus A310-300's you are someone SPECIAL to our cabin crew.

To them, you are not just a passenger on their aircraft, but a guest in their country.

And that gives us the greatest pride of all.

Kenya Airways
The pride of Africa

the fish recognition pennants that fishermen fly when they have landed a catch. The local colours are yellow for shark, black for tunny, light blue for marlin, green for bonito and white for any other. Big game fishing is organised here by Mr and Mrs Slater, who have two boats and can be contacted through the Ocean Sports. Charges run from Shs 3,500/- a day up to Shs 6,000/- for the more luxurious boat. The author Wilbur Smith has been among their many international clients.

A few miles south of Watamu, within the national reserve, is Mida Creek, one of the best places for bird and marine life on the entire coast. Carmine bee eaters roost here and in March/April and November/December hundreds of species of migrating shore birds pass through. Near the mouth of the creek are Tewa Caves, partly underwater, where giant groupers (up to 363 kilograms or 800 lbs) and rock cod can be seen close to by skin divers.

Watamu has several hotels. The Ocean Sports, mentioned above, has comfortable rooms in thatched bandas and a noted buffet lunch on Sundays. Next door is the Seafarers (Three star. PO Box 182 Malindi; telephone Watamu 6), recently greatly improved, with a good swimming pool and a pleasant bar. There are also two massive package tour hotels in the vicinity, The Turtle Bay Beach Hotel (Three star. Bookings PO Box 40503, Nairobi) and the Watamu Beach (Three star. Private bag, Malindi). Both these have plenty of organised entertainment, excursions and car-hire desks. But if you want to do your own thing, the smaller two would be more enjoyable. Watamu is about twenty minutes drive from Malindi airport. Taxis are available from Malindi.

Malindi
Malindi, despite international recognition and recent expansion, is still a relaxed small resort with almost everything one could want. There are a few Arab ruins, a single main shopping street, an attractive old town with tall white-washed houses and quiet shadowy byways, and a real beachcombing atmosphere. The bay runs in a wide sweep of sand on to which a break in the reef lets the rollers in (but not the sharks) so it's a good place for surfing. Old timers remember when the beach was much closer to the village, but that was before the sand bar near the mouth of the Sabaki River just north of the town broke, changing the character of the bay and turning the nearer parts of the beach into a brownish coloured sand. However there is no lack of the original beautiful white coral sands out towards Casuarina Point. The other major change is that whereas Malindi used to be rather sleepy, it now offers plenty of hectic evening entertainment.

Historically, Malindi probably dates back to the 9th century. Arabs occupied the site from the 13th century onwards, following

Kenya

Mombasa's example in giving a hostile reception to the Portuguese explorer, Vasco da Gama, although he left a permanent memento of his call in the shape of the white pillar which now stands outside the town on the way to Casuarina Point and is one of the oldest European monuments in Africa. After holding off Turkish and other attacks in the 16th century, Malindi went into decline following the transfer of the Portuguese headquarters to Mombasa, and the Arabs recovered domination. For nearly three centuries slaves were sold in front of the pillar tombs which stand by the Juma Mosque. The taller of these tombs dates from the 15th century. Malindi's present status began with the building of the first beach hotels in the 1930s, when it started to become popular with British settlers' families, though the tourist boom did not occur until after Independence in the 1960s.

One of the principal events of Malindi's year is the Sea Festival with its fishing contests, held during November. In the last week of January, when the marlin and sailfish are running far out beyond the reef, the International Billfish competition takes place, with participants from all over the world. Details can be had from the Malindi Sea Fishing Club (PO Box 364, Malindi; telephone 20410). The hotels can arrange game fishing for you. For goggling and marine life you want to go some four kilometres (three miles) south to Casuarina Point to the Malindi Marine National Park, which has magnificent coral gardens. Normal park entry fees are payable and glass-bottomed boats are usually waiting for clients — remember that it's a lot cheaper to go in a group. Also out in this direction is Mark Easterbrook's snake farm, open every day, where you can watch the snakes being fed on Fridays at 1630. Sports available are golf at the course just north of the town, riding at the Palm Tree Club near the golf course and, of course, windsurfing at any of the hotels, and squash at the Driftwood Club.

The telephone dialling prefix for Malindi is 0123. Numbers should have five digits.

Malindi's Hotels

Malindi's hotels used to be around the centre, where the better ones still are. Lately the resort has expanded with two hotel clubs, geared to German and Italian tour operators, and a number of quasi-hotels run by tour firms along towards Casuarina Point. These latter are not listed or officially classified.

The hotels along the main street used to back onto the sea 20 years ago, but the ocean's retreat has left a 200-metre swathe of sand dunes between them and the breakers. The most sophisticated hotel, with English connections, is the Arab style Sindbad (Four star PO Box 30 Malindi; telephone 20880). It has an attractive pool. The others, all three star, are the banda-style Lawfords (PO Box 20

Malindi; telephone 20440) which holds frequent beach barbecues; the Blue Marlin (PO Box 20 Malindi; telephone 20441) and the Eden Roc (PO Box 350 Malindi; telephone 20480). These, like the Suli Suli Club (PO Box 360 Malindi; telephone 317) and the Palm Tree Club (unclassified. PO Box 180 Malindi; telephone 20397) out to the north, all have swimming pools and there is a disco at one or the other every night.

Three kilometres south of the town, off the road to Casuarina Point, is the completely different Driftwood Club (PO Box 63 Malindi; tele-phone 20155) which does not take package tours, has one of the best restaurants in the area, accommodates guests in simple chalets (some air-conditioned) and has its own scuba diving school. Finally, on the road to Casuarina Point, is the Indian Ocean Lodge, a stunning looking and expensive establishment, not open to non-residents. The Lodge (bookings PO Box 171 Malindi; telephone 20394), is a beautiful white Arab style house, situated on a small promontory above a magnificent beach. It has its own pool and gardens and the all-in charge of Shs 5,200/- double a day includes all food and drink, its own fast boats for big-game fishing and trips to the Galana Lodge.

At the other extreme, if you want to stay very cheaply, there are a number of Shs 60/- to Shs 100/- a night African hotels in the old town, such as the New Kenya, the Lamu, and the New Safari. There is also a Youth Hostel. It's a bad idea to try sleeping rough on the beach. The part of the old Town near the market and the bus stopping place is where to look for cheap accommodation.

Tours and Transport
The main tour and travel firms, and the Kenya Airways office, are in or off the main street. Among them are Pollmans (PO Box 384 Malindi; telephone 20128) in Lamu Road and UTC (PO Box 365 Malindi; telephone 20040) in Harambee Road. Hertz shares an office with UTC and as well as the Avis office (telephone 20513) there are several local car-hire firms. Hire vehicles at the coast are often not in prime condition and you should check that yours has such basics as a spare wheel and a jack.

There are normal taxis and there are the shared 'taxis', as distinct from matatus, which ply up along the coast. For cheap transport, go to the old town and near the market you will easily find the Malindi Taxi Services office, which runs reliable minibuses and taxis down to Mombasa, usually leaving when they are full rather than to a timetable. There is a daily conventionally sized bus to Lamu, crowded and not comfortable, but you get there.

Kenya Airways operates daily flights to Mombasa and Nairobi. There are excursion fares. The airline's town office telephone is 20237 and the airport number 20192. It is essential to reconfirm bookings 48 hours beforehand. There are daily flights to Lamu which any travel agent can book for you.

As from Mombasa, UTC and others operate one- to three-day air excursions to Amboseli and Tsavo National Parks and even to the Masai Mara. A variety of days' outings are possible, including the air excursion to Lamu. One of the more amusing is the dhow safari on the dhow Tasubiri, which takes people out for a picnic lunch to a secluded beach. Another is to have lunch at Robinson Island, mentioned in a moment, or visit 'Hell's Kitchen' on the north bank of the Sabaki River, see below. Rather closer, only 13 kilometres (8 miles) to the north is Mambrui, a small fishing village of the Bajun tribe, with an old mosque and its attractive replacement. The other obvious trip is south to see the Gedi ruins and the Marine National Park at Watamu, already described. Tours are starting to feature visits to local farms, schools and dispensaries, where anyone interested will discover something of ordinary African life: not all traditional dancing and beach boys.

Restaurants
Eating out in Malindi is no problem. One of the best restaurants is the Umande, off the road to Casuarina Point, which has French cuisine. It is advisable to book. The Suli Suli Inn serves Italian food and the Palm Garden has Indian dishes. The restaurant at the Driftwood Club has excellent seafood. For nightlife, although all the hotels have discos, the Stardust is outstanding, with lighting effects which would do credit to London or New York.

Medical Facilities
In case of illness, Malindi has several resident doctors and a small hospital (telephone 20490).

Garsen, Che Chale, Robinson Island
The road north from Malindi ceases to be tarmac outside the town and is quite rough. The most distinctive feature of the coastline is the promontory called Ras Ngomeni, further on than Mambrui, which juts out into the Indian Ocean to form one boundary of the huge crescent shaped Ungwana Bay (Formosa Bay).

Past Mambrui there are turn-offs from the main Garsen road which lead to Che Chale and to Robinson Island, both mini-resorts in their own right, while inland the road along the north bank of the Sabaki River leads to 'Hell's Kitchen'. This is a miniature Grand Canyon, with multi-coloured rocks and pinnacles, created by erosion: the same savage effects of rushing water that elsewhere strips Africa of its fertile topsoil and threatens famine, although some experts argue that Africa has been eroding for millions of years and the real problem is population growth. Either way, you reach 'Hell's Kitchen' by following the road signed to Marafa.

Che Chale
By contrast, what man can make successfully of sand is on view at Che Chale, one of the ultimate 'get away from it all' places. This beach lodge is set among casuarina trees on a long and effectively private beach on Ras Ngomeni. Created by a former hunter, Johnny Aniere, the accommodation is in thatched cottages, the walls of which are made of sewn palm matting, keeping them cool. The cuisine is excellent. Che Chale takes only a dozen people at a time and is expensive. The cost includes full board, wind-surfing, goggling and transfers from Malindi. Deep sea fishing and trips to the nearby coral gardens along the reef are extra. Bookings PO Box 492, Malindi or through Abercrombie and Kent (PO Box 59749, Nairobi; telephone 334955: or in London). Che Chale is 20 kilometres (12 miles) from Malindi, off the Garsen road, but needs four-wheel drive and is very difficult to find without directions.

Ras Ngomeni itself offers a paradise of tide-shaped driftwood for beachcombers, while the saltpans between it and the main road are a haunt of waterbirds: you can see pelicans, yellow-billed storks, egrets, pied kingfishers and ospreys. Both the sand on the beaches and the sea water glitter with mica or 'fool's gold' as its called. Offshore to the north is the launching platform for an Italian-American space rocket programme.

Robinson Island
This is a small island in Formosa Bay, really called Kinya'ole, which has made its reputation by serving enormous seafood lunches — oysters, crabs, lobsters, prawns and baked fish — on an otherwise deserted beach, where guests swim or sunbathe afterwards. The idea is a good old Mediterranean one and presumably only the British influence has prevented it being followed more often on the Kenya coast. Robinson Island is offered as a tour by most travel agents, but you can perfectly well find it yourself. The turn off is 20 kilometres (12 miles) from Malindi on the Garsen road. You then drive seven kilometres (four miles) to the shore, where there is a car park, and a boat takes you across for the feast. It might be advisable to book your table through a Malindi travel agent beforehand. The island, understandably, is not on the telephone. The season is August to April.

Garsen to Lamu
The remainder of the 111 kilometres (69 miles) from Malindi to Garsen has little noteworthy. As mentioned in the Eastern Kenya section Garsen itself is a small town on the Tana River, populated by Somali, Orma and Pokomo people. From here the murram road goes on to Lamu via a ferry, but it can be impassable in the rains. Near Garsen

Kenya

is a heronry, where breeding birds can be seen from May to September. A diversion up-river from Garsen, turning left before the ferry, takes you to Wenje 58 kilometres (36 miles) and the Tana River Primate Reserve, already described. The principal road, after you have crossed the ferry, continues alongside the Tana River delta and near new settlement schemes until it reaches Mokowe where you take a boat across to Lamu. If you fly into Lamu, the plane lands on Manda island and there are usually boats waiting to ferry you across the creek. Cars are not allowed on Lamu Island.

Lamu

Lamu, together with its sister islands of Manda and Pate, has been inhabited for over a 1,000 years. Each constituted a state, despite the relative smallness of the archipelago, and they dominated each other in turn, engaging in wars which reputedly were interrupted if the tide brought in a big run of fish. Today 65 per cent of the people depend on fishing for their livelihood, catching barracuda, kingfish and sea tilapia, though not shellfish. The other principal occupation has always been trade and the dhow trade with Muscat and Saudi Arabia remains more important to Lamu than to any other port on the coast. The picturesque waterfront (shown in the drawing in this section) sees a constant coming and going of boats and there are sometimes great stacks of mangrove poles lying on the quayside awaiting shipment to Arabia. The point about the mangrove is that it grows in swamps by the sea — you pass through mangroves taking the boat from the airfield — and so its wood is impregnated with salt, which deters white ants from eating it. The wood is also hard. For centuries it has been favoured for the construction of houses in

Dhows lying off Lamu

142

Arabia, the length of the average mangrove pole determining the span of ceilings. However Arabian oil wealth has replaced the traditional mangrove poles with steel and concrete and the trade is dying.

Equally the dhows are being replaced by small merchant ships, though dhow building is still important to Lamu. There is a shipyard in the town, with the main one round the other side of the island at Matondoni, and the launching of a new dhow occasions at least two days of celebration. The dhows themselves are made of mahogany. The smaller dhow-like fishing boats — as in the foreground of our illustration — are called *mashuas*. They all have similar triangular sails, but the dhow has a high bow and stern and a deck, as befits a cargo carrier. A large dhow can have a deadweight of 120 tons, carry 400 tons of freight and by local standards cost a fortune to build — three or four million shillings. The original Lamu dhow was the *mtepe*, the 'sewn boat', the planks being literally sewn together with cord because the people mistrusted iron nails. You can see a model of one in the museum. Making dhow models is a local speciality.

Overall, Lamu is a unique blend of tradition and informality: the latter making it something of a haven for drop-outs from Europe. Twenty-five years ago the town had no proper hotel and was 'undiscovered'. Now it has several and tourists on excursions from Mombasa or Malindi may fail to appreciate that beneath the sleepily relaxed exterior, the people are strongly Moslem and proud of their individuality. They do not normally drink and will, for example, be offended if you take alcohol with you for a picnic trip on one of their boats. The Riyadha Mosque in the town is a centre of learning and in January there is a tremendous celebration for the feast of Maulidi, when thousands of Moslems converge on Lamu and the shops run out of everything. Traditionally three visits to Lamu for Maulidi equal one pilgrimage to Mecca.

Town Tour
If you tour the town you must look out for the museum, which is on the waterfront. Among its prize exhibits are two huge brass and ivory ceremonial horns, or *siwas*. The area between the museum and the fort, an unmistakable castellated structure on a slight hill, is the 17th century town. The fort itself was originally an Omani palace, was fortified by the Portuguese and is now the prison. The narrow streets of the old town have many shops selling carvings. Some of the best buys are brass inlaid chests and silver ornaments. The wood for the traditional Lamu doors comes from the Witu Forest, near the Garsen Road. One good shop to ask for is called Scanda. You should also seek out the makers of model dhows to see their craft, as well as seeing the full scale shipyard. Two books on Lamu are 'An Historical Guide to the Lamu Archipelago' by Esmond and

Kenya

Chrysee Martin and 'Lamu Town' by James de Vere Allen, who founded the museum.

Hotels

The main hotel in the town is Petley's Inn (Three star, Box 4 Lamu; telephone 48) which is on the waterfront with delightful views from the dining room and has a swimming-pool two floors up. The food is good, but the downstairs bar is apt to be noisy. There are a number of cheaper hotels, with no air-conditioning, in the town's back streets — where it can be stifling in hot weather. Probably the best of these is the New Mahrus. The other good hotel is in the totally different surroundings of Lamu's other village, Shela, where many miles of superb beach stretch around the point. This is Peponi (Three star, PO Box 24 Lamu; telephone 29). With a long terrace overlooking the sea, Peponi's is spread out among coconut groves, its accommodation being largely in chalet bedrooms. The food is excellent. Nearby is the old Shela mosque and some very photogenic scenery. You can take a boat from the Lamu waterfront to Shela for about Shs 50/- or walk along the shore, which takes 45 minutes.

Manda Island

Manda Island has two places to stay, both on the beach, though very different in facilities and price. Opposite Shela, across the creek, is the Ras Kitau Beach Hotel, unjustifiably not classified and not on the telephone (bookings through Flamingo Tours PO Box 83321, Mombasa; telephone 311978: or through Flamingo or Bunsons in Nairobi). This is a pleasant hotel with recommended Italian cooking, though the banda rooms become rather hot. It is reached by boat from the airstrip, not overland, and lays on a shopping boat to and from Lamu town every morning. The beach here is excellent. At the north end of Manda Island is one of the most exclusive and isolated beach establishments on the entire coast, the Blue Safari Club (not classified. Bookings PO Box 41759, Nairobi; telephone 338838. Telex Blue Safari FMC 22708 Nairobi. Or through Archer's Tours or Abercrombie and Kent in London). The Club was started by a Kenyan Italian, Bruno Brighetti, who is an honorary game warden, as a private resort for rich friends. The maximum accommodation is for 24 people. The cuisine is Italian. There is every kind of watersport, including scuba diving, deep-sea fishing and bird-watching. The Italian girls who get invited are also worth looking at. Priced in Swiss francs at SwFr 500 a day, the seasons advised by Brighetti are November to mid-December and mid-February to mid-April, when the sea water is at its clearest.

Excursions

The obvious trips from Lamu are all by boat and there is no lack of craft on the waterfront available for hire. One pleasant trip is to go fishing, then sail to a beach on Manda Island where the boatmen cook the fish and you swim until late afternoon. Prices are entirely by negotiation. But be warned; if you decide to go further and sail to Pate — a rewarding visit — remember that you go through the creeks and that *mashuas* require wind to move. We went up to Pate once in three hours — and took seven hours getting back, including being caught on a mudbank when the tide went out.

Pate and Siyu
Sailing to Pate in the creeks behind Manda Island you pass the Blue Safari Club on Manda Bay, where you may be allowed to call in for a drink. Pate itself, like Siyu on the same island, is very run down, but with interesting traces of former glory, such as shards of the Chinese porcelain which once decorated house walls. Both were centres of Arab colonisation in their hey day. Gold ornaments are a local speciality. The journey there, past mangrove swamps and creeks alive with birds, makes the trip additionally worthwhile, and there are such curiosities as crabs with a single giant claw which deserve to feature in a thriller film.

Kiwaiyu and Kiunga Marine National Reserve
Beyond Pate is a whole archipelago of coral islands, notably Kiwaiyu Island, of considerable beauty and offering magnificent scuba-diving and sailing. They can only be reached effectively by a power boat, or if you are feeling rich, you could hire a floatplane down at Kilifi and fly up for the day. There are two places to stay, both expensive: the Kiwayuu Island Lodge on the island, and the Kiwayu-Mlango wa Chanu Safari Village on the mainland. Why both spell their names differently to the accepted map spelling of Kiwaiyu is unclear: commercial competition perhaps. Either way, the island lies some 65 kilometres (40 miles) north east of Lamu and is on the edge of the Kiunga Marine National Reserve. The chain of coral islands in this 250 sq kilometre Reserve not only shelter outstanding marine life and coral gardens, they are also home to bushbuck and other game: not so surprising perhaps when you remember that the Dodori National Reserve is on the mainland opposite. If reindeer can swim out to islands in northern Norway why should not bushbuck do the same in these much warmer waters? Turtles lay their eggs on the coral beaches and 150-year-old giant clams lie near the reef.

The Kiwayuu Island Lodge (Unclassified. Bookings Empire Tours, PO Box 86606, Mombasa; telephone 20663), has nine rooms, a lounge and bar, set on 10 kilometres of deserted beach. Kiwayu-Mlango wa Chanu (Bookings Musiara Ltd, PO Box 48217, Nairobi; telephone 331871 or through Let's Go Travel) used to be the Kiwayu Safari Village until is was acquired by the owners of Governor's Camp and upgraded. It has 17 thatched suites, each with its own bathroom. All water sports except scuba-diving and deep-sea fishing are included in the tariff of Shs 2,000/- per person, double. It's been described as 'Tahitian' in atmosphere. The words *Mlango wa Chanu* are the local name for the entrance to Kiwayu harbour. *Mlango* means equally 'gate' or the gap in a reef. Past patrons have included Mick Jagger and the Prime Minister of Italy.

There is a daily air service from Nairobi's Wilson airport operated by Air Kenya Aviation Ltd. The fare is Shs 2,000/- one way or Shs 3,670/- return.

The Coast South of Mombasa

The south Kenya coast has deservedly come into its own. The fine white coral beaches here are mostly better than those north of Mombasa and the natural delights are swimming, goggling (snorkelling) and big-game fishing, though there is less marine life along the reef, not least owing to the depredations of shell and coral souvenir sellers. Although you have to cross Mombasa Harbour on the Likoni ferry, which runs every ten minutes, you are then on a good tarmac road to some 40 kilometres (25 miles) of international class hotel developments, as yet well spaced out.

Likoni Ferry to Tiwi

Just south of the ferry at Likoni is the enlarged Shelly Beach Hotel (Two star. PO Box 96030 Mombasa; telephone 451221), a pleasant place to go for a drink or a meal. The reef is more interesting here than further south, though the swimming is not so good. Specimens you may expect to find in the clear greeny-blue water around the reef include brittle stars, a kind of starfish whose arms break off but grow again, and a variety of conch shells, among them the rare foot-long giant spider conch. Along Shelly Beach there are also a children's resort centre and a camping site.

Between the villages of Waa and Tiwi a road branches off inland to the village of Kwale and the Shimba Hills National Reserve, known for its handsome sable antelope and described below. The main gate is 17 kilometres (10½ miles) from the turn-off. There is now a lodge.

Along Tiwi Beach, as further down the coast, there are beach cottages to rent at anything from Shs 400/- a day for two bedrooms in simple style, to Shs 1,500/- for luxury with servants included. There is no single local agent, so the best plan is to book through one of the major Nairobi tour operators. Let's Go Travel (PO Box 60342, Nairobi; telephone 29539) specialises in self-catering accommodation and can provide a priced list of beach cottages at different coastal resorts.

Tiwi Beach is separated from the celebrated Diani Beach by the estuary of the Mwachema River. On the south side, close to the sea, is a well preserved ancient Persian mosque in a grove of giant baobab trees. Persian, Arab and Portuguese ships all used the estuary for shelter if they could not reach Mombasa. A word of warning, however, do not walk here or anywhere away from the hotels either alone or carrying valuables. There have been many robberies.

Diani Beach

The five kilometre (three mile) stretch of white coral sand fringed by palm trees known as Diani Beach has seen more recent development than any other part of the coast. It has a tarmac access road signed from the main road just before Ukunda, where there is an airfield, a small shopping complex with a supermarket, bank, boutiques and an amusement centre. The Diani Beach telephone dialling prefix is 01261.

Among the longer established hotels which are favourites of English visitors are the Trade Winds (Three star. PO Box 8, Ukunda; telephone Diani Beach 2016), which has been expanded but retains its comfortable informality; and the Two Fishes (Four star. PO Ukunda; telephone Diani Beach 2101). Another family hotel is the Jadini, greatly improved to a Four star standard (PO Box 84616, Mombasa; telephone Diani Beach 2051). The most luxurious hotel is the Diani Reef (Five star. PO Box 35, Ukunda; telephone Diani Beach 2175). Like most of the others it has all the facilities you would expect in a Mediterranean resort hotel, as have the Leopard Beach (Five star. PO Box 34, Ukunda; telephone Diani Beach 2111). The Africana Sea Lodge (Five star. PO Box 84616, Mombasa; telephone Diani Beach 2052), and the Sheraton Golden Beach (Five star. PO Box 31, Ukunda; telephone Diani Beach 2172). However, the five star rating is given more for such physical attributes as swimming pools and razor sockets in the rooms than for cuisine or atmosphere and none of the hotels — except perhaps for the Diani Reef and the Leisure Lodge — is significantly different to package tour hotels anywhere else: except that they are in Kenya. They all have pools, discos, tour operator's desks, shops, watersports and heavily organised programmes of entertainment. Not all encourage outside visitors to come in for as much as a drink. The Robinson's Baobab, for example, despite its English name, is effectively a German club while the Leisure Lodge Club, adjoining the Leisure Lodge Hotel, is a fully-fledged one, bookable only in Munich. All the hotels organise excursions to Mombasa, the average bus fare being Shs 130/-. There is a diving school at the Jadini Hotel.

If you do not want to stay in a package tour hotel there is the Nomad Beach Hotel (PO Box 1, Ukunda; telephone Diani Beach 2155) which has thatched bandas and is a south coast equivalent to the Driftwood Club at Malindi, with water sports and a first-class restaurant. It charges Shs 1,000/- double, which is substantially cheaper than the other hotels and can also be booked through Let's Go Travel. It has a campsite.

Beach Cottages
A second alternative is to rent a cottage. About the best of these, very well situated on a bluff overlooking the beach and catching the sea breeze, are the Warrandale Cottages (PO Box 40521, Mombasa; telephone Diani Beach 2186). Spanish styled, these vary from taking two to six people. Seacrest Cottages can be booked in Nairobi at Agip House (PO Box 44053, Nairobi; telephone 22728). These and a number of other villas can also be booked through Let's Go Travel. The local Wailes Agency for Galu Cottages has an office near the Leopard Beach Hotel. Further down the coast, at the spot called Four° Twenty' South, after the parallel of latitude, there are cottages rentable through Kenyavillas (PO Box 57046, Nairobi; telephone 29161). Further on there are beach cottages at Msambweni, the Seascape Beach Villas, again bookable through Let's Go Travel.

Restaurants
The Nomad's restaurant can be heartily recommended for seafood. So can Ali Barbour's, established in a natural coral cave by Diani Beach. It is open for dinner only. Otherwise, if you want a night out the best answer is a taxi to Mombasa.

Around Diani
Apart from the Shimba Hills National Reserve, there are relatively few inland attractions near Diani, and many holidaymakers take flying safaris to the Mara or to Tsavo. Of minor interest is an extraordinary baobab tree near the Trade Winds Hotel. Baobabs are said, in local legend, to have been pulled up and re-planted upside down by the devil, which is why the branches look like roots. This giant specimen of a common coastal tree is estimated to be 500 years old, has a girth of 21.69 metres (71 ft 2 ins.), and is protected. Cashew nut trees are also common down here, while in the nearby Jadini Forest you will find innumerable butterflies, birds and monkeys. Look out specially for the black and white colobus monkey, with long white hair round its head and shoulders.

Big Game Fishing
For fishing enthusiasts the greatest attractions down here are out in the Indian Ocean, where black and striped marlin, sailfish, barracuda, shark, tunny, five-fingered jack, kingfish, wahoo and bonito cruise in the almost unexploited deep water beyond the reef. The main Diani fishing expert, with several boats and full tackle, is John Bland (PO Box 47, Ukunda; telephone Diani Beach 2087), who operates from the Jadini Hotel. Other boats are run by Nomad Boats, (telephone Diani Beach 2156) at the Nomad Beach Hotel. Costs are around Shs 450/- per hour per boat. Count on at least four hours. John Bland also hires out diving equipment and has a glass bottomed boat for viewing the reef.

The Shimba Hills National Reserve
Geographically the 192 sq kilometre (74 sq miles) Shimba Hills
National Reserve lies directly inland from Diani, at altitudes of up to
448 metres (1,471ft). The Kidongo Gate can be reached from a road
through Niele. However, it is preferable to drive back towards
Mombasa on the main road and turn off to Kwale at the road junction
between Waa and Tiwi, already mentioned. From the turn off it's
half an hour's drive through Kwale village, where you are 365 metres
(1,200 ft) above sea level. It's better not to take the earlier entrance,
before Kwale, as it does not lead into the main circuits of the reserve,
which are well signposted. The area is largely thick tropical forest,
inhabited by many animals including the small forest elephant, the
rare roan and black sable antelopes, buffalo and leopard. However,
we only saw herds out on the Lango Plains near Giriama Point,
where the trees give way to rolling parkland along an escarpment.
This is one of the few reserves where you are allowed out of your
car, but forest elephant have a reputation for ill-temper, so keep
your distance. Camping sites are available (ask at the gate) and in
late 1987 a 'tree hotel' was opened. Like Treetops, the Shimba Hills
Lodge is constructed on stilts, with walkways above ground, overlooking a waterhole and salt lick in a forest glade. Guests transfer
at the Park gate into a four-wheel drive vehicle and are escorted to
the Lodge by the resident naturalist. The tariff (not set at the time
of writing) includes tea, dinner and breakfast. Bookings through Block
Hotels (PO Box 47557, Nairobi; telephone 335807) or local Mombasa
travel agents.

Diani to Shimoni
To continue down the coast you must return to the main tarmac
road at Ukunda. Pending new developments, there is little noteworthy except fine beaches near Gazi and Funzi. The beach cottages
at Four Twenty South and at Msambweni have already been mentioned. At Msambweni there is a reasonably stocked village shop
and there are certain to be hotels eventually, if only because it is
so unspoilt.

Then, some 80 kilometres (50 miles) from Mombasa, you reach the
village of Ramisi and the sign to the world-famous Pemba Channel
Fishing Club, (PO Box 44, Ukunda; telephone Msambweni 5Y2). The
last 16 kilometres (10 miles) from Ramisi is rough going, but that
will hardly deter enthusiasts, because the Pemba Channel offers
some of the finest fishing in Africa and many records have been
established here, especially for marlin and shark. Furthermore the
Manager, Mr Pat Hempill, lets you keep the catch or else will sell it
for you and credit your account. This is not usually possible
elsewhere. The rooms are chalets with bath or shower. Recently a
competitor has opened in the shape of the Shimoni Reef Fishing
Lodge, which has makuti-roofed cottages available either on a half-
board or a self-help basis. Bookings through Flamingo Travel (PO

Box 44899, Nairobi; telephone 28961). Rates are around Shs 1,100/- double, half-board.

Kisiti National Marine Park

From Shimoni you can take a boat to snorkel in the 28 sq kilometres (11 sq miles) Kisiti National Marine Park, which encompasses four reef islets and their coral gardens, with the tiny Mpungiti National Reserve adjoining it. Wasini Island, just offshore, has a restaurant with a good reputation for its seafood, amongst the dishes being crab and fish cooked Swahili style in coconut milk and spices. An Arab dhow makes the short trip across and places can be booked in advance for a full day tour through Thorn Tree Safaris in Kaunda Street, Nairobi (PO Box 42475; telephone 25641). You sail through the islands, visit the coral gardens for goggling and have time to see Wasini village, with its old Arab tombs.

South of Shimoni is the Tanzania border. If you were to cross, you would continue on the main tarmac road from Ramisi and eventually reach Tanga.

Lions taking their siesta near Lake Manyara

Northern Tanzania

The Country	152
National Parks and Reserves	153
Transport and Safaris	154
Hotels and Game Lodges	156
Arusha, Arusha National Park, Mount Meru	157
Moshi and Mount Kilimanjaro	161
Lake Manyara, Tarangire, Ngorongoro Crater	164
Olduvai Gorge, the Serengeti, Mwanza	168

The Country

The highest, the longest, the deepest, the most vast, the most numerous — all these adjectives can be applied to the many attractions which Tanzania offers to the visitor. The first recorded mention of it occurs in the 'Periplus of the Erythraean Sea', a detailed mariner's guide to the East African coast dating from the first century AD. This document refers to the island of Menouthias, probably Zanzibar or Pemba, and the mainland town of Rhapta, possibly Pangani or another town in the Rufiji River delta.

A number of settlements were made on the coast by Arabs and possibly Persians, the most famous and best preserved being Kilwa in the south. Bagamoyo, a small town just north of Dar es Salaam, was the favourite jumping-off spot for the 19th century explorers, including Livingstone, Stanley, Burton and Speke, as well as being the start and end of the great slave caravans from the interior.

As Tanganyika, the country became a sovereign state on December 9, 1961. Previously it had been a German colony from the 1880s until 1916, and after that a United Nations Trusteeship administered by Britain. It became a republic within the Commonwealth exactly a year after *Uhuru* (Swahili for independence), under the Presidency of Dr Julius Nyerere, who was the country's first Prime Minister. Then on April 27, 1964, a union was formed between Tanganyika and the islands of Zanzibar and Pemba, taking the name of the 'United Republic of Tanzania'. Mwalimu Dr Nyerere became President of this new state, being succeeded in 1985 by Ali Hassan Mwinyi, former President of Zanzibar. *Mwalimu,* incidentally, means Teacher; ministers and officials are called *Ndugu* or Comrade. A new capital city is currently being laid out at Dodoma, for completion in the late 1980s, but Dar es Salaam will remain the commercial centre.

Today the country's 937,062 sq kilometres (361,705 sq miles) are the home of over 120 different tribes, the largest being the Sukuma. The total population is 22 million, including a small percentage of Arabs, Asians and Europeans.

Within Tanzania's borders lie Africa's highest mountain, Kilimanjaro; its deepest and longest freshwater lake, Tanganyika; and the largest game reserve in the world, the 41,440 sq kilometre (16,000 sq miles) Selous; as well as the finest concentration of wildlife in the world on the Serengeti Plains. Overall 247,535 sq kilometres (95,548 sq miles) of land is permanently set aside for the preservation of wildlife. However both the most spectacular and the most accessible areas lie in Northern Tanzania, on which this chapter concentrates.

The north has often been described as a microcosm not just of

Tanzania but of East Africa as a whole. Its scenery ranges from the vast, golden plains of the Serengeti to the snow-capped peaks of Mount Kilimanjaro, from wild bush country to neatly tended farms and plantations, from tumbling mountain streams to lakes pink from the flamingoes flocking round them, over rolling grasslands and through tropical rain-forests. Among the people are prosperous African farmers, operating highly mechanised farms, peasant cultivators still using the primitive digging stick and pastoral nomads like the famous warrior tribe, the Masai.

The main attraction is, of course, the unsurpassed concentration of wildlife, the greatest in Africa. Almost wherever you go, even on the main highways, you can generally expect to see zebra, wildebeest, ostrich and antelope. In fact, one of the most frequent road signs on the Arusha-Moshi road is 'Danger — game area', illustrated by a leaping buck. Trips to the incomparable Serengeti Plains, Kilimanjaro, Lake Manyara and the Ngorongoro and Ngurdoto Craters can be made in a short tour, since they are not far apart although the roads can be poor, especially during the rains.

The Kilimanjaro International Airport at Sanja Juu, 56 kilometres (35 miles) from Arusha, means that visitors can fly straight from overseas into the heart of Tanzania's safari country.

Climate
Northern Tanzania is a semi-temperate region with two rainy seasons a year, the long rains in April and May and the short rains in either October or November. This means that the best seasons for safaris are July to October and December to February. Mean temperatures vary between 17° C and 30° C (62° F and 85° F) and there is frost and snow on high ground. The nights are cool. In the evenings, especially from June to October and during the rainy seasons, warm clothing is necessary. There is low humidity and the area is virtually free from mosquitoes, though mosquito nets are provided in some hotels.

National Parks and Reserves
President Nyerere's Arusha Manifesto back in 1967 was a landmark for African game conservation, 'Wildlife is an integral part of our resources', he said. Today 25 per cent of the country's area is devoted to parks and reserves. The famous ones in the north, all described in the text, are:

Arusha National Park
137 sq kilometres (53 sq miles). Combines three formerly independent sanctuaries — the 1½-mile-wide Ngurdoto Crater, the Mount Meru Crater, and the Momella lakes, scene of many films. Elephant, rhino buffalo and smaller game. Open all the year.

Northern Tanzania

Lake Manyara National Park
330 sq kilometres (128 sq miles) in the Rift Valley south west of Arusha, 230 sq kilometres (89 sq miles) being lake. Noted for its 340 species of birds and for the lions that take their siestas in its trees. Open all the year.

The Ngorongoro Crater
The floor area of this fantastic 2,000 ft deep volcanic crater is 113 sq kilometres (44 sq miles). It is the centre of a 8,290 sq kilometre (3,200 sq mile) conservation area which is a pioneer experiment in reconciling the interests of wildlife and forests with the needs of the local Masai tribe. Large herds of plains game.

The Serengeti National Park
About 14,760 sq kilometres (5,700 sq miles) between Arusha and Lake Victoria, it contains the most spectacular concentration of plains game anywhere in the world. Open all the year. Lodges.

A useful series of 50 to 70-page booklets on Tanzania's National Parks was published in 1986 by the National Parks in co-operation with the African Wildlife Foundation. Only available within the country, they include outline Park maps and are worth specifically asking for at Park entrances or Lodges.

Entry fees to the Parks and Reserves must be paid in foreign currency by non-residents and are US$10 per person per day. The use of campsites costs US$6 per person per day, except in the Ngorongoro Crater where the charge is US$30. Vehicle entry fees are additional, depending on weight and start at around £5 sterling or US$8.

In the past it used to be possible to fly into certain Park airstrips from outside the country. Immigration and customs facilities have now been restored at Lake Manyara and at Seronera in the Serengeti, but the landing fee for a foreign registered aircraft is US$400.

Transport and Safaris

Scheduled Air Services
Air Tanzania Corporation, the State airline, operates services from Kilimanjaro Airport near Arusha to Dar es Salaam, Musoma, Mwanza and Tanga. Dar es Salaam is the connecting point for services to other towns. The fare from Arusha to Dar es Salaam is Shs 2,500/-, but visitors are likely to be asked for the foreign currency equivalent. Departure times of air services are unreliable and it can be difficult to book the return flight. Air Tanzania has offices in Arusha (PO Box 740; telephone 3201) and in Moshi (PO Box 1436; telephone 3061). The regional office in Kenya is in Chester House, Koinange Street, Nairobi (PO Box 20077, Nairobi; telephone 336397).

Air Charter
Light aircraft can be chartered in both Arusha and Dar es Salaam.
In Arusha Tanzania Game Tracker Safaris (PO Box 2782, Arusha;
telephone 7700) operate several aircraft. In Dar es Salaam Tanzanian
Air Services Ltd (PO Box 364, Dar es Salaam; telephone 051-42101)
can provide planes for visiting the southern Reserves. Charter rates
are between US$2 and US$3 per mile.

Rail
Trains run on both the original railway system linking Dar es Salaam
with Arusha, Mwanza, Kigoma and the intermediate towns, while
the Tazara Railway from Dar to Zambia passes through Mbeya. Train
tickets are cheap. The fare from Arusha to the capital is Shs 500/-and
you could pay that in local currency. But this service only runs once
a week on Sundays and is very slow.

Buses
There are extensive local bus services, which are cheap, but crowded.

Car Hire
Car hire is available in Arusha, through the travel agents listed below,
but seldom on a self-drive basis. Payment must be in foreign
currency and rates are around 60 US cents per kilometre. However
the charge for the driver will be modest. Petrol is not always available
and costs Shs 50/- a litre. If you do drive yourself you must have
an International Driving Licence and local Tanzanian vehicle
insurance. Vehicles are also available in Moshi (see under Moshi
below).

Safaris
Major hunting and photographic safaris have in part already been
dealt with in the Safaris section. However, it bears repeating that
Arusha has been a starting point for safaris for the better part of
the century and that 21 of the 29 species of game which may be
shot by the holder of a general game licence are to be found in
Northern Tanzania, while some of the rarer species are more easily
obtained here than anywhere else in East Africa, especially the
greater kudu and the sable antelope. The hunting season is from
July to December. Complete hunting or photographic safaris are
organised by Tanzania Wildlife Corporation (PO Box 1144, Arusha)
who handle taxidermy and the shipping of trophies. Private firms
which organise hunting in conjunction with the Wildlife Corporation
include Tanzania GameTracker Safaris Ltd (Private Bag, Arusha;
telephone 057-6986). Photographic safari specialists include Ker and
Downey, contactable in the USA, as is GameTracker Safaris, through
Sporting International, 7701 Wilshire Place Drive, Suite 504, Houston,
Texas 77040; telephone 713-744-3527. Abercrombie and Kent,
addresses in the next paragraph, also organise photographic safaris.

Northern Tanzania

Do-it-yourself Safaris

You can only organise your own safaris in Tanzania with difficulty. You would have to hire a vehicle in Arusha and probably pay all the anticipated charges in advance. The hassle of paying bills in foreign exchange can be considerable, since you will often find the hotels do not have change in foreign currency. Normally the travel agent or tour operator deals with this. However, if you are determined, it can be done.

Note that to wear camouflage clothing of any kind is illegal.

Tour Operators and Travel Agents

Recently more private tour operators and safari firms have been permitted to operate in Tanzania and to open lodges and camps. Nevertheless the largest organisations remain the government owned State Travel Service (Head Office PO Box 1369, Arusha; telephone 057-3300), represented overseas by the Tanzania Tourist Corporation (TTC). At the time of publication the Tanzania Tourist Representative was planning to open an office in London. There is no longer an office in New York.

The main private firms now operating in Arusha are Abercrombie and Kent (PO Box 427, Arusha; telephone 057-7803), located at Room 348, Ngorongoro Wing, Arusha International Conference Centre; Bush-trekker Safaris, whose head office is in Dar es Salaam, have a desk at the New Arusha Hotel; Subzali Tours and Safaris (PO Box 3061) and Emslies (PO Box 24, Arusha). Simba Safaris rent out cars. There are a number of others in Arusha including Bobbys Tours and Travel, Executive Tours, Khan Tours, Ranger Safaris and Shah Tours. George Dove Safaris (PO Box 1182, Arusha; telephone 057-3265) used to operate in co-operation with the Tarangire Tented Camp and retains useful connections.

Hotels and Game Lodges

A chain of hotels and game lodges is run by the Tanzania Tourist Corporation, who run a centralised booking system through their Dar es Salaam office (PO Box 2485; telephone 27671/4; telex 41061). These hotels are indicated by (TTC) in the text. Their standards are variable and had become decidedly low until renovations began in the 1986/87 seasons, so there is hope of continued improvement. TTC hotels and lodges have tariffs set in US dollars. At the time of writing the norm was US$38 single bed and breakfast, and US$46 double, with five per cent service and 10 per cent sales tax added. Meals in TTC lodges were US$6.25. They would sometimes accept local currency in payment for meals and drinks.

A number of new privately-owned lodges are being built, while other

rundown ones like the Ngorongoro Crater Lodge were being renovated. There is no official classification system.

Hotels in towns are cheaper than lodges. The norm is around US$15
to $25 single and US$25 to $40 double. By law visitors must pay
accommodation bills in foreign currency. The official rate at the time
of writing was Shs 100/- to £1.00 and Shs 62/- to US$1.00. In southern
Tanzania hotels will take only US dollars.

The cost of meals varies widely. Outside Dar es Salaam and Arusha,
menus are likely to be simple, except of course in the game lodges.
A snack will cost up to Shs 200/-, while a full meal in a good restaurant will be Shs 400/- or more. Beer costs Shs 80/- a bottle and soft
drinks almost as much. Tanzania also makes her own Dodoma rosé
and red wine.

Arusha, Arusha National Park, Mount Meru

Driving from Kilimanjaro Airport, which is where most people will
arrive, you fork left for Arusha and right for Moshi, while Kilimanjaro
rises — probably into cloud — on your right and Mount Meru is to
the left.

Arusha

Arusha is an old trading post that is now the most important town
in Northern Tanzania, the administrative headquarters of its region,
and the place where President Nyerere set out the famous 'Arusha
Manifesto' on game preservation. Its position on the Great North
Road, halfway between Cairo and the Cape, is marked by a plaque
near the New Arusha Hotel, and it is also the exact geographical
centre of East Africa.

Despite its recent rapid growth, Arusha has managed to retain a
pioneering air, yet in places is paradoxically reminiscent of an English
Town. Behind it tower the slopes of Mount Meru. Its avenues are
riotous with Nandi flame-trees and blue-flowering jacarandas, while
brightly dressed Africans walk proudly through the busy streets,
gathering in the markets, where they will usually consent to be photographed — for a small fee.

There are modern shops in the northern part of the town and in
the Arusha International Conference Centre, but it is also worth visiting the bustling, colourful bazaar. Among the best local buys are
wood carvings by the famous Makonde tribe of southern Tanzania;
skin articles like wallets and handbags, meerschaum pipes, which
are made locally; and various semi-precious stones mined in the
country. You may find rubies, sapphires, zircons, moonstones,
tourmalines, garnets and tanzanite, a beautiful blue semi-precious
stone. Unfortunately the best stones seldom come into the shops,

they tend to be smuggled out of the country. The town has chemists, outfitters and other shops concerned with the safari business, though stocks of European products are very limited and prices high. The National Bank of Commerce has branches in Uhuru Road and Clock Tower Square. There is a ladies hairdresser in the New Arusha Hotel. On Sundays services are held at a number of churches and if you are ill there is the small Mount Meru Hospital.

Tour operators and travel agents are listed in the earlier Transport and Safaris section. Taxis are available in the town.

Hotels in Arusha
Arusha has a number of hotels. About the best is the spacious Mount Meru Hotel (TTC), set in beautiful grounds a kilometre from the centre of the town, overlooking the slopes of the mountain. It has a swimming-pool and is adjacent to a well maintained golf course. The Hotel Seventy Seven (TTC), also slightly out of town, is constructed like a village, with tennis, swimming and golf and is much patronised by government officials. The New Arusha Hotel (PO Box 88; telephone 3241) also has a pool and gardens stretching down to the river. The less expensive New Safari Hotel (TTC) is famous. In the bar innumerable photographs of game, leopard skins, Masai shields and spears, and the long, shining copper bar top, create an atmosphere well known to Ernest Hemingway on his visits. The hotel was extended and modernised in 1978. Other places to stay include the Hotel Equator (adjacent to the New Arusha and under the same management), the attractively positioned Tanzanite Hotel (PO Box 3063; telephone Usa River 32) nine kilometres (six miles) out on the Moshi road which is cheap and popular with back-packers, and the YMCA behind the New Safari Hotel.

Standards of cuisine are not high. The New Safari Hotel is one of the better places for lunch and there is a Chinese restaurant in the town.

Sports
Local sports include fishing for trout in the Temi River for which a licence has to be obtained from the New Arusha Hotel. There is a 9-hole golf course at the Gymkhana Club. Mountaineering enthusiasts can tackle Mount Meru (14,978 ft) in a day, starting from an advanced point reached by car, or they can do it at a more leisurely pace, taking three days. The climb is little more than a stiff scramble. Legend has it that Mount Meru was once higher than Kilimanjaro, but volcanic activity made it subside. On a clear day you can see that it has a lesser peak. The two are known locally as 'Big Meru' and 'Little Meru'.

Safari Circuits
The main northern Tanzania safari circuit runs westwards past Lake

Manyara and the Ngorongoro Crater to the Serengeti Plains, while the road going north leads to the Kenya border. First, however, we describe Arusha's National Park, the neighbouring town of Moshi and Mount Kilimanjaro.

Arusha National Park and Ngurdoto Crater

The tarmac road from Arusha to Moshi stretches across the Sanya Plains, and several species of game are usually seen on the drive between the towns.

Around Arusha, the scenery is very tropical, with banana plantations along the road, and the thickly forested slopes of Mount Meru beyond. Thirteen kilometres (8 miles) from Arusha there is a turn-off for Lake Duluti, a very pretty and fairly deep crater lake, where you can swim and fish for tilapia. Numerous waterbirds can be seen among the lakeshore and among the reeds. About 21 kilometres (13 miles) from the town is the turn-off for the 137 sq kilometre (53 sq mile) Arusha National Park, which includes the Momella Lakes, the Ngurdoto Crater, and the former Mount Meru Crater National Park.

The great attraction of the Arusha National Park is that within its small area it contains such a variety of scenery, including lakes and the ancient forest on Mount Meru's slopes. The park is only 50 kilometres (31 miles) from Arusha, can easily be visited inside a day, and is open throughout the year. The best months to see it are from July to March. Most of the Park roads are passable in ordinary cars, though they can become treacherous in the rainy seasons of October to November and March to May. There are numerous observation points and picnic sites.

The Park's 137 sq kilometres (53 sq miles) incorporate three distinct areas, the Ngurdoto Crater, Momella and Mount Meru, ranging in altitude from 1,500 metres (4,980 ft) to Meru's dramatic summit at 4,566 metres (14,980 ft). Geologically, Ngurdoto was a subsidiary vent of the greater Meru volcano, one side of which was blown out, releasing the ash, lava and mud deposits in which the Momella lakes eventually formed. This happened relatively recently, so far as geologists are concerned: 250,000 years ago. Whereas Ngurdoto is extinct, Meru is merely dormant and produced a lava flow around 100 years ago.

Aftor entering the Park you come to a fork in the road. The left branch goes to Momella and the right to Ngurdoto and after that to the Momella lakes. The guide published by the National Parks and the African Wildlife Foundation has a useful sketch map.

Ngurdoto Crater

Ngurdoto is a beautiful miniature crater about two and a half kilometres (one and a half miles) across and a few hundred feet deep.

Northern Tanzania

A ring road gives access to several vantage points on the crater rim but visitors are not allowed into the crater itself. The crater walls are heavily forested and on the well-watered floor almost every type of animal can be seen through binoculars while the visitor picnics in glades on the wooded rim. It was described by Sir Julian Huxley, the naturalist, as 'a gem of a park'. One curiosity of the area is that the only resident predators are leopards. Lions come in, but never stay, having been effectively eliminated by the early farmers and hunters.

From the crater rim you have to return to the Ngurdoto Gate to take the road past several pools and Kampi ya Fisi to Momella. *Fisi* is Swahili for hyena and there is indeed a hyena den nearby.

Momella
Momella was run as a farm from 1907 by the Trappe family. The remarkable Mrs Trappe was the first woman to become a professional hunter in East Africa and both her grandsons are hunters today. She made part of Momella into a sanctuary in German times and it became a National Park in 1960. It is a most beautiful area which includes seven lakes, tranquil and untypical of Africa, with a tremendous amount of birdlife and a heavy concentration of wildlife, including elephant, buffalo, giraffe, waterbuck, bushbuck, hippo and colobus monkey. It lies in a saddle between Mount Meru in the west and Kilimanjaro in the east and is spectacularly lovely on a clear day when the mountains can be seen high in the sky.

When Count Teleki, the Hungarian who was both the first European to reach Lake Turkana in Kenya and to see these lakes, came here in 1876 he remarked on the large numbers of hippo and rhino here. Hippo there still are, especially in the small Momella lake. Poaching has reduced the rhino to a reported single animal.

Mount Meru
The road from Momella joins the direct road from Arusha near the Momella Gate and goes on to Mount Meru, the Momella Lodge, described in a moment, being to the north off the Ngare Nanyuki road. You must be accompanied by an armed Park ranger if you intend to go on foot anywhere in the Mount Meru part of the Park. On the way you pass waterfalls and through montane forest, emerging to find the 1,500 metre (nearly 5,000 ft) cliff face of the volcano facing you. The trees in the lower montane forest are mainly African Olive and in the higher forest are Juniper and Podo. There are elephant, buffalo and many birds, including tawny eagles, the brilliant green trogons and turaco. This is one of the best places to find black and white colobus monkeys, usually high in a tree and looking as if they are shrouded in a black and white cape.

Lodges and Camping
The Arusha National Park is served by a rustic hotel called the
Momella Lodge, just outside the northern boundary near the
Momella Gate of the park. Originally constructed as a film set, the
lodge has since been rebuilt and is an ideal place for someone who
does not want the strain of a strictly scheduled tour, but prefers to
have a base from which to make sorties into the surrounding country
as the mood takes him. However, the road is rough and four-wheel
drive is recommended.

Within the Park there is a self-help rest-house, sleeping five, near
the Momella Gate. It can be booked through the Park Warden (PO
Box 3134, Arusha) or the State Travel Service. There are four
campsites, all with water, lavatories and fuel-wood. Three are near
the Momella Gate and the fourth is close to the Ngurdoto Gate.
Additionally there are two large huts for climbers on the upper slopes
of Mount Meru, the Miriakamba Hut and the higher Saddle Hut.
Fuel-wood is available at both. South of the Park there are two
other privately run lodges, both well run, one with its own game
sanctuary, now described.

Mount Meru Game Sanctuary
Approximately 20 kilometres (12 miles) from Arusha, off the Arusha
to Moshi road, is the Mount Meru Game Sanctuary, which shelters
leopard, elephant, warthog, buffalo and buck, among other species.
Its Mount Meru Game Lodge is clean, comfortable and strongly recommended. Founded by a great local character, the Hungarian Dr
von Nagy, the sanctuary and lodge are now run by Abercrombie
and Kent (Bookings PO Box 427, Arusha; telephone 057-7803). Not
far away, down a mile of bad road off the main road near the Usa
River, is the German-run Ngare Sero Mountain Lodge, also recommended. Bookings through any travel agent. Riding safaris are
operated from the Lodge.

Moshi and Mount Kilimanjaro

Moshi
Moshi is the principal centre of the Tanzanian coffee industry, and
buyers from all parts of the world attend the coffee auctions there.
It is also the administrative headquarters of the Kilimanjaro region,
with one million inhabitants, mostly from the Chagga tribe, who
run notable coffee-growing co-operatives. The Chagga are known
for the beauty of their women. In fact they live at one end of what
has often been described as Tanzania's 'bolt of beauty' stretching
from the Chagga of Kilimanjaro to the Wabondei of Tanga, with the
Wapere of Pare in between. The town is slightly larger than Arusha
and is connected with Nairobi by rail (the line does not operate at
present), while a branch runs from it to Arusha. Fine views of the
snows of Kilimanjaro can be had from the Moshi Hotel, a large,

airy hotel, run by the TTC which charges US$25 single and US$34 double per night. Other, cheaper places to stay are the Coffee Tree Hostelry and the Waremi Hotel, while the YMCA on the Moshi-Arusha road is very active. It has a swimming-pool, tennis, and organises mountain climbs.

Minibuses and cars can sometimes be hired through the State Travel Service office in the Moshi Hotel. Reliable taxi services are operated by Aziz Taxis and Kilimanjaro Tourist Cabs. Air charters can be arranged through the travel agents, Emslies Ltd (telephone Moshi 2071). There are daily scheduled flights to Dar es Salaam by Air Tanzania.

The Moshi Club has a golf course facing Mount Kilimanjaro, and there are tennis courts at the Gymkhana Club.

Mount Kilimanjaro National Park
The 19,340-ft Kibo Peak of Mount Kilimanjaro dominates Moshi, where daily life is closely linked with the mountain. Climbing expeditions start from the town and many people are drawn here by the magnificence and mystery of this, the highest mountain in Africa, lying only three degrees south of the Equator yet crowned with a permanent icecap. Often the only visible sign of the mountain is the great, snow-mantled shoulder of Kibo (19,340 ft) and the rugged crags of Mawenzi (16,890 ft) thrusting through a ring of cloud. The lower slopes and forests are hidden.

The roof of Africa ranks among the highest volcanic mountains of the world, consisting of three separate volcanoes of different ages which have been welded into one great mass covering an area of 89 kilometres by 61 kilometres (56 miles by 38 miles). The oldest of these volcanos, known as Shira (13,140 ft), is 12 kilometres (7½ miles) to the west of Kibo, while Mawenzi is 28 kilometres (17½ miles) to the east. Kibo is the youngest of the volcanoes.

The National Park's 1,665 sq kilometres (643 sq miles) encompasses all but the lower slopes of the mountain and therefore a great variety of both flora and fauna from the snow caps down through tundra and moorland to thick rain-forest. On the moorland are the extraordinary plants that characterise the East African mountains: the giant groundsel and lobelias that have seemingly evolved in response to freezing cold at night and hot tropical sun by day. As in the Arusha National Park, the vegetation is protected. Animal life includes buffalo, rhino, eland, colobus and blue monkeys, and the rare Harvey's and Abbott's duiker. Elephant have been seen at 16,000 ft, and the skeleton of a leopard found above the snowline, where there are known to be wild dogs too. The Park attracts more visitors than any other in Tanzania, quite a few for the mountain climb.

Climbing Kilimanjaro

One of the main attractions of the ascent of Kilimanjaro is that it does not require mountaineering experience, nor is any special climbing equipment needed for Kibo if the normal route is followed. The climb can be done by any normally healthy person, though considerable physical endurance is required over the five days needed to make the ascent. Almost any time is suitable, except during the long rains in April and May. The best months are January, February, September and October, when there are very often cloudless days.

The first European to see Kibo was Johannes Rebmann in 1848 and the first to reach its highest point was Hans Meyer, in 1892. Climbers traditionally follow the route taken by most of the early explorers. They start from Marangu — which means 'many waters' — where the Kibo Hotel (PO Box 102, Moshi) and Marangu Hotel (PO Box 40, Moshi) are situated, 5,000 ft up and 40 kilometres (25 miles) from Moshi. Neither hotel is expensive and both have been arranging safaris for more than 30 years. Costs are reasonable, with reductions for large parties. This includes everything from guides downwards; though clothing, which the hotels can provide, is extra. The guides — absolutely essential for any safari — and porters are very experienced, many having made more than 100 ascents each. However it is sensible to bring your own sleeping-bag and a torch (flashlight) with spare batteries since batteries can be unobtainable locally and the final stage of the climb starts in the dark. In all other respects the mountain guides are well organised. The mountain huts, built by the Norwegians, are large and equipped with bunks, mattresses and cooking facilities. You carry your own food and sleeping bags, both of which the hotels can provide. Obviously you need warm clothing, gloves and sunglasses.

Around the hotels there are plantations of coffee, maize and bananas. From here, climbers pass through the forest belt which ends at 10,000 ft. The first night stop is made at the Mandara Hut (9,000 ft) with room for up to 100 people. Then they emerge on to the grasslands, near a volcanic cone known locally as *Kimangi Marangu* — 'the small chief of Marangu' — which until not long ago was the site for rainmaking ceremonies.

The second night stop is made at the even larger Horombo Hut (12,300 ft), near the start of the moorlands, glaciers and snow. Dotted around are giant lobelia and groundsel. On the third day, climbers reach Kibo Hut, 3,000 ft below the summit. The final ascent usually begins about 0300 so that Gillmans Point (18,635 ft) can be reached by about dawn, when there is a good chance of a clear view of the plains below and of the glorious sunrise behind Mawenzi.

New routes up have also been developed. For instance one can drive up to 15,000 ft on the Shira plateau, seeing the game in the national park, then climb this 'plateau route'.

Mawenzi, however, should only be attempted by experienced mountaineers, using normal Alpine climbing gear. Advice for those wishing to attempt this climb can be obtained from the Kilimanjaro Mountain Club (PO Box 66, Moshi), the TTC, or the Director of National Parks (PO Box 3134, Arusha). The TTC can provide a route map for climbers.

Around Marangu and Kilimanjaro's lower slopes
Many places of interest can be visited from Marangu, such as the Ura River with its spectacular waterfalls and the Msumbe Spring, said to have been the home of a snail endowed with powers to revive warriors killed in battle. There are fine walks and visitors often find themselves being accompanied by friendly Chagga children, who like to invite their newfound friends into their homes.

Fishermen can find plenty of sport in the mountain streams and trout rods can be hired from either of the hotels.

Kilimanjaro, 'the shining mountain', has its legends, like all other mountains. *Kibo,* pronounced by the old people 'kiboo' as an exclamation of wonder, has a cave at its foot known as *Nyumba ya Mungu* — 'The House of God'.

The ancient stones of Umbo, situated at Machame and Uru, pillars about six feet above ground level and rammed deeply into the earth, are said to have been places of initiation. The story is told at Uru that they were put in by white people with broad shoulders who reached Kilimanjaro from the west in great numbers, searching for cedarwood and ivory with which to build and decorate the palace of their King, Semira. In this legend they found cedar; at Nanjara in Usseri near the eastern part of Kilimanjaro; the King was actually Solomon and his palace the temple at Jerusalem.

Lake Manyara, Tarangire, Ngorongoro Crater
For the first 75 kilometres (46 miles) towards Manyara you are on a tarmac road, but after the turn off to the right at Makuyuni you come on to a murram surface and the going is much rougher from here on right through to the Serengeti. The only entrance to the Lake Manyara National Park is 50 kilometres (31 miles) from the turn-off. The extent of the Park has recently been enlarged slightly and it is now 330 sq kilometres (128 sq miles), two thirds of it water, one third dry land.

Before game conservation became of international concern, the country around Lake Manyara was one of the most popular hunting grounds in East Africa because of the profusion of wildlife. The protection afforded by its present status has resulted in a spectacular concentration of animals for such a small area. The Park takes in the northern half of the lake, which lies at the foot of the dramatic escarpment of the Rift Valley's western wall. Small as the land area is, it includes five distinct vegetation zones, explained in detail in the National Park booklet. At the entrance gate you are among the high trees of a tropical forest, known as 'ground water forest' because it is not fed by rainfall, and frequented by elephant and troops of baboons. Continuing you pass through light woodland, scrub and open plains to marshland. If you make an early start, and hire a ranger guide, you should easily see three of the 'Big Five' game animals in a day, though in wet conditions you will need a four-wheel drive vehicle to get down the escarpment.

The lions in Manyara have the habit of spending most of the day spread out along the branches of acacia trees, as is shown in the illustration at the start of this chapter, presumably because it is cooler 10 or 20 ft up than on the ground. The Park is also famous for its elephant, which now number around 450 — the highest density of elephant population in Africa. They particularly like the sparse woodland by the escarpment, which is where the naturalist Ian Douglas-Hamilton and his wife Oria gained the experiences for their book 'Among the Elephants'. He predicted that the elephants' habit of stripping the bark off the acacia tortilis trees for food would kill them in a decade. However the elephant have largely stopped doing this and a regeneration of the woodland is taking place: which prompts the thought that they may be more intelligent about their limited habitat than the humans who have denuded the farmland around the Park of trees. Manyara is also an excellent place to see hippo. Since the level of the lake began to fall in 1978, thus increasing the salinity of the remaining water, the hippo have moved to find fresher water and now congregate where the Simba River flows into the lake. They number at least 200.

Manyara is as famous for its birds as its animals, and a small hide has been built on the edge of the soda lake for the use of enthusiastic birdwatchers. At certain times of the year, thousands of flamingoes form a solid line of shimmering pink, stretching many miles down the lake, while among the 340 species are duck, waders, jacanas, egrets, ibises and storks. In the acacia woodlands and along the open grasslands are kingfishers, plovers, coursers, larks and wagtails.

Park Accommodation
The Lake Manyara Hotel (TTC) is just outside the Park boundary, perched on the edge of the Rift Valley wall with magnificent views over the lake. Buffalo, elephant and other game can be seen from the hotel grounds. This is probably the best of the TTC hotels. It

has a swimming-pool and gift shop. Vehicles can sometimes be hired and guides are available at the Park gate. Bookings can also be made through Serengeti Safari Lodges Ltd (PO Box 3100, Arusha; telephone 057-3849). At the time of writing construction of a lodge in the Park was being planned by Ranger Safaris of Arusha.

Near the Gate are ten self-help bandas, with common cooking and dining huts. Firewood is provided. Bookings through either the National Parks Head Office (PO Box 3134, Arusha) or through Manyara's Chief Park Warden (PO Box 12, Mto Wa Mbu). There is also a hostel for groups at the Gate (bookings as for the bandas) and two campsites in the forest close to the Gate. The campsites have water, showers and toilet facilities. A further special campsite is situated at Mahali pa Nyati, near the Hippo Pool, for which permission is required from the Warden.

Gibbs Farm
A pleasant alternative to staying at Lake Manyara, or at Ngorongoro, is Gibb's Farm, near Karatu on the road from the lake to the Ngorongoro Crater, 25 kilometres (16 miles) from the Manyara Gate. Set high among coffee estates, the farm was originally a German settler's house. Now operated by Mrs Margaret Kullander (formerly Gibb) it has accommodation for 24 guests, serves food from the farm and has its own waterfall, salt lick and walking tours. Bookings through Abercrombie and Kent (PO Box 427, Arusha; telephone 057-7803).

Onwards from Lake Manyara
From Lake Manyara you can either return to the main road and head south or continue westwards to Ngorongoro and Serengeti, passing Karatu and Gibb's Farm. The first route, which leads to Dodoma and Southern Tanzania, brings you to the Tarangire National Park, an area of more than 2,600 sq kilometres (1,007 sq. miles), designated as a park particularly to protect rhino, oryx and lesser kudu. Unfortunately many tour operators regard Tarangire as being too far off the recognised northern circuit, disregarding its attractions.

Tarangire National Park
The Tarangire National Park lies due south of Lake Manyara and its entrance gate is 107 kilometres (67 miles) from Arusha, eight kilometres from the tarmac road to Dodoma. It is the only place in Tanzania where you can view fringe-eared oryx easily and during the dry season the river attracts large concentrations of ungulates — whereas in the Serengeti wildebeest, zebra and others are more dispersed. Other big game is plentiful and includes elephant, buffalo, lion and greater kudu. During the rains, however, especially from March onwards, the herds move away from the Tarangire river and spread across some 20,000 sq kilometres of Masai country. Only

resident animals like waterbuck remain behind. The National Park guidebook contains a diagram of these dispersal routes and of the Tarangire eco-system, which is defined by the migration routes. A wildlife census — done by specialist aerial photography — assessed the numbers of animals in the eco-system during the 1980 wet season as including 32,000 zebra, 30,750 impala, 25,000 wildebeeste, 6,000 buffalo and 3,000 elephant.

The Park consists mainly of grasslands and floodplains, some wood-lands and rocky hills. There are several circuits, and ranger guides are available. The Park headquarters is at the extreme northern tip of the Park. On a short visit the areas of the Tarangire river and Lemiyon are likely to offer the best game viewing. Less happily, both mosquitoes and tsetse fly are prevalent. One of the best protec-tions against tsetse is an American 'Shoo-Bug' jacket, available from sporting goods shops in the USA, but not, alas, in Africa or Britain.

Accommodation at Tarangire
The Tarangire Safari Lodge is privately run (Bookings PO Box 1177, Arusha; telephone 057-3090). It is situated 10 kilometres (6 miles) from the main gate, by the Tarangire river. Basically tented — each tent has its own bathroom — there are some permanent buildings and the whole camp has recently been renovated.

There are three campsites, with toilet facilities at one. It is necessary to book during the dry season through the Park Warden in charge, Tarangire National Park, PO Box 3134, Arusha.

The Park has an airstrip, garage facilities at the Park HQ, a petrol pump — without petrol at the time of writing — and a first-aid dispensary.

Neolithic rock paintings
This part of Tanzania is noted for neolithic graves and rock paintings. Some of the best and most accessible paintings are at Kolo at the foot of the Rift Wall. Kolo is 249 kilometres (156 miles) south of Arusha on the Great North Road. Visitors must be accompanied by one of the government guides who are there. There are 11 protected sites in the area, out of more than a 1,000, many not yet fully examined.

The paintings, associated with various Stone Age cultures, are usually dark red and depict animals, hunting scenes and various symbols. At least a dozen styles are discernible and the earliest work is perhaps 3,000 years old, the newest only 200. But no one knows for sure who did the paintings. A good selection can be seen in a day, before driving on to Dodoma.

Few if any organised tours go as far south as this, however. They normally return north to rejoin the road past Lake Manyara to the Serengeti plains, which winds up through spectacular scenery to the Ngorongoro Crater.

The Ngorongoro Crater

This unique volcanic crater is the heart of a 8,290 sq kilometre (3,200 sq mile) conservation area which contains the greatest permanent concentration of wildlife in Africa in a setting of unequalled grandeur. Some 10,000 Masai live near Ngorongoro with their 100,000 cattle, sharing the land with the wildlife. The fantastic crater itself, a *caldera* or 'collapsed' volcano, is 2,000 ft deep and its flattish floor is 18 kilometres (10 miles) wide. You need four-wheel drive to go down into it, but once there you find one of the wonders of Africa, where approximately 14,000 wildebeest, 5,000 zebra and hundreds of gazelle graze, while the Ngorongoro lions are almost as famous as those of the neighbouring Serengeti. With luck an early morning visitor will see at least one lion and his mate tearing at a kill of wildebeest or zebra, with the attendant scavengers, hyena, jackal and vultures hovering nearby. The State Travel Service operates Land Rovers into the crater, charging in foreign currency. Their vehicles are frankly in poor condition. A better bet is to hire a Toyota Land Cruiser from the small fleet maintained by Abercrombie and Kent at the Wildlife Lodge. Either way it will cost around US$75 a half-day or US$100 for a full day. If you have your own vehicle you should consult the Conservator about taking it down, as about camping there.

Ngorongoro has two lodges, both overlooking the crater. The better used to be the privately owned Ngorongoro Crater Lodge (Bookings PO Box 751, Arusha; telephone 057-3530), which became very rundown and is currently being renovated with a possibility of new management. It has a log cabin style dining room, lounge and bar. Most other buildings are of log construction, their rural aspect contrasting with the comfort inside. Warm clothing is advisable for early mornings and evenings as the lodge is nearly 8,000 ft above sea level. At the time of writing, however, the TTC's Ngorongoro Wildlife Lodge had already been renovated and was definitely preferable. Bookings through the State Travel Service. More simple accommodation is available at the Ngorongoro Rhino Lodge (PO Box 445, Arusha) which is owned by the Conservation Authority. The campsites on the crater floor can be booked direct through the Conservation Authority (PO Box 776, Arusha). The camping fee is US$30 per person per night.

Olduvai Gorge, the Serengeti, Mwanza

From Ngorongoro it is well worth stopping at the Olduvai Gorge en route to the Serengeti, which is 57 kilometres (36 miles) along the gravelled, but rough, road.

Olduvai has been called the cradle of mankind. Here very early human remains, 1¾ million years old, forming what has become known as the Nutcracker Man, were found by Dr L. S. B. Leakey. The skull of *Zinjanthropus boisei,* to give it its scientific name, is now in the National Museum in Dar es Salaam. In late 1963, Dr Leakey and others found remains which are believed to be even older than the Nutcracker Man. Fossils were first seen here by a German butterfly collector in 1911. There is a small museum where guides and publications are available. Many of the other finds from Olduvai are also in the National Museum. There is no accommodation.

If you are interested in pre-history you should also visit Laetoli, where there are fossilised human footprints 3.6 million years old and a small Museum is being created.

The Serengeti National Park
At Olduvai you are close to the eastern boundary of the Serengeti National Park which encompasses the largest migratory concentration of plains game to be found anywhere in the world. The northern boundary adjoins the famed Mara game country of Kenya, while to the west the Park stretches in a long 'corridor' to within two miles of Lake Victoria. Its total area is around 14,760 sq kilometres (5,700 sq miles) and even so it does not include all the territory across which the great migratory routes pass.

The terrain within the park varies from the treeless, central Serengeti Plains to savannah-type stretches dotted with flat-topped acacia trees and interspersed with magnificent rock outcrops or *kopjes* while riverine bush, thick scrub and forest grow in the north and along the Mara River.

Although the Serengeti is best known for its magnificent lions, it contains over 35 species of plains game as well as some 500 species of birds. A wildlife population of more than two million large mammals has been recorded. According to recent estimates, there are more than three million animals in the Serengeti, including 1.4 million wildebeest, 250,000 gazelle and 200,000 zebra.

The annual movement in May or June of wildebeest and zebra from the central plains to the permanent water of the western corridor and their return in November or December is one of the most remarkable and inspiring sights of Africa. The great herds gather in the central plains and then move steadily westwards, six or seven abreast and often forming a line several miles long. At the tail end of the procession come the cripples and those too old to keep up, with the inevitable following of lion and other carnivores. Thousands and thousands of wildebeest and zebra pass through the central Itonjo Range, gradually dispersing throughout the length and breadth

169

of the corridor until many are up in the northern Serengeti and move into the Mara area of Kenya.

Recognition of the Serengeti's wildlife started in the early 1920s when professional hunters began to take clients there: and when the human population was very much smaller and did not interfere with the aeons-old movements of the wildlife. The word 'Serengeti' simply means 'open space', which is what it always was. In 1929 a part of the central Serengeti around Seronera was designated as a game reserve. In 1950 certain species became totally protected and in 1951 it was made a National Park, which at that time incorporated Ngorongoro. Despite changes, it manages to retain the wild, untamed atmosphere of Africa, leaving even the most blasé visitor with a haunting memory of its primeval beauty.

International understanding of the importance of the Serengeti only came around the time of Tanganyika's independence with the publication of the late Dr Bernhard Grzimek's book 'Serengeti Shall Not Die'. This was written jointly with his son Michael, who was tragically killed flying their zebra-striped light aircraft on the Salei Plains, south-west of Lake Natron. Its wreckage still lies there. Dr Grzimek, who was the Director of the Frankfurt Zoo, campaigned throughout his life for the Serengeti, eventually coming to live in Tanzania. He died in 1987. His book remains a classic.

There are many game viewing circuits in the Serengeti, although at the time of writing driving could often be restricted by shortages of fuel. The main fuel supply is at Seronera, where cars are sometimes limited to 20 litres. Some routes have restrictions. For example, you may not enter the Seronera Valley, renowned for its leopards and lions, unless accompanied by a ranger guide. Again, the National Parks booklet is invaluable.

Lodges in the Serengeti and their Surroundings
There are several lodges, all of which have suffered from lack of supplies in recent years. If you are coming from Ngorongoro on the main road towards Seronera, the Ndutu Lodge is reached by a turn-off before the Naabi Hill Gate. Situated just outside the Park on the edge of the long grass plains and by the small Ndutu lake, this used to be a tented camp but now has permanent buildings. It is associated with Gibb's Farm (see above) and can be booked through PO Box 1501, Karatu; telephone 25. Still very basic, it has been described by one visitor as 'relaxed but falling apart'. Ndutu's great virtue is that it is a superb place for game viewing during the December to March period of the migration cycle. There is also a campsite at Ndutu, though with poor facilities.

Seronera
Forty kilometres (25 miles) north west from Ndutu is Seronera (TTC),

about the best known of the Serengeti lodges and in the centre of the Park. This is a well-constructed, permanent lodge by a *kopje,* built of pleasant coloured stone, with a swimming-pool, shop and airstrip. Immigration and Customs facilities are available. However the lodge has suffered grievously from neglect. In July 1987 it had no water, either in the taps or the pool, although it had been due for renovation back in 1984 with the aid of the World Bank. Petrol is sometimes available. None the less, the place is justly famous. You can hear the lions roaring at night, while topi, kongoni, gazelles and other game are normally seen near the lodge and a dawn game-run from Seronera is unforgettably beautiful. Lodge bookings are done through Serengeti Safari Lodges Ltd (PO Box 3100, Arusha; telephone 057-3849).

Seronera has four campsites, controlled by the Park Warden there and fees are payable at the Gate or Park office. There is a Tourist Centre, where Park guides can be hired.

While at Seronera it is worth visiting the unique Serengeti Research Institute. This internationally staffed centre studies the wildlife and vegetation of the area, plots the migration of animals, and improves conservation methods. It is situated 3 kilometres (two miles) east of the Lodge. Its activity had declined, but lately has increased again. It is closed on Sundays.

Lobo
About 64 kilometres (40 miles) from Seronera towards the Kenya border is Lobo Wildlife Lodge (also TTC), ingeniously set on a natural rock promontory, with a swimming-pool, shop, airstrip and good game viewing. Although in a beautiful setting, Lobo is often considered by tour operators to be out of range. It can be booked through Serengeti Safari Lodges Ltd, as above. There is a campsite. The country here is upland bush, with some woodland, now much frequented by elephant, probably as a result of agricultural expansion in areas which they used to inhabit outside the Park.

Fort Ikoma
Fort Ikoma, a remarkable 'Beau Geste' type of fort built by the Germans in 1904 north west of Seronera, was made into a lodge in the 1970s but has now reverted to military use.

The Western Corridor and Camps
The Western part of the Park is crucial to the migrations, since the great columns of wildebeeste, zebra and gazelle surge down here before turning north outside the Park to head up toward the permanent water of the Mara in Kenya. Much of the corridor has the notorious black cotton soil which becomes sodden and impassably slippery during the rains. But you will see the herds are moving through here in the dry period of June to October. A road

runs from Seronera along the corridor to the Ndabaka Gate, Lake Victoria and eventually to Mwanza.

South of the corridor the Park is adjoined by the Maswa Game Reserve, where hunting is permitted and in which Tanzania Game Trackers have established a first-class tented camp at Mamarehe, close to the Park boundary. The camp can be reached from Seronera by road on a circuitous route via the Moru *kopjes,* where there is a campsite. Being outside the Park, night drives are permitted at Mamarehe and so are walking safaris. The rates are US$75 a night, plus US$35 taxes. Bookings Tanzania Game Trackers (Private Bag, Arusha; telephone 057-6986). You need four-wheel drive to reach the camp. It has an airstrip.

A further tented camp is planned within the Western corridor near Kirawira. Information from the National Parks.

Mwanza

Immediately west of the Serengeti is the huge expanse of Lake Victoria, the second largest lake in the world and the size of Ireland. There are two towns on this side of it, Musoma and Mwanza.

Mwanza is a thriving commercial town on the shore of Lake Victoria, with low hills behind it. It is one of the principal ports of the lake, though steamers no longer ply to Kisumu in Kenya. The climate is

Sukuma dancers of Tanzania

hot but not so humid as on the coast. A well-known sight near Mwanza is the Bismarck Rock, a huge rock which has been poised as if about to fall for as long as anyone can remember. There are two hotels, the New Mwanza (TTC) and the Lake (PO Box 910, telephone 3263), while a cheaper place to stay is the Mwanza Guest House (PO Box 971). The New Mwanza charges US$34 single per night and US$40 double.

Half a mile from Mwanza, and a short boat trip away, is Saanane Island, a game sanctuary where many species of animals can be seen at close quarters. Rhino and buffalo are kept separate from the public, but antelope and other non-dangerous game are allowed to roam freely. Speke's Gulf near Mwanza is named after the explorer, who caught his first glimpse of the lake from the village of Mwanza in 1858.

One attraction in the area is the Sukuma Museum at Bujora about 10 kilometres (6 miles) from Mwanza. This was the first of Tanzania's tribal museums and it has many fascinating mementoes of the chiefs and the traditional rites of the Sukuma people, Tanzania's largest tribe. Furthermore once a year, just after Saba Saba Day in July, the tribe's most famous dancers gather at Bujora for a mammoth *ngoma* or dance festival.

When in this East Lake region you can visit the famous Williamson Diamond Mines at Mwadui, though arrangements must be made well beforehand with the company. Mwadui is 137 kilometres (86 miles) from Mwanza by road but can also be reached by air charter.

East Africa's Wildlife

If you want to known more, visit the wildlife exhibition in the Nairobi Museum and try some books from the bibliography at the end of this book. We are grateful for permission to reproduce some of these drawings by Rena Fennessy from the 'Shell Guide to Wildlife,' unhappily out of print at present.

Here is some of the game you are most likely to see on safari.

Swahili names are given in italics

The **African Elephant,** *Ndovu* or *Tembo,* is larger than the Indian, particularly its ears. An average bull weighs up to six tons and stands 10-11 ft at the shoulder, while a cow elephant weighs five tons. The heaviest recorded single tusk, from Tanzania, reached 228 lbs. Elephant are intelligent, live in herds and are vegetarians. They inhabit both the bush and the mountain forests. Their life span is about 70 years.

The **Hippopotamus,** *Kiboko,* whose name is Latin for 'river horse', is really of the pig family. Hippos congregate in 'schools' and spend most of the day submerged in water up to their nostrils. They come ashore to feed on grass at night. A grown hippo weighs two and a half tons, yet can outrun a man. Male hippos fight each other to the death.

The **African** or **Black Buffalo,** *Nyati* or *Mbogo,* has been forced to live in the forests and thick bush by encroaching civilisation, despite its basic food being grass. Buffalo stay in herds, and though shy are one of the most dangerous Big Game animals. A grown bull will weigh 1,800 lbs and the span of its horns may be 50 inches.

The **Black Rhinoceros,** *Kifaru,* weighs about two tons and is a solitary animal, fond of the thorn scrub. It has poor sight but good smell and hearing. Although a vegetarian, it is bad-tempered. The rare **White Rhino** (not illustrated) is larger and better tempered, but not white. Its name derives from the Dutch *weit,* meaning wide, which refers to its distinctive square jaw. The rhinos' horns are composed of tightly packed hair, not real horn. Because of their horns' value rhinos have been so hunted as to be an endangered species.

The **Giraffe,** *Twiga,* the tallest mammal, grows to 18 ft and weighs over a ton. It browses on leaves, especially acacia, likes open country and is inoffensive. Its small horns are covered in skin and soft hair. The **Reticulated Giraffe** is so called because its markings are square, within a network of whitish lines, instead of star-shaped.

The **Common Zebra**, *Punda Milia*, is found in open country over most of Kenya and Tanzania, always managing to look sleek and well fed. Zebra move in herds, often with giraffe, eland and other animals. They feed on grass, leaves and, if necessary, shrubs. A male zebra stands five ft high at the shoulder and weighs 700lbs. The rarer **Grevy's Zebra** is taller, has larger ears and narrower stripes.

The **Lion**, *Simba*, is found in open country throughout East Africa. A full-grown male weighs 400-500 lbs. The lioness has no mane. 'Prides', or families, of lion doze in the shade during the day and hunt at dusk, springing on the backs of the zebra, buffalo, wildebeest or whatever they have stalked. They kill only when hungry, once in three or four days.

The **Leopard**, *Chui*, hunts by night, is wary, and extremely dangerous when wounded or cornered. It makes its lair in cliffs, or among rocks in thick bush. Its favourite food is baboon, though if hungry it will eat rodents and even insects. An average male weighs 170 lbs. and measures about seven and a half ft from nose to tail.

The **Serval Cat**, *Mondo*, is short-tailed, long-legged and spotted, with large ears. It looks like a cross between a small leopard and a lynx. It hunts at night, feeding on birds and small mammals. The serval is widespread, particularly liking places that are marshy or near water.

The **Cheetah,** *Duma,* looks like a leopard, but with longer legs and smaller head. Also its spots are isolated, not grouped in a pattern. It hunts by day and is the fastest mammal in the world — it has been timed at 60 mph. Cheetahs stand three ft at the shoulder and are about seven ft long. They are easily tamed and have been raced against greyhounds in Europe.

The **Wart Hog,** *Ngiri,* is named after the warts on its grotesque head. It feeds on the plains in families, or 'sounders', and lives in holes. During the day it crops grass, or digs for roots with its tusks, while kneeling on its forelegs. It is related to the Giant Forest Hog, largest of the African pigs, which weighs over 300 lbs.

The **Spotted Hyena,** *Fisi,* is a night-time scavenger. Though its jaws can crush bones it is a coward and only attacks small, weak or aged animals. Its colour varies, usually being tawny or greyish, it weighs up to 170 lbs. and is the size of a large dog. Hyenas have a characteristic, unpleasant howl and they 'laugh' when lions are around.

The **Baboon,** *Nyani Mkubwa,* is a large dog-faced monkey seen in many parts of East Africa. It lives on the ground, usually moving in troops under the leadership of a big old male, and goes into the trees to sleep at night. Baboons will eat practically anything, animal or vegetable. The babies ride on their mothers' backs.

The **Patas Monkey,** *Kima,* roams in troops of ten or 12, like the baboons. It normally stays on the ground, using low trees or anthills as observation points. Its habitat is the dry savannah of north-west Kenya and of Tanzania. In colour it is reddish, with white underparts and white side-whiskers on its face.

The **Colobus Monkey,** *Mbega,* is jet black in colour, with a magnificent white mantle round its back, a white face and a white-tipped bushy tail. It lives in highland forests, like the Aberdares of Kenya, eats leaves and very rarely descends from the trees.

Sykes Monkey, *Kima,* often called the Blue Monkey, is dark blue-grey in colour, with black forelimbs, hands, feet, crown of head and tip of tail, it eats fruit and greenery, and inhabits forest near water. It is known for its friendliness. Variants of the species are called Silver and Golden Monkeys, from their colouring.

The **Lesser Bush Baby,** *Komba,* is a nocturnal relative of the monkeys, and lives mainly in acacia bush. Driving at night you often see its large eyes winking red at you out of the darkness. It is very active, climbing and making tremendous leaps in search of insects and fruit. During the day it sleeps, whole families cuddling together in hollow tree trunks.

Grant's Gazelle, *Swala Granti,* likes dry open grassland or even desert. It has graceful lyre-shaped horns, which both sexes carry, and is pale buff in colour, with a white rump and underside and a chestnut streak down the centre of the face. The male stands about 32 inches high at the shoulder. Gazelles are a species of antelope, with slender legs.

Thomson's Gazelle, *Swala Tomi,* known as the 'Tommy', is more reddish in colour than the Grant's Gazelle which otherwise it is like, and has a distinctive black band running along its flank. It also has a habit of twitching its small tail. The Tommy lives in large herds on the plains.

The **Gerenuk,** or Walter's Gazelle, *Swala Twiga,* has a delicately incongruous long neck and a giraffe-like head. It is a dark rufous colour, paler on the flanks, and with white bands over its eyes. It stands 36 to 41 inches high at the shoulder and weighs about 100 lbs. Only the males have horns. Gerenuk wander in small groups, browsing on leaves in acacia thorn country.

The **Dikdik,** *Dikidiki* or *Suguya,* stands only 15 inches high and weighs 12 lbs. It lives in the driest thorn scrub and is usually seen in pairs. In colour it is grey or grizzled brown, has a shaggy coat and a distinctively long nose. The **Klipspringer** is in many ways similar, but larger, standing about 21 inches high at the shoulder.

The **Uganda Kob,** of north-west Kenya, and Uganda, stands three ft high at the shoulder. It has a sleek red-gold coat, with white underparts and white rings round the eyes. The kob drinks daily, so is never far from water. It stays in herds and the males fight savagely to master their harems.

The **Impala,** *Swala Pala,* is a timid, medium-sized antelope, famous for leaping in the air when alarmed — it can jump 30 ft and rise ten ft above the ground. Impala move in large herds. They have smooth chestnut-coloured coats and tufts of black hair on the hind legs above the hooves. Only the males carry horns. Found in acacia bush and scrub country.

The **Common Waterbuck,** *Kuro,* is a large and handsome antelope found in eastern Kenya and Tanzania, usually near water. A bull may lead a herd of up to 30 cows, who have no horns. Their coats are shaggy, greyish brown, and with a white ring on the rump.

The **Sable Antelope,** *Palahala* or *Mbarapi,* is a splendid animal, standing nearly five ft high, almost black, and bearing great scimitar-shaped horns. It is white on the underparts, rump, and face. In East Africa it is only found in a few coastal areas of Tanzania, and near Mombasa in the Shimba Hills National Reserve. It likes lightly wooded country and stays in small herds.

The **Oryx,** *Choroa,* one of the most handsome, powerful and fierce antelopes, is found in varying species from Ethiopia to the Kalahari. It is reddish brown in colour, with black and white face markings. The female grows longer horns than the male — up to 40 inches. Oryx stand four ft high at the shoulder and weigh up to 450 lbs. They move in small herds. Amboseli and Tsavo are good places to look for them.

The **Greater Kudu,** *Kandala Mkubwa,* likes rocky and mountainous bush. A male stands five ft high at the shoulder and weighs about 600 lbs. The female has no horns. Kudus' bodies are a lavender grey colour, with white stripes. The **Lesser Kudu,** *Kandala Ndogo,* is rather smaller and has no fringe of hair running down its throat. It lives in thick bush and scrub.

Coke's Hartebeest, usually known as the *Kongoni,* is widely distributed in Kenya and Tanzania. It stays in large herds, grazing, while one animal acts as sentinel. When surprised it snorts, stamps a foreleg and gallops away. Its colour is light fawn, and its bracket-shaped horns and steeply sloping hindquarters make it easily recognisable.

The **Wildebeest** or **Gnu,** *Nyumbu,*
seen in vast herds migrating across
the Serengeti Plains every year, is
one of the commonest antelopes in
open country all over East Africa. It
has a dark grey body, a white beard,
a shaggy mane, and a clumsy gait.
Its horns look slightly like a
buffalo's. It stands about five ft high
at the shoulder.

The **Eland,** *Pofu* or *Mbunja,* the
largest of the antelopes,
congregates in large herds, often
alongside zebra and giraffe. They
are found in open country in both
Kenya and Tanzania. Both sexes
carry heavy twisted horns. A full-
grown bull weighs over 1,050 lbs
and stands six ft high at the
shoulder. The colour is greyish
brown, with light stripes.

The **Bushbuck,** *Mbawala* or *Pongo,*
is a beautifully marked small
animal, with a white underside to
its tail. It prefers forest thickets to
open country, is shy, and lives in
families, not herds. A male stands
three ft high at the shoulder and
weighs about 100 lbs. The
Sitatunga, *Nzohe,* is a swamp-
dwelling variant of the same
species.

The **Bongo,** same name in Swahili,
is the largest of the forest antelopes,
though smaller than an eland. It
stands four ft high at the shoulder
and both sexes carry horns. In
colour it is bright reddish chestnut,
with vertical white stripes. Bongo
live only in the mountain forests,
are very shy and seldom seen.

183

The **Ostrich,** *Mbuni,* one of the sights of Africa, cannot fly but has a kick that can kill a man and can run at 45 mph. Fully grown, it can be eight ft high. It lays eggs in clutches of 14 or more. You often see it on the plains among herds of animals. True to stories it does sometimes hide its head on the ground when approached.

Birds

Kenya and Tanzania shelter over 1,200 species of birds, if all the winter migrants coming from Europe are included, and bird watching will take you into some of the most fascinating areas. Most safari firms incorporate bird watching in their game viewing arrangements.

At the coast in March and April plovers and sandpipers migrate north en masse and there are always a multitude of waterbirds: curlews, white egrets, green backed herons, cormorants and others.

On the inland lakes you will find pelicans and storks and, of course, the million-strong flocks of flamingoes which frequent the Rift Valley lakes of Bogoria, Nakuru and Natron, turning the shores pink.

In plains country you find everything from ungainly ostriches to the brilliantly coloured Paradise flycatcher, from lilac-breasted rollers and tiny sunbirds to vultures and the long-legged, snake-eating, secretary-bird. Even in Nairobi gardens there is a spectacular variety of birdlife.

Bibliography

Animals

There is a vast literature on game in Africa. A useful handbook for game watching is:

'A Field Guide to the Larger Mammals of Africa' by Jean Dorst and Pierre Dandelot, published by Collins.

'Know Kenya's Animals', by Jonathan Scott and published in Nairobi, is a smaller local handbook.

For general reading we recommend the following, all of which were in print at the time of writing:

'Born Free' and 'Living Free', both about the lioness Elsa by the late Joy Adamson and published by Collins.

'The Marsh Lions — the story of an African Pride', by Brian Jackman and illustrated (with photographs and drawings) by Jonathan Scott, published by Elm Tree Books. An excellent account of a group of lions studied for two years in the Masai Mara.

'The Leopard's Tale' by Jonathan Scott, published by Elm Tree Books, is also based on Scott's researches in the Masai Mara.

'Among the Elephants' by Iain and Oria Douglas Hamilton, published by Collins/Harvill. A world-famous account of the elephants in Tanzania's Lake Manyara National Park.

'Elephants at Sundown. The Story of Billy Woodley' by Dennis Holman, published by W. H. Allen. Account of a renowned Kenya game warden's conservation efforts. Billy Woodley is at present Warden of Tsavo West National Park.

Two classics which should be available in libraries are:

'No Room in the Ark' by Alan Moorehead, published by Cassell.

'Serengeti Shall Not Die' by Bernard Grzimek, published by Fontana. First published in 1960, this account of Serengeti's wildlife before Tanganyika's independence helped create the present Serengeti National Park.

Birds

The definitive reference book on birds is:

'Birds of Eastern and North Eastern Africa' by Mackworth Praed and C. H. B. Grant, published by Longmans in two volumes.

A handier reference book, easy to carry on safari, is:

185

Bibliography

'A Field Guide to the Birds of East Africa', by J. G. Williams and N. Arlott, published by Collins.

'Birds of Africa' by John Karmali, published by Collins, is more of a coffee-table book, though with superb photographs.

Butterflies

The definitive work is:

'Butterflies of the Afrotropical Region' by Bernard D'Abrera, published by Lansdowne Editions. This is a large and comprehensive volume.

'A Field Guide to the Butterflies of Africa' by J. G. Williams, published by Collins, is a handy reference book.

Snakes

'Poisonous Snakes of Eastern Africa and the Treatment of their Bites' by A. and J. Mackay, is useful, if morbidly titled.

General

A beautifully produced introduction to Kenya is:

'The Book of Kenya' by Gerald Cubitt and Eric Robins, published by Collins/Harvill.

'The Cradle of Mankind' by Mohammed Amin, published by Chatto and Windus, is an illustrated account of the Samburu and Turkana people and the wildlife of Lake Turkana.

'Africa Adorned' by Angela Fisher, published by Collins, is a magnificently illustrated study of African women's make-up and jewellery.

'Vanishing Africa' by Mirella Ricciardi, published by Collins, is a deservedly best-selling photographic essay on Kenya's tribes.

'The Battle of the Bundu' by Charles Miller, published by Purnell, describes the World War 1 campaign of the great German General von Lettow-Vorbeck and the British attempts to defeat him in Tanganyika.

'Journey through Kenya' by Mohammed Amin, Duncan Willetts and Brian Tetley, published by the Bodley Head. Magnificent colour photographs.

'The Flame Trees of Thika' by Elspeth Huxley, published by Penguin Books. The story of the author's childhood in Kenya.

'Out of Africa' by Karen von Blixen (Isak Dinesen), published by Random House, New York, and Penguin, London. The classic about her life on a Kenya farm in the 1920s.

'Africa's Rift Valley' by Collin Willock, published by Time-Life Books.

'White Mischief' by James Fox, published by Penguin, is a recently-filmed reconstruction of Kenyan settler life in the 1930s and the murder of Lord Erroll.

No book prices are quoted because they vary widely, being higher in game lodges than they are in city bookshops.

East African Wildlife Society

The Society's bookshop on the mezzanine floor of the Hilton Hotel, Nairobi, is an excellent place to buy wildlife literature, and the Society's monthly magazine, 'Swara', is an inexhaustible source of information on current wildlife topics and local developments. Back numbers are obtainable at the office.

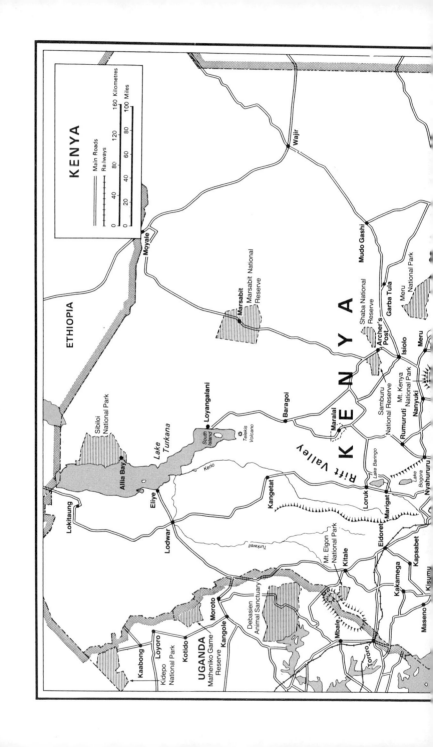

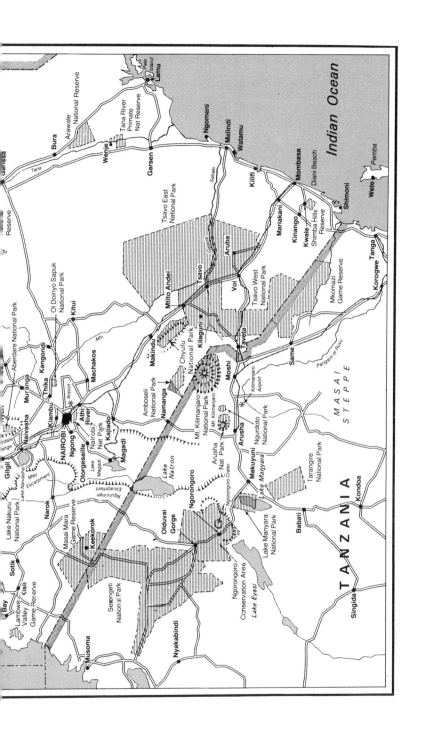

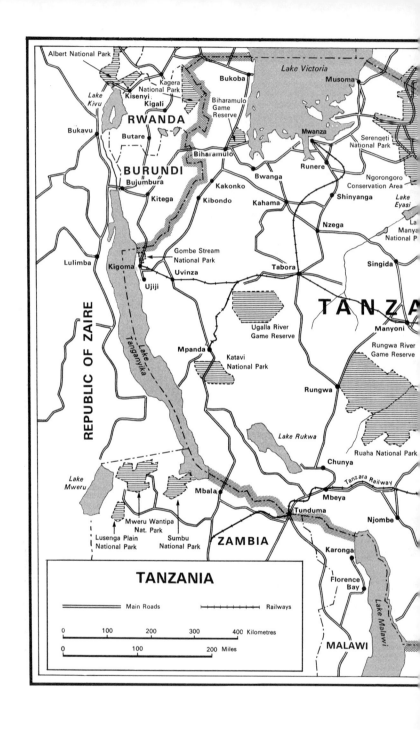

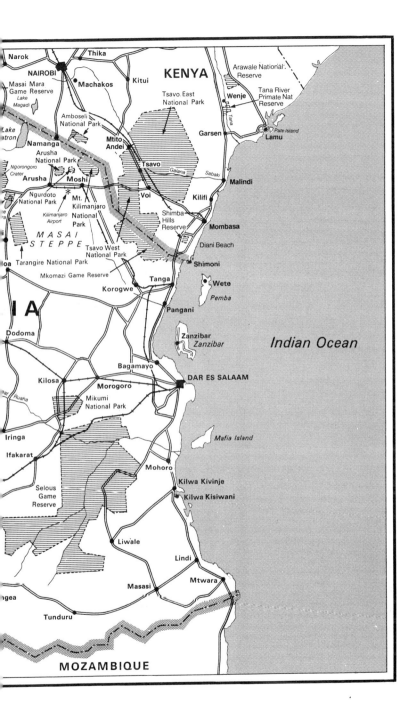

Index

AA of Kenya 13, 47
Aberdare Forest 90, 91
Aberdare Mountains 41, 73, 88, 92, 94, 106
Accommodation 14, 39-41, 157
Adamson, George 70, 98
Adamson, Joy 69, 70, 94, 98, 102
Aero Club of East Africa 46
African Wildlife Foundation 8, 31, 154, 159
Agricultural Show, Nakuru 72
Air Charters 12, 45-46, 155, 162
Air Tanzania 10, 154
Airlines 9, 10, 12, 43-46, 84, 154, 162
Airports 9, 10, 11, 122, 128, 154
Air Rescue 33
Albizia 74
Alia Bay 105
Altitude 14
Ambatch wood 74
Amboseli see National Parks
Amber 53
American Cultural Centre 57
Aniere, Johnny 141
Antelope 90, 119, 153, 173
Arab Sultanates 8, 37
Arab Traders 71
Arabs 121, 122, 125, 130, 132, 137-138, 146, 150, 152
Arboretum, Nairobi 58
Archer's Post 101-103
Aruba 118, 119
Arusha 11, 154, 157-161, 167
Arusha International Conference Centre 157
Arusha Manifesto 8, 154, 157
Athi Plains 50, 60, 108
Athi, River see also Sabaki 89, 109, 119

Baboon 60, 178
Baden-Powell, Lord 90
Bagamoyo 152
Bajun People 140
Ballooning 81, 82
Banking 15, 16, 52, 158
Baobab Trees 114, 148
Batian 95, 96
Beaches:
  Bamburi 129, 130
  Diani 146-149
  Four Twenty South 149
  Funzi 149
  Gazi 149
  Kenyatta 129
  Nyali 130
  Ras Kitau 144
  Shanzu 129
  Shela 144
  Shelly 146
  Tiwi 146
Beach Cottages 148
Big Game Fishing see Fishing
Bird Shooting 30
Bird Watching 69, 70, 71, 94, 165
Birds and Birdlife 74, 75, 81, 87-89, 95, 98, 102, 104-106, 110, 117, 132, 141, 142, 145, 148, 160, 165
Bismarck Rock 173
Bland, John 148
Blixen, Karen 50, 59
Bogoria, Lake see National Parks
Bomas of Kenya 38, 58, 63
Bombolulu Gardens 130
Bongo 36, 91, 183
Boran 103, 104
Brighetti, Bruno 144
British Council 57
Buffalo, Cape 30, 36, 60, 70, 87, 89, 90-92, 101, 110, 117, 119, 149, 153, 160, 162, 166, 173, 175
Buffalo Springs 102
Buibui 124, 125
Bujora 173
Bush Baby 179
Bushbuck 89, 160, 183

Camel Safaris 31, 97, 99, 103
Camps see Lodges and Camps
Campsites 49, 74, 75, 98, 102, 105, 112, 147, 149, 161, 166, 167, 171
Car Hire 13, 46-47, 128, 137, 139, 155, 162,
Caracal 110
Carmine Bee Eaters 131, 137
Carr Track, Mount Kenya 96
Casinos 54, 55, 127
Casuarina Point 137, 138, 139
Central African Republic 12
Chagga People 89, 161, 164
Chania Falls 89
Chanler's Falls 103
Che Chale 140
Cheetah 60, 78, 80, 97, 110, 117, 177
Cherangani Hills 88
Chogoria 97
Chuka Drummers 37
Churchill, Winston 88
Chyulu Hills 112-114
Cigarettes 21
Cinemas 56, 128
Civet Cat 110
Climate 14, 122, 153
Clothing 52
Clubs see Lodges

Coffee Estates 88, 161
Coke's Hartebeest *see* Kongoni
Colobus Monkey 77, 87, 91, 107, 148, 160, 162, 178
Complaints 14, 15
Coral *see also* Reef 121
Cosmetics 17, 18, 26
Cottar, Glen 82
Crescent Island 69
Crocodiles 60, 74, 75, 80, 101, 102, 106, 117, 118, 119
Crocodile Point 118
Currency 15, 16, 52, 157
Customs Duties 16

Dancing, Traditional 37-38, 63, 95, 174
Dar es Salaam 7, 11, 152-155, 169
Dhows 140, 142, 143, 150
Do It Yourself Safaris 49
Diamond Mines 173
Diani Beach 146-148, 149
Dikdik 180
Diplomatic Representation 16, 17, 129
Diving School 147
Dodoma 152, 166, 167
Douglas-Hamilton, Ian and Oria 165
Dress 17, 18, 27
Drink 19, 20, 21, 157
Driving 13, 33, 155
Dunga 84

East African Wildlife Society 8, 43, 51
El Karama Ranch 92
El Molo Tribe 37, 105
Eland 60, 79, 87, 91, 114, 183
Eldoret 44, 76, 83, 86, 87
Electricity 18
Elephant, African 23, 36, 87, 90, 91, 98, 101, 104, 110, 114, 117, 119, 149, 153, 160, 165-167, 174
Elgeyo Escarpment 76
Elsa's Camp 98
Elsamere 70
Eliye Springs 99, 105
Embu 97, 106
Empash 110
Enamishera Hill 110
English Point 124
Enkongo Narok Swamp 110, 112
Entasekera 77
Equator 94, 96, 163
Esoit Oloolulu (Siria) Escarpment 77
Ethiopia 7, 106
Etiquette 18
Ewaso Narok River 93

Ferguson's Gulf 99, 105
Fischer's Tower 70
Fishing 27, 28, 32, 69, 83, 84, 90, 92, 94, 97, 120, 121, 122, 127, 131, 137, 139, 141, 144, 146, 149, 158, 159, 164
Fishing Camps 94
Fishing Safaris 32
Flamingoes 62, 71, 73, 153, 165
Flying Doctor Service 22
Food 19, 20, 55, 127, 140, 148, 150, 157, 158
Forest Animals 90
Formosa Bay *see* Ungwana Bay
Fort Hall *see* Murang'a
Fort Ikoma 171
Fort Jesus 125, 131
Four Twenty South 148
Fourteen Falls 89
Foxes 97
Freretown 124, 129
Funzi 149

Galana River *see also* Sabaki 114, 118, 119
Gamble's Cave 71
Game Conservation 43
Game Reserves *see* National Parks and Reserves
Game Trophies 16
Garissa 107
Garsen 107, 108, 140, 141
Gasohol 47
Gate of Mists 96
Gazelle 60, 69, 70, 78, 80, 168, 169, 171, 179-180
Gazi 149
Gedi 128, 132, 140
Gerenuk 97, 101, 110, 117, 180
Geysers 64
Giant Forest Hog 90
Gilgil 71, 93
Gillman's Point 163
Giraffe 60, 72, 92, 98, 101, 104, 119, 160, 175
Giraffe Manor 58-59
Giriama Tribe 37, 131
Gnu *see* Wildebeeste
Gold 86, 145
Golf 27, 56, 83, 84, 86, 138
Grant's Gazelle 179
Gratuities 29
Great Rift Valley 7, 36, 60-76, 91, 93, 99, 100, 165
Greater Kudu 73, 155, 166, 182
Gregory, John 62
Grevy's Zebra 176
Groundsel, Giant 87, 91, 95, 162, 165
Grzimek, Dr Bernhard 78, 170
Gulf of Winam 85
Gura Waterfall 91
Gwasi Hills 86

Index

Haggard, Rider 71
Hairdressers 52, 158
Hartebeest 72, 86
Health 21, 22
Hell's Gate 69, 70
Hell's Kitchen 140, 141
Hemingway, Ernest 158
Hippo Point 84
Hippopotamus 60, 74, 78, 80, 106, 160, 165, 174
Hitch Hiking 47, 122
Homa Bay 85-86
Hot Springs 70, 74
Hotels, General:
  Kenya 39-41
  Tanzania 156-157
Hospitals 22, 128, 140
Hunter's Antelope 107
Hunting Safaris 30, 31, 155
Huxley, Elspeth 89
Hyena 60, 78, 177
Hyrax 81
Hyrax Hill 71

Immigration 22, 23
Impala 60, 72, 89, 114, 167, 181
Impala Point 60
Information Bureau 51
International Bill Fish Competition 138
Isiolo 96, 98, 99
Itonjo Range 169
Ivory Room 126

Jackal 80
Jadini Forest 148
Jilore Forest 120
Jomo Kenyatta Airport 9, 10, 43
Juja Farm 89
Jumba La Mtwana 131

Kabarnet 74, 75, 76
Kaisut Desert 103
Kajiado 109
Kakamega 86
Kakamega Forest 86
Kalenjin People 37, 76
Kamba People 37, 108
Kampi ya Fisi 160
Kampi ya Moto 74
Kanamai 131
Kangas 51, 124, 126
Kangethwa Dam 114
Kapenguria 88
Kapkimolwa 77
Kapsabet 86
Karatu 165, 166

Karen 50, 55, 59
Kariandusi 71
Karisia Hills 100
Karura Waterfall 91
Kavirondo see Winam Gulf
Kedong Valley 63
Keekorok 77, 80, 81
Kentrout Trout Farm 96
Kenya Airways 9, 10, 12, 43, 44, 122
Kenya Association of Hotel Keepers
  & Caterers 15, 38
Kenya Association of Tour Operators
  15
Kenya Marineland 130
Kenyatta, Mzee Jomo 38, 88
Kenyatta Conference Centre 50
Kericho 46, 83, 84
Kerio Valley 74, 75, 76, 87
Kiambu 88
Kibo 110, 162-164
Kibukoni 108
Kibwezi 113
Kichwa Tembo 77, 80
Kigoma 155
Kijabe 38
Kikambala 131
Kikoi 51, 124, 126
Kikuyu Tribe 37, 88
Kilaguni 114
Kilifi 121, 130, 132
Kilgoris 83
Kilimanjaro International Airport
  11, 153
Kilimanjaro Mountain Club 164
Kilwa 152
Kimana Gate 109
Kimangi Marangu 163
Kinangop Plateau 70, 91
Kipepeo 130
Kipsigis People 77
Kisii 83-85
Kisumu 83-84
Kitale 86-87
Kitengi 51
Kitengela Corridor 60
Kitui 37
Kitum Cave 87
Kiunga 121
Kiwaiyu Island 44, 145
Klipspringer 114
Konigsberg, Cruiser 57, 125
Kolo 167
Kongelai Escarpment 88
Kongoni 60, 70, 114, 182
Koobi Fora 36, 61, 105
Krapf, Dr. Ludwig 95, 129
Kudu 30, 73, 114, 117, 155, 166, 182
Kwale 146, 149

Laetoli 169
Laikipia 75, 92
Laisamis 103
Lakes:
  Amboseli 110
  Baringo 30, 72, 73-76
  Bogoria 71, 72, 73-76
  Chala 117
  Duluti 159
  Elementeita 69, 71
  Jipe 117
  Magadi 62
  Manyara 30, 164-166
  Naivasha 30, 63-70
  Nakuru 30, 69, 71-72
  Natron 62
  Ndutu 172
  Rudolf *see* Lake Turkana
  Tanganyika 7, 61, 152
  Turkana 30, 36, 45, 61, 75, 88, 99,
    104, 105
  Victoria 7, 37, 72, 76, 84, 172
Lammergeyer 70
Lambwe Valley 85, 86
Lamu 44, 45, 124, 130, 139, 140, 141,
  143, 145
Langata 58
Lango Plains 149
Language 23
Lavatories 24
Leakey, Jonathan 75
Leakey, Dr. Louis 57, 61, 105, 169
Leakey, Richard 36, 57, 61, 105
Lenana 95
Leopard 30, 60, 77, 80, 97, 98, 149, 176
Leopard's Rock 98
Lesser Kudu 166
Lewa Downs 103
Libraries 57, 59
Likoni 146
Limuru 63
Little Serengeti 115
Lion 30, 60, 78, 82, 91, 95, 117, 165,
  169, 171, 176
Livingstone, David 152
Lobelias, Giant 91, 95, 162, 163
Loboi Gate 74
Lodges and Camps, Kenya:
  Aberdare Country Club 91
  Amboseli New Lodge 112
  Amboseli Serena Lodge 112
  The Ark 30, 91
  Aruba Lodge 119
  Baomo Lodge 107
  Buffalo Springs Tented Lodge 102
  Bushwhackers Camp 113
  Bwatherongi Bandas 98
  Cottars Camp 77, 81

Crocodile Tented Camp 119
Eliye Springs Campsite 105
El Karama Ranch 92
Fig Tree Camp 81
Fisherman's Camp 69
Galana Game Ranch Lodge 120, 139
Governor's Camp 77, 81
Island Camp 75
Keekorok Lodge 77, 80
Kichwa Tembo Camp 81
Kilaguni Lodge 114
Kilimanjaro Buffalo Lodge 112
Kilimanjaro Safari Lodge 112
Kimana Lodge 112
Kitani Lodge 115
Kiwayuu Island Lodge 145
Kiwayu Safari Village 145
Kongoni Farm 70
Lake Baringo Club 75
Lake Nakuru Lodge 71, 72
Lake Turkana El Molo Lodge 104
Lake Turkana Fishing Lodge 105
Lion Hill Hotel 102
Little Governor's Camp 81
Mara Intrepids Club 81, 82
Mara River Camp 81
Mara Serena Lodge 80
Mara Serova 82
Mara Sopa Lodge 81
Maralal Safari Lodge 100
Marsabit Lodge 104
Masai Lodge 60
Meru Mulika Lodge 98
Meru Mount Kenya Lodge 97
Meteorological Station Chalets 97
Mount Elgon Lodge 87
Mount Kenya Safari Club 94
Mountain Lodge 93
Naro Moru River Lodge 94
Ngulia Safari Camp 115
Ngulia Safari Lodge 115
Oasis Club 104
Salt Lick Lodge 117
Samburu Game Lodge 101
Samburu River Lodge 101
Sangare Ranch 120
Secret Valley 93
Shaba Tented Camp 102
Shimba Hills Lodge 149
Taita Hills Lodge 117
Thomson's Falls Lodge 93
Treetops 90
Tsavo Safari Camp 119
Voi Safari Lodge 119
Lodges and Camps, Tanzania
  Gibbs Farm 32, 166, 170
  Lake Manyara Hotel 165
  Lobo Wildlife Lodge 171

Index

Momella Lodge 161
Mount Meru Game Lodge 161
Ndutu Lodge 170
Ngare Sero Mountain Lodge 161
Ngorongoro Crater Lodge 168
Ngorongoro Rhino Lodge 168
Ngorongoro Wildlife Lodge 168
Seronera Wildlife Lodge 154, 170
Tarangire Safari Lodge 167
Lodwar 88, 100
Loginye Swamp 110
Loita Hills 62, 77
Loita Plains 64, 80, 179
Loitokitok 109
Loiyangalani 100, 104, 105
Lolgorien 83
Lolokwe 103
Lorian Swamp 99
Lorochi Plateau 100
Losiolo Escarpment 100
Lugard Falls 118, 119
Luo People 84
Luya People 37

Machakos District 37, 108
Machame 164
Magadi 61, 62
Magado 103
Magado Crater Lake 103
Mail *see* Postal Services
Maji ya Moto 73
Makindu 113
Makingeny Cave 87
Makonde Carvers 51, 157
Makupa Causeway 122, 129
Makutano 109, 113
Malindi 45, 119, 120, 121, 122, 128, 137, 138, 141
Malindi Sea Fishing Club 138
Mamarehe 172
Mambrui 140
Manda Island 142, 145
Mandera 106
Mangabey 107
Mangroves 132, 142, 143, 145
Manyani 118, 120
Maps 24
Mara River 78, 81, 169
Mara River Bridge 77
Mara Triangle 80
Marafa 141
Maralal 75, 91, 93, 100, 101
Marangu 163, 164
Marigat 73, 74, 76
Marsabit 99, 103-104
Masai Mara 44, 61, 72, 76-83
Masai People 37, 62, 77, 108-110, 153, 158

Mashuas 143, 145
Matatus 46, 139
Mathews Range 103
Matondoni 143
Mau Forest 84
Mau Summit 72, 76, 78, 83
Maulidi 143
Maua 98
Mawenzi 110, 162-164
Mayer's Ranch 38, 58, 62
Mbagathi River 60, 89
Mboya, Tom 85
McMillan, Sir Northrup 89
McMillan, Lady 89
Menengai Crater 72, 73
Meru 96, 97
Mtepe, or 'sewn boat' 143
Mida Creek 132, 137
Migration, Serengeti 78, 169-171
Ministry of Tourism & Wildlife, Kenya 38, 42
Mnarani 132
Mogotio 73
Moi, President Daniel arap 38, 76
Moi International Airport 9, 10, 122, 128
Mokowe 142
Molo 75, 83
Mombasa 7, 45, 121, 122, 129, 138, 145, 147
Momella 160
Momella Lakes 153, 159
Monkeys 69, 81, 148, 162
Morijo 77
Moshi 159, 161, 163
Moslems 18, 19, 99, 143
Mount Elgon 87
Mount Homa 85
Mount Kenya 36, 89, 96
Mount Kenya Game Ranch 95
Mount Kilimanjaro 7, 110, 152, 153, 158, 161, 163, 164
Mount Kulal 104
Mount Longonot 64
Mount Meru 158, 160
Mount Meru Crater 159
Mount Shaba 102
Mountain Club of Kenya 87, 96
Mountain Guides 163
Mountain Huts 96, 161, 163
Mountains of the Moon (Ruwenzori) 7
Moyale 106
Msambweni 148
Msumbe Spring 164
Mtito Andei 113, 114, 119
Mtito Andei Gate 115
Mtwapa Creek 129, 132
Mudanda Rock 118
Mukatan Swamp 75

Murang'a (Fort Hall) 88, 89
Murka 115
Museums:
  Fort Jesus 125, 131
  Karen Blixen 59
  Kariandusi 71
  Kenya Railway 57
  National, Dar es Salaam 169
  National, Nairobi 57
  Olduvai 169
  Olorgesaillie 62
  Sukuma 173
Musiara Airstrip 81
Musoma 172
Muthaiga 50
Mwachema, River 146
Mwadui 173
Mwanza 172
Mweiga 90, 92
Mwinyi, Ali Hassan 152
Mzima Springs 114

Naabi Hill 170
Naivasha 64, 91
Naivasha Vineyards 70
Nakuru 72, 83
Namanga 109
Nandi Hills 86
Nanjara 164
Nanyuki 45, 94, 95
Naro Moru 94, 96
Narok 72, 76, 77
National Christian Council of
  Kenya 131
National Parks & Reserves, Kenya
  41-43
  Aberdare National Park 91
  Amboseli National Park 30, 42, 44,
    109-112, 139
  Arawale National Reserve 107
  Boni National Reserve 108
  Buffalo Springs Reserve 101
  Dodori National Reserve 108, 145
  Hell's Gate National Park 64, 70
  Jilore Forest Reserve 132
  Kakamega National Park 86
  Kerio National Reserve 76
  Kisiti National Marine Park 150
  Kiunga Marine National Reserve 145
  Kora National Reserve 98
  Lake Bogoria National Reserve 73-74
  Lake Nakuru National Park 43
  Lambwe Valley National Park 86
  Losai National Reserve 103
  Malindi Marine National Park 121,
    138
  Maralal National Sanctuary 100
  Marsabit National Reserve 104

Masai Mara Game Reserve 13, 30,
  42, 64, 77-82, 139, 169
Meru National Park 42, 97, 98
Mpungiti National Reserve 150
Mount Elgon National Park 87
Mount Kenya National Park 43, 95-96
Nairobi National Park 36, 43, 59, 60
Nakuru National Park 71
Ol Doinyo Sapuk National Park 89
Rahole National Reserve 106
Ruma National Park
  see Lambwe Valley
Samburu National Reserve 30, 43,
  75, 99, 101-102
Saiwa Swamp Park 87, 88
Shaba National Reserve 102, 146,
  148, 149
Sibiloi National Park 105
South Island National Park 105
Tana River Primate National
  Reserve 107
Tsavo National Park 30, 43, 113,
  114-119, 139
Watamu Marine National Park 140
National Parks & Reserves, Tanzania
  153, 154
  Arusha National Park 153, 159, 161
  Kilimanjaro National Park 162
  Lake Manyara National Park 32, 153,
    154, 164, 165
  Maswa Game Reserve 172
  Mkomazi Game Reserve 117
  Mount Meru Crater National Park
    153, 159, 161
  Ngurdoto Crater 153, 159, 160
  Ngorongoro Crater 30, 153, 154,
    166, 168, 170
  Saanane Island 173
  Selous Game Reserve 152
  Serengeti National Park 30,
    152-154, 166, 169, 170
  Tarangire National Park 166
National Theatre, Nairobi 56
Ndawe Escarpment 115
Ndorobo 36
Ndoto Hills 103
Nelion 95, 96
Ngobit River 92
Ngong 59
Ngong Hills 59, 60, 61, 82
Ngorengore 77, 83
Nguruman Escarpmont 62, 77
Niele 149
Nightlife 56, 127, 128, 137, 139, 147
Nile River 12
Nile Perch 81, 85, 104
Njau, Elimo 89
Njemps People 74, 75

Index

Njoro 83
Njorowa Gorge (Hell's Gate) 69-70
Nutcracker Man 169
Nyahururu 71, 72, 90, 92
Nyali 127, 130
Nyambeni Hills 102
Nyanza 84-85
Nyerere, President Julius 8, 152, 157
Nyeri 45, 89, 90
Nyika see Taru Desert
Nyumba ya Mungu, Cave 164

Ol Doinyo Sapuk 89, 119
Ol Donyo Lengai 61
Ol Kalou 93
Olmelepo Gate 81
Ol Pegeta Ranch 92
Ol Tukai 110
Olduvai Gorge 61, 168, 169
Olorgesaillie 62
Orma People 108, 141
Oryx 30, 101, 105, 117, 166, 182
Ostrich 60, 153, 184
Overland Treks 12
Oyugis, Pelicanry 85

Pare 117
Patas Monkey 178
Pate Island 142, 145
Pelicans 71, 85
Pemba Channel Fishing Club 149
Photographic & Specialist Safaris 31
Photography 24, 25, 31
Places of Worship 56, 57
Pokomo People 107, 108, 141
Pokot People 87
Postal Services 25
Prehistoric Sites 71, 105, 167, 169
Prince Charles 100
Prince Philip 90, 104
Ptolemy 7, 36, 122
Public Holidays 26
Pyrethrum 83

Rabai 129
Railways 46, 83, 84, 116, 122, 155, 161
Ramisi 149
Ranches, Private 32, 72, 91, 92, 120,
   166, 170
Ras Ngomeni 140, 141
Rebmann, Johannes 114, 129, 163
Red Colobus Monkey 107
Red Sea 7
Reedbuck 72, 91, 114
Reef, The Coastal 120-122
Rendille People 106
Reserves see National Parks
   & Reserves

Restaurants, Kenya 54, 55
Restaurants, Tanzania 157
Reticulated Giraffe 175
Rhinoceros 36, 72, 90, 91, 153, 160,
   162, 166, 173, 175
Riding Safaris 31
Rift Valley see Great Rift Valley
Riyadha Mosque 143
Roan Antelope 80
Roberts, Mrs David 75
Robinson Island 140
Rock Paintings 167
Root, Alan 82
Rufiji River 57, 152
Rumuruti 91, 93
Rusinga Island 81, 85
Ruwenzori 7

Saanane Island 173
Sabaki River 137, 140
Sable Antelope 30, 149, 155, 181
Safaris, Kenya 29-33, 95
Safaris, Tanzania 29-33, 155, 156, 158
Safari Rally 56, 97
Sagana 97
Sagante, Singing Wells 104
Saguta 91
Saiwa Swamp 88
Sala Gate 119, 120
Salaita Hills 115
Salei Plains 170
Samburu 36, 45, 96, 97, 100-101
Sand River 78
Sangare Ranch 32, 92
Sanya Plains 159
Satima 91
Scott, Jonathan 81, 185
Scuba diving 28, 130, 131, 139, 144
Sea Festival, Malindi 138
Sea Transport 12
Security 26
Semi-precious stones 27, 51, 118, 157
Serengeti Plains 8, 78, 82
Serengeti Research Institute 171
Seronera 170-171
Seven Forks Power Station 106
Shanzu 129
Shela 144
Sheldrick, David 119
Shetani Lava Flow 61, 112
Shimoni 149, 150
Shira Plateau 162, 164
Shopping 26, 27, 51-52, 157
Simba River 165
Sirimon Track 96
Sitatunga 88, 184
Siwas 143
Siyu 145

Snake Parks 57, 75, 130, 138
Solio Ranch 72, 91
Somalis 106, 108, 141
Sonachi Crater Lake 69
Sotik 83, 84
South Horr 104
South Island 105
Souvenirs 27, 63, 126, 157
Space Rocket Programme 141
Speke's Gulf 173
Sport 27, 56, 127
State Travel Service, Tanzania 11,
    156, 162
Subukia 93
Sukuma People 172, 173
Sultan Hamud 109, 113
Suswa 77
Swahili, Language 23-24
Sykes Monkey 178

Taita Hills 117, 118
Taita People 118
Talek Gate 80
Talek River 78
Tambach 76
Tana River 98, 106, 108, 141
Tana River Primate Reserve 142
Tanga 150
Tanzania Tourist Corporation 156
Tanzania Wildlife Corporation 30, 31,
    154
Tarangire 166-168
Taxis 58, 128, 139
Taveta 115, 117
Tea 83
Telegraphs 25
Teleki, Count 105, 160
Telephones 25, 26
Temi River 158
Tewa Caves 137
Theatre 56, 128
Thesiger, Wilfred 100
Thika 88
Thomson, Joseph 93
Thomson's Falls see Nyahururu
Thomson's Gazelle 179
Timau 96
Time 28
Tiwi 146, 149
Topi 80, 105
Transport and Tours Kenya 14, 43-47,
    58, 128. Tours Tanzania 156
Trappe family 160
Travel Agents 12, 48, 49, 128, 138,
    139, 156
Tsavo, River 114, 115, 119
Tugen Hills 75, 76

Tugen People 74, 76
Turkana People 105, 106

Uasin Gishu Plateau 76, 83
Uaso Ngiro River 77
Uaso Nyiro River 99, 101, 162, 163
Uganda 7, 83
Uganda Kob 180
Ukunda 147, 149
Umbo 164
Ungwana Bay 140, 141
Ura River 164
Uru 164

Vasco Da Gama 122, 138
Voi 115, 118
Von Lettow-Vorbeck, General Paul
    115, 125

Waa 146, 149
Wabondei Tribe 161
Wajir 106
Waliangulu 37
Walter's Gazelle see Gerenuk
Wamba 101, 103
Wamunyu 108
Wanderobo People 83
Wapere People 161
Wart Hog 60, 119, 177
Wasini Island 121, 150
Watamu 121, 128, 132, 137
Waterbuck 69, 72, 91, 101, 105, 110,
    114, 119, 160, 167, 181
Watta People 108
Weights and Measures 28
Wenje 107, 142
Western Corridor, Serengeti 171
West African Forest 86
Westlands 63
West Pokot 88, 99
White Rhinoceros 175
Wild dogs 162
Wildebeest 60, 78, 183
Wildlife Conservation & Management
    Department, Kenya 60
Wilson Airport 9, 44, 45, 146
Winam Gulf 85
World Wildlife Fund 8, 56, 60
World War I 116, 125
Worsessa Look-out Hill 119
Wundanyi 118

Yatta Plateau 118-119

Zanzibar 7, 37, 122, 124, 125
Zebra 78, 82, 98, 101, 114, 153,
    166-168, 176
Zebroid 92

NOTES